The Peculiar Afterlife of Slavery

ASIAN AMERICA
A series edited by Gordon H. Chang

The Peculiar Afterlife of Slavery

THE CHINESE WORKER AND
THE MINSTREL FORM

Caroline H. Yang

STANFORD UNIVERSITY PRESS
STANFORD, CALIFORNIA

Stanford University Press
Stanford, California

Printed in the United States of America on acid-free, archival-quality
paper

Library of Congress Cataloging-in-Publication Data

Names: Yang, Caroline H., author.
Title: The peculiar afterlife of slavery : the Chinese worker and the
    minstrel form / Caroline H. Yang
Other titles: Asian America.
Description: Stanford : Stanford University press, 2020 | Series: Asian
    America | Includes bibliographical references and index
Identifiers: LCCN 2019033251 (print) | LCCN 2019033252 (ebook) |
    ISBN 9781503610378 (cloth) | ISBN 9781503612051 (paperback) |
    ISBN 9781503612068 (ebook)
Subjects: LCSH: American literature—19th century—History and
    criticism. | Foreign workers, Chinese, in literature. | Minstrels in
    literature. | Race in literature. | Racism in literature. | West (U.S.)—
    In literature.
Classification: LCC PS217.F66 Y36 2020 (print) | LCC PS217.F66
    (ebook) | DDC 813/.395073—dc23
LC record available at https://lccn.loc.gov/2019033251
LC ebook record available at https://lccn.loc.gov/2019033252

Cover design: David Drummond, Salamander Hill

Text design: Kevin Barrett Kane

Typeset by Newgen in 11/14 Garamond

For my mother, Juliana Kwija Yang (1946–2014)

Contents

Acknowledgments

This book has taken a long time to write, and I have received a lot of help along the way. I began to think about the ideas in the book after reading W. E. B. Du Bois's *Black Reconstruction in America* in graduate school at the University of Washington. I thank Moon-Ho Jung for recommending it and giving me the foundation for my own book through his scholarship and guidance. Caroline Chung Simpson, Chandan Reddy, and Steve Sumida gave shape to my ideas with their brilliance and mentorship. Caroline, in particular, guided me with humor and care for which I will always be grateful. I am still trying to master the art of gracious reading that I learned from Chandan's exemplary readings and actions. I am also thankful for friends who gave me intellectual and emotional sustenance during grad school: Ryan Burt, Jim Chin, Jeff Chiu, David Cho, Marsha Elliott, Dokubo Goodhead, Kristine Kelley, Jina E. Kim, Tamiko Nimura, Michael Oishi, Amy Reddinger, Vince Schleitwiler, Ji-Young Um, and most of all, Seema Sohi, without whom my life as a grad student would have been unthinkable.

My Chancellor's postdoctoral fellowship in Asian American studies at the University of Illinois at Urbana–Champaign (UIUC) allowed me to think of myself as a book writer. I thank my fellow postdoc Victor Mendoza for his friendship and humor. My immense gratitude goes to the entire roster of core faculty in Asian American studies when it was a program: Nancy Abelmann, Pallassana Balgopal, Lisa Cacho, Augusto Espiritu, Susan Koshy, Soo Ah Kwon, Esther Kim Lee, Martin Manalansan, Lisa Nakamura, Fiona Ngô, Mimi Nguyen, Kent Ono, Yoon Pak, and Junaid Rana. I am grateful for the meaningful conversation I shared with each and every one of them, both as a postdoc and as a new faculty member. Mary Ellerbe, Viveka Kudaligama, Pia Sengsavanh, and Christine Lyke provided indispensable help with administrative concerns. I also received help from the amazing library system at UIUC, and Tessa Winkelmann and Joanna Wu provided essential research help. I am grateful for Youngji Jeon, Sandra Lee, and Michelle Salerno, my former students at UIUC. Nancy Abelmann, with her indefatigable enthusiasm and generosity, missed by all, helped my book writing tremendously with institutional support. She helped me put together a successful application for the visiting fellowship at the James Weldon Johnson Institute (JWJI) for the Study of Race and Difference at Emory University, which was crucial to my work on the book. I thank the other visiting fellows and Tyrone Forman, who was directing the institute at the time.

I have found the University of Massachusetts Amherst the most enjoyable place to work, with wonderful colleagues. I am especially grateful to Jane Hwang Degenhardt for her enduring friendship and support since my arrival and for reading some of my earliest and roughest drafts. Asha Nadkarni has been so helpful and generous throughout my writing process, and I'm grateful to call her a friend. I thank Sarah Patterson for providing invaluable feedback after reading multiple chapters at the most crucial time. For her cheer and help, I thank Rebecca Lorimer-Leonard. For the gift of time and poetry, I thank Ocean Vuong. Randall Knoper has been the most supportive mentor and department chair, and I am grateful for his helpful reading of my chapter on Mark Twain. I am also grateful to Donna LeCourt for stepping up as interim chair during a crucial semester and guiding me through various deadlines. For their encouragement, support, and advice, I thank Jen Adams, Nick Bromell, Rebecca Dingo, Laura Doyle, Laura Furlan, Haivan Hoang, Emily Lordi, Rachel Mordecai, Mazen Naous, Hoang Phan, TreaAndrea Russworm, Daniel Sack, Malcolm Sen, Jenny Spencer, and Ron Welburn. I am also grateful to my colleagues who attended my department colloquium presentation and helped sharpen my ideas. It is with much pride that I thank my former and current graduate students at UMass who inspire my thinking: Jae Young Ahn, Xu Li, Pat Matthews, Tom Poehnelt, Chamila Somirathna, and Porntip Twishime. I also thank Wanda Bak, Meg Caulmare, Mary Coty, Patty O'Neil, Tom Racine, and Celeste Stuart, the wonderful staff in the English department. Research for this book was supported by the Research Intensive Semester leave, and financial support was provided by the Office of the Vice Chancellor for Research and Engagement at the University of Massachusetts Amherst.

I have received research help from many libraries, institutions, and people. I thank Beth M. Howse for helping me browse through the Charles Chesnutt Collection at Fisk University. The staff and librarians at the Du Bois Library at UMass are miracle workers: Michael James, Jim Kelly, Laura Quilter, and especially Annie Sollinger, who skillfully obtained high-quality images and sources for me. I also thank S. T. Joshi for his speedy and helpful response on the bibliographical and biographical details on Ambrose Bierce; Peter Davis for answering my question on "spectacular extravaganza" that changed the course of the book; Esther Kim Lee for telling me about Dave Williams's *The Chinese Other*; Judy Tsou for pointing me to images on sheet music on the Chinese; Mary Chapman for generously sharing her writings on Sui Sin Far and research findings on Walter Blackburn Harte; Yashika Issrani for her meticulous assistance with the bibliography; and Martin Zehr for generously sharing his image of "The New Heathen Chinee." My work, from the title of the book to the ideas in it, is greatly influenced by Saidiya Hartman's writings, and I am grateful for her inspiring scholarship.

This book benefited vastly from conversations with colleagues outside my own institution. I thank the organizers and participants at various presentations: Cathy Schlund-Vials and Jason Chang for inviting me to present at the Pacific New England meeting; the members of the Five College Asian/Pacific/American Program—Floyd Cheung, Richard Chu, Iyko Day, Robert Hayashi, Ren-yo Hwang, Miliann Kang, Jina B. Kim, C. N. Le, Asha Nadkarni, and Franklin Odo—whose engagement with my scholarship since my arrival in the valley I have valued greatly; Todd Tietchen and the American Studies Program at UMass Lowell; and Min Hyoung Song and Julia Lee for inviting me to present the beginning iteration of this book at their institutions. In addition to those already mentioned, smart and generous people whom I respect greatly have read various portions of the book and provided elucidating comments: Rick Bonus, Kimberly Juanita Brown, Iyko Day, Lezlie Frye, Laura Fugikawa, Gordon Hutner, Julia Lee, Josephine Lee, Kimberlee Pérez, Seema Sohi, and Elda Tsou. For his essential feedback on the entire book, I am immensely grateful to Moon-Ho Jung. Remaining errors are all my own.

At Stanford University Press, I thank Margo Irvin, whose ablest hands guided this book to fruition. From her encouraging words about my book proposal to her keen reading of my revised introduction, Margo has been a dream of an editor, and I cannot thank her enough. For answering all my questions and shepherding the book to production, I thank Faith Wilson Stein, Cindy Lim, and Nora Spiegel. For their help and expertise during and beyond the production stage, I thank Jessica Ling, Rebecca Logan, and Stephanie Adams. I also thank Gordon Chang, the Asian America series editor, for his time and unwavering support. I am grateful to the anonymous reviewers for the press, all of whom made this book much stronger. Outside SUP, I am grateful for the editorial advice and enthusiasm of Sara Cohen and the time that Tony Tiongson took to champion my book.

I thank my mentors, colleagues, friends, and family from near and far who supported me over the years. Anne Eggebroten gave me the best piece of advice in college that set me on this path. I am grateful for the mentorship of Ann duCille, J. Kēhaulani Kauanui, Susan Koshy, and Colleen Lye, who have each provided support in key moments during the creation of this book. Before I knew what my book was about, Elda Tsou spent a whole day helping me think through my ideas. This book benefited so much from her all-around fabulousness, and I thank her deeply. Lezlie Frye, Laura Fugikawa, and Kimberlee Pérez, my beloved writing group (ROT) members, made it possible for me to reclaim writing as an important part of my life, and I can't thank them enough. Kimberlee's encouragements to keep going have been my lifelines; I would be utterly bereft without her friendship and her extraordinary intuition and acumen. Even from far away, Lezlie inspires me with her wisdom and commitment to building community, and Laura continues to be one of my most trusted readers and allies. I thank Iyko Day for talking through some of my crudest ideas with me, pointing me in the right direction, and providing much cheer and support along the way. I am grateful to go through this process with my comrade Christine Ho. I also thank Kiran Asher, Mari Castañeda, Rebecca Dingo, Jonathan Hulting-Cohen, Miliann Kang, Chan Young Park, Jacqueline Wallace, Wes Yu, and all the awesome women of the Potluck Book Club—each and every one an amazing person who has made it possible for me to feel at home and have fun in the valley. Friends and colleagues from afar also provided good cheer and support over the years: Jennifer Chung, Seema Sohi, Jina E. Kim, Julia Lee, Stephen Sohn, Yu-Fang Cho, Naomi Paik, Esther Kim Lee, David Eng, Min Song, and Barbara Kessel and the Men's Movie Critic. I am grateful for Loïc Egyed, Mai Nako, Mary Nguyen, Eric Bennett, João Vargas, Amanda Lewis, Tyrone Forman, Catherine Rottenberg, Neve Gordon, and especially Nga Tang, friends who allowed me the necessary respite from work in sunny locales, mostly with their sunnier company. I am inspired by and happy to have my nieces-in-law Mina and Seri Jung in my life. For her unbounded generosity and expertise in artistic matters, I thank Juliana Sohn. I am so grateful for my extended family—my *eemos* and *eemobus*, *keun umma*, and cousins and all their kids: the Sohns in New Jersey and New York, all the Kim sisters in Korea and their daughters and son, the Yis and Yangs in California and Korea, and those who passed while I was writing this book—my maternal grandmother, Yoo Byung Hee; my maternal grandfather, Kim Sam Yong; my *keun appa*, Kwang Sin Yang; and my beloved *gomo*, Christine Miran Yi.

My big thanks go to Matthew and Madeline's parents, Frank Yang and Jarnette Lee, for making me a *momo*, and Matthew and Madeline, for making my trips to Los Angeles the best parts of the year. I thank Jarnette for all the FaceTime calls with and pictures of M&M that never failed to spark joy and brightened even my gloomiest writing days. My brother's fancy (to me) congratulatory texts have meant more to me than he could ever imagine. I thank my dad, Joseph Kwang Il Yang, for his steadfast love and support. I am perpetually grateful for Hyejin Cho, who teaches me how to be a good friend and person by being the best best friend anyone could ever hope for. I simply can't imagine my life without her. My biggest love and gratitude go to my partner, Moon-Kie Jung, for having nourished me with joy and laughter, date nights, and the world's most delicious fried egg throughout all the years that I was working on the book. He has read approximately one thousand drafts, often in record time, and I am so grateful for all the countless ways that he made this book possible.

Finally, even more than myself, my mom, Juliana Kwija Yang, would have been *so relieved* that the book is finally complete. For being my best teacher and my first and most generous reader, I dedicate this book to her with all my love and gratitude.

The Peculiar Afterlife of Slavery

Introduction

The Chinese Question in the Early Afterlife of Slavery

In June 1870, just months after the U.S. Congress ratified the Fifteenth Amendment to the Constitution, the Republican-leaning *New-York Tribune* published an essay proclaiming that "the Chinese question has become the living question of the hour" (Swinton 1). The article categorically opposed the presence of Chinese labor on the "grounds of race" (1), implying that the most pressing race issue five years after the end of the U.S. Civil War was not the "Negro problem" but the "living" "Chinese question": whether or not Chinese labor was beneficial to the development of the United States. The article's writer was mostly concerned with delineating the "Chinese race" as diametrically opposed to the "European race" of the "dominant American people," which he also distinguished from the "African race" and the "Indian race" (1). Nevertheless, the alarm bell that he rang regarding Chinese labor was at this time part of a rising concern, much of which consisted of arguments for or against that labor in comparison to Black labor. In one of the earliest writings on the topic published outside California during the Reconstruction period after the Civil War, journalist Henry George wrote in May 1869 that the Chinese worker posed a threat to white labor because the former was not like the Black worker, who was akin to "an ignorant but docile child" and "a simple barbarian with nothing to unlearn" ("Chinese Question" 2). Instead, the Chinese worker was like "a grown man, sharp but narrow minded, opinionated and set in character" (2), which made him unassimilable. In contrast, Willie Wild, a California correspondent for the

New Orleans *Daily Picayune*, wrote in July 1869 that the Chinese "work well and faithfully, and I would prefer them every time to black labor" (Wild 12).

Though there was no consensus in the arguments that compared Chinese and Black workers, the unequivocal result was that the period of Reconstruction in the United States ushered in a period of Chinese exclusion. Indeed, while various journalists were writing about the merits or evils of Chinese labor, lawmakers participated in a similar discourse in Congress as they discussed the Chinese question in connection to the "Negro problem." Almost immediately after ratifying the Fifteenth Amendment in 1870, which resulted in the enfranchisement of Black men, Congress engaged in a heated debate over the revision of the 1790 law that had restricted naturalized citizenship to "free white person[s]." Charles Sumner, a Radical Republican from Massachusetts, proposed that in the true spirit of mending the nation, the word "white" should be taken out in the revised wording. Many lawmakers interpreted Sumner's proposal to mean that the "immense, teeming, swarming, seething hive of degraded" Chinese, "who are slaves," could potentially become U.S. citizens and balked at the prospect, reasoning that just because they performed "an act of justice" and "enfranchised the colored man," who was "an American," they were not obligated to surrender the institution of U.S. citizenship to the Chinese (*Congressional Globe* 1870, 5125). Sumner's proposal did not pass, and the naturalization law retained whiteness as the original and authentic marker of citizenship and added those of "African nativity and persons of African descent" (5176). The 1870 naturalization law debate was just one prelude to the string of anti-Chinese immigration laws that were passed around the official end of Reconstruction in 1877 and well beyond.

Scholars in the field of Asian American studies have substantiated the connection between the anti-Chinese discourse and Reconstruction, undertaking in the process the important work of challenging the master narrative of the history of the United States as a nation of immigrants, particularly one that erases the history of Asian exclusion and posits the Asian as a model immigrant (see Moon-Ho Jung; Wong; Torok; Saxton; Aarim-Heriot; Paddison). In particular, Lisa Yun, Lisa Lowe, and Edlie Wong, along with Moon-Ho Jung, have ascertained the way in which the racialized Chinese worker figure of the "coolie" necessitates a reframing of the history of the transatlantic slavery, coolie trade, and empire in a transnational and comparative context. They have shown that the coolie is not just a post-slavery figure in the United States but also deeply imbricated in the history of global racialization of labor in the development of racial capitalism, revealing what Lisa Lowe calls the "intimacies of four continents" (4). In making their important historical interventions, these scholars focus mainly on the history of the racialization of the Chinese worker and how the Chinese were compared to Black people, as I also do in the examples above.

The important transnational history of the Chinese worker, however, does not fully account for the specificity of enduring antiblackness after slavery in the United States. What strikes me about the above examples comparing the Chinese with Black people, whether or not they were comparing the latter favorably to the former, is the undeniable similarity in how Blackness is represented—as childlike, sometimes wayward, and always dependent—which evinces a preservation of the mode of antiblack representation from slavery. And so, when we study what Edlie Wong calls the "dialectical configuration of black inclusion/Chinese exclusion" during Reconstruction (3), we need to ask what it means that Black people were viewed as "American" in contradistinction to the Chinese, who were labeled as "slaves." In the course of equating and excluding Chinese workers as "slaves" in the comparative racialization of the Chinese and Black people after emancipation, what happened to the racial logic of antiblackness from slavery?

To answer the question, I turn to the most popular and influential form of representing Blackness in the United States during and after slavery: blackface minstrelsy.[1] At a time when journalists and politicians routinely compared the Chinese with Black people, a minstrel song by Harry F. Lorraine with the derogatory title "Nigger Versus Chinese" (1870) asked its own version of the Chinese question: "What can all de Chinese do Along side ob de Nigger?" (4).[2] Like the majority of the newspaper writers and lawmakers of the period, the song links the presence of the Chinese to the end of slavery, as it states, "Since niggerman had been made free, De Chinee hab come ober" (3), and ultimately answers that Black people are more desirable than Chinese workers. But the song's reason is unlike any that a journalist or lawmaker would have given. The song suggests that the Chinese are undesirable because they "cannot learn to play the fiddle, Or pick the ole Banjo, Or stave de head ob de [t]am-bo-rine, Dey are so mighty slow" (4). Naming musical instruments that were customarily associated with Black people and minstrel shows, the song deems Black people to be preferable because of their ability to play such instruments. In doing so, it provides an insight that can be gleaned only in a study of cultural representations. Though its main point seems to be about Chinese unassimilability as the basis for exclusion, the song also effects Black racialization as the basis for inclusion through its statement that the Chinese "cannot learn" the musical skills associated with Black people. Assumed in the song is not only Black people's natural predilection for music and entertainment but also their desire to serve as objects of enjoyment for white people, which was the antiblack racial logic of slavery that birthed blackface minstrelsy and the antebellum caricature of the "happy slave." As the lyrics are purportedly sung by a Black figure, the knowledge that Blackness and the minstrel form are one and the same is meant to be understood as being produced and proclaimed by Black people themselves, and this knowledge is the song's basis for including them and excluding the Chinese.

The Peculiar Afterlife of Slavery exposes the process through which the antiblack racial logic of slavery remained meaningful through the minstrel form *and* the figure of the Chinese worker in cultural representations after emancipation. For this investigation, Lorraine's song provides a point of departure in three ways. First, "Nigger Versus Chinese" underscores how inseparable minstrelsy was from slavery and what Saidiya Hartman calls its "afterlife"—the enduring antiblackness and violence derived from "a racial calculus and a political arithmetic that were entrenched centuries ago" that continued to imperil Black lives after emancipation (*Lose* 6). The song's pronouncement that the Chinese cannot be a minstrel figure is followed by the complaint that the Chinese have "got no pret-ty yellow gals [with] nice lit-tle su-gar lips" (Lorraine 4). Demonstrating that the term "yellow" would not be associated with Asians until later in the nineteenth century, the song's invocation of the "yellow girl" to describe a mixed-race Black woman reveals the legacy of slavery and sexual violence against Black female captives.[3] As the "yellow girl" was a popular topic of many minstrel songs, which I discuss in Chapter 4, the song emblematizes the way in which the violence of slavery is both disclosed and disavowed in minstrelsy. Second, the song's publication year of 1870 points to the significance of the Reconstruction period in the nationalization of the Chinese question, especially through the phenomenon of comparative Black and Asian racialization that Colleen Lye has termed the "Afro-Asian analogy" ("Afro-Asian" 1735). Third, despite the song's dissociation of the Chinese from minstrelsy, yellowface performances of the Chinese worker appeared in minstrel shows as early as the 1840s, as Krystyn Moon has shown. During Reconstruction, the Chinese worker character became a national *literary* figure, mainly because of the success of Bret Harte's poem "Plain Language from Truthful James" (1870), which I discuss in Chapter 1. Arguing for reading Harte's Chinese character as a minstrel figure, *The Peculiar Afterlife of Slavery* tracks the figure of the Chinese worker and the minstrel form in subsequent chapters on writings by Mark Twain, Ambrose Bierce, Sui Sin Far, and Charles Chesnutt, who each and differently employed the minstrel form in conjunction with their literary representations of the Chinese worker.

. . .

By studying representations of the Chinese worker as demonstrating the persistence of antiblackness in and through the minstrel form, I am underscoring the inseparable link between formal minstrel representations of race and the structure of white supremacy in slavery and its afterlife. Specifically, minstrelsy provides the means to understand the racial capitalism of slavery. As coined by Cedric Robinson, "racial capitalism" refers to the ways in which the "development, organization, and expansion of capitalist society pursued racial directions," so that "racialism would inevitably permeate the social structures emergent from capitalism" (Robinson 2). Locating racism as a product of racialism in the "'internal' relations of European peoples" in the development of capitalism (2), Robinson underscores race as a mechanism of differentiation key to capitalism. That is, as Jodi Melamed explains, "capitalism *is* racial capitalism," since accumulation of capital requires "loss, disposability, and the unequal differentiation of human value," and "racism enshrines the inequalities that capitalism requires" (Melamed 77; emphasis in original). In line with scholarship that calls for studying slavery as a part of—rather than apart from—the development of U.S. capitalism,[4] examining minstrelsy through the framework of white supremacist racial capitalism blurs the line between the slaveholding South and the non-slaveholding North and West and reveals how racial differences and relations of inequality were produced and reproduced all across the United States through the proliferation of minstrel shows. Claiming to be an authentic replication of Black life in the South during slavery, the minstrel show originated in the Northeast before the Civil War and was popularized by performers in the North (see Green). Minstrelsy, whose "birthplace," according to Robert

Toll, was New York City, became a "national institution" (Toll 32, 26) as a by-product of the minstrel troupes' travels as they set to stage the vagaries of slavery in the South.

The birth of minstrelsy as staged entertainment occurred in the 1830s and 1840s, in what Eric Lott calls "the most politically explosive moment of the nineteenth century" (*Love* 37). This period saw the rise of industrialization, urbanization, and wage labor in the North and working conditions that increasingly challenged the definition of such laborers as "free." As scholars such as Lott and David Roediger have established, minstrelsy was crucial to the formation of white working-class male identity as white and free, especially in debates about workers', as well as women's, rights in the nineteenth century. As Roediger states, "Blackface minstrels were the first self-consciously *white* entertainers in the world" (*Wages* 117; emphasis in original). The minstrels performed their whiteness into being through the production of what it meant to be Black, by impersonating what they imagined to be Blackness. Cultural expropriation is therefore minstrelsy's "central fact," as Lott reminds us (*Love* 19). But even more important, the production of white working-class identity as white and free through the cultural expropriation of Blackness served two critical functions that buttressed the racial logic of slavery. First, as Douglas Jones, Jr., writes in *The Captive Stage*, antebellum minstrelsy cultivated a collective *national* white "proslavery imagination" (7). Jones builds on Tavia Nyong'o's problematization of the "increasingly orthodox" (Nyong'o 8) understanding of the history of minstrelsy—that it had a more radical beginning as part of a working-class culture and politics in the 1830s and 1840s before it was co-opted by the middle class and became mainstream in the 1850s, when it turned more proslavery. Minstrelsy was always proslavery, regardless of its class identification and geographic location, which means that the white identity produced through minstrelsy was always steeped in a proslavery imagination. Second, minstrelsy functioned to "regulate the course of black freedom and counter the aims of black activism" (Jones 7), particularly in urban areas with a large free Black population, many of which were outside of the deep South.

This twin function of early antebellum blackface minstrelsy can be seen in a *Baltimore Sun* issue in November 1837. In one column, the *Sun* reported on a show by "Jim Crow," the stage persona of Thomas D. Rice, who popularized the song and dance of the same name and whose nickname, "Daddy

Rice," alluded to his status as a forerunner in the history of staged minstrel shows. In a paraphrased speech that he delivered as Jim Crow, Rice stated that he had been touring in England and Ireland to correct the misguided abolitionist belief that "negroes were naturally equal to whites" ("Theater" 2). Referring to his performance in blackface, he claimed, "I effectually proved that negroes are essentially an inferior species of the human family, and that they ought to remain slaves" (2). The article states that Rice's antiblack, proslavery declaration was met with "some murmurs of disapprobation from the boxes, which was quickly put down by the plaudits of the pit" (2). Dismantling the notion that the white workers who patronized antebellum minstrel shows felt an affinity with those enslaved, the "plaudits of the pit" indicates the proslavery attitude of those workers, as the equation of "negroes" and "slaves" on the minstrel stage enabled the belief that as "not-slaves," they were free. The "murmurs of disapprobation" are further silenced with the audience's subsequent "tremendous applause" and "immense cheering" for Rice's speech, particularly when he claims that he was proud of the fact that "I was an American, and that my country was in some degree benefitted by my performance" (2). Rice's linking of his performance as Jim Crow and his invocation of his national identity as an American— "I have been of such signal service to my country!!" (2)—underscores the essential role that the performance and definition of Blackness on the minstrel stage played in the definition of whiteness as a proslavery and national identity.

The "murmurs of disapprobation" in the article also bring light to the fact that the proslavery imagination was promulgated through minstrelsy amid the rise of Black abolitionism. As minstrelsy was the first and most successful popular cultural form in the antebellum United States, the cultural practice of white men performing in blackface needs to be understood as a defense of slavery and white supremacy against arguments for Black freedom. Black activists in places such as Baltimore challenged the rightfulness of slavery through their antislavery efforts. An example of such actions can be seen in the *Baltimore Sun* issue discussed above. In the column next to the article on Jim Crow's performance was an article with the subtitle "Negro Samuel Robinson vs. Edward Townsend." The article states that Samuel Robinson sued for his freedom by citing the 1817 act of the Maryland assembly, which declared that "no sale of any servant or slave, who is or may be entitled to freedom after a term of years . . . shall be valid and effectual in law" ("Proceedings" 2). As he was held "as a slave for a term of years," Robinson claimed that he was entitled to freedom after that term. The jury ruled in his favor, and the article concludes with the pronouncement that Robinson was "accordingly liberated" (2). The side-by-side placement of the Jim Crow speech and the Robinson article demonstrates that against the presence of Black activists like Robinson, who claimed their freedom, blackface minstrelsy actively sought to negate that freedom with a performance that posited Black inferiority and justified slavery.

Black abolitionism also extended to a critique of blackface minstrelsy. A study of minstrelsy therefore has to keep in mind the "complex responses that black activists and abolitionists had to the genre, almost from its beginning," as Ngyong'o stresses (8).[5] Frederick Douglass, who emancipated himself from slavery in Baltimore in 1838, less than one year after the publication of the above *Sun* article, attested to the dialectical relationship between the proslavery imagination of blackface minstrelsy and antislavery activism during slavery. In the October 28, 1848, issue of the *North Star*—itself a powerful venue of abolitionism—Douglass wrote a trenchant criticism of a white reviewer who had panned the performance of the Hutchinson Family, a group of white antislavery singers, in Rochester, New York.[6] Calling the reviewer a "pro-slavery and narrow-souled demon," Douglass surmised that the reviewer would not "object to the 'Virginia Minstrels,' 'Christy's Minstrels,' the 'Ethiopian Serenaders,' or any of the filthy scum of white society, who have stolen from us a complexion denied to them by nature, in which to make money, and pander to the corrupt taste of their white fellow-citizens" (Douglass, "Hutchinson"). Alluding to the lucrative profitability of blackface minstrelsy, Douglass's comment pushes us toward a "critique of the national popular" in the nineteenth-century study of minstrelsy (Nyong'o 9).[7] If white Northerners were at a crossroad between slavery and abolitionism, the entertainment provided by minstrel shows eased the choice of the majority to adopt the proslavery imagination, as evidenced by the widespread and domineering popularity of such shows as a national cultural institution.

Minstrel shows staged Black freedom as apocryphal and thus defined freedom as limited to white people. Slavery, as the indispensable backdrop to any minstrel show, was naturalized in the course of such shows. The minstrel form, therefore, was one of the means through which racial differences were justified and concretized in slavery through performances in blackface.

The minstrel form naturalized the social relationship of white supremacy through the creation of a racial hierarchy in which "blackness [became] the mark of subjects who should be most captive, while whiteness marked those who should be most free" (Jones, *Captive* 19). The minstrel form proliferated in the antebellum United States as a performance and justification of slavery that relied on "Black" endorsement of slavery and nullified Black activism and freedom.

Here I am thinking of *form* not as a passive product of structure but as an active component of it, as literary theorist Caroline Levine suggests (xi). That is, rather than see the minstrel form as merely mirroring the reality of slavery, I am proposing to conceive of it as having created a particular sociality in slavery. More specifically, instead of thinking that the minstrel form is a reflection of the violence of slavery, we might see that it is constitutive of the specific kind of violence of slavery that produced Blackness and Black people as commodities. "It is not merely the content of minstrelsy to which we must attend," as Nyong'o instructs, "but its commodified and professionalized form" (109). Accordingly, we must consider "the ability to put on blackness . . . in the context of chattel slavery and the economy of enjoyment founded thereupon"—an economy predicated on the "fungibility" of the enslaved as a commodity, "specifically its abstractness and immateriality" (Hartman, *Scenes* 26). A crucial component of racialization under slavery, the popular consumption of minstrelsy and performance of Blackness can be understood as a part of the process through which human beings became commodities. As Stephanie Smallwood writes, citing Arjun Appadurai's definition of the commodity, "Turning people into slaves entailed more than the completion of a market transaction . . . [for] the economic exchange had to transform independent beings into human commodities whose most 'socially relevant feature' was their 'exchangeability'" (35). If the market selling enslaved people was crucial to the process of turning a person into a commodity and another person into a property owner, as Walter Johnson has shown (*Soul*), the minstrel form, which animated the social relationship of slavery, enabled the pleasure of ownership beyond the market.

The minstrel form thus reveals the social relationship at the heart of slavery that reduced enslaved people to a fungible commodity in an "economy of enjoyment." In such an economy, we see traces of the minstrel form in everyday practices of violence in slavery, as the captive became an object of labor *and* entertainment for the enslaver. Thomas Rutling, who was born into slavery in Tennessee, stated in an interview in 1872 that as soon as he was "large enough," his mistress "made [him] bring wood and water, play with the children to keep them quiet, and sing and dance for her own amusement" (qtd. in Blassingame 616), demonstrating the way in which forced labor and entertainment existed on a continuum. Solomon Northup, who was stolen into slavery for twelve years, likewise wrote in his autobiography:

> No matter how worn out and tired we were, there must be a general dance. . . . "Dance, you d—d niggers, dance," Epps would shout. Then there must be no halting or delay, no slow or languid movements; all must be brisk, and lively, and alert. . . . Epps' portly form mingled with those of his dusky slaves, moving rapidly through all the mazes of the dance. Usually his whip was in his hand. . . . Frequently, we were thus detained until almost morning. Bent with excessive toil—actually suffering for a little refreshing rest, and feeling rather as if we could cast ourselves upon the earth and weep, many a night in the house of Edwin Epps have his unhappy slaves been made to dance and laugh. (125–26)

The intermingling of violence of the whip and the injunction to dance, as well as the "mingling" of Epps's body with "his dusky slaves," demonstrates the intimacy of slavery that Christina Sharpe says can be characterized only as "monstrous" (*Monstrous* 2). Combined with Epps's projection of his enjoyment to those in his enslavement who would rather weep or rest, Northup's description demonstrates the inseparability of the violence of slavery and the "economy of enjoyment." That the captives were "actually suffering" and "bent with excessive toil" does not register in such an economy. The ascription of enjoyment to a captive position was at the heart of "scenes of subjection" (Hartman, *Scenes* 4), such as Epps's house, in which dancing took place, but they were not limited to those spaces. The minstrel form was also present at the auction block. William Wells Brown, a Black activist who liberated himself from slavery and penned the first African American novel, *Clotel* (1853), as well as the first African American play, *The Escape; or, A Leap for Freedom* (1858),[8] recalled of those enslaved in pens that "some were set to dancing, some jumping, some to singing, and some to playing cards. This was done to make them seem cheerful as possible" (qtd. in W. Johnson, *Soul* 130).

In all the above examples, the captives are not just envisioned as "vehicles for white enjoyment" (Hartman, *Scenes* 23). They are also made to perform the "simulation of agency and the excesses of black enjoyment" (22). Such performance of purported agency was at the heart of a minstrel show, in which white participants not only derived pleasure at the cost of the suffering of the Black captive but also ascribed *enjoyment* of that suffering to the enslaved. Particularly through the proliferation of popular minstrel songs, such ascription crossed the boundary between the stage and actual enslavement. In an interview conducted for the Federal Writers' Project on narratives of formerly enslaved people, Eda Harper recalled, "My old master mean to us. . . . He used to come to the quarters and make us chillun sing. He make us sing Dixie. Sometimes he make us sing half a day. Seems like Dixie his main song. I tell you I don't like it *now*. But have mercy! He make us sing it" (qtd. in Rawick 164; emphasis in original).[9] The song "Dixie," also called "(I Wish I Was in) Dixie's Land," was written around 1859 by Dan Emmett, a popular blackface minstrel who wrote the song for Bryant's Minstrels. Told from the purported viewpoint of a captive who sings, "I wish I was in de land ob cotton, / Old times dar am not forgotten," "Dixie" was set to upbeat music and included the chorus, "I wish I was in Dixie, Hooray! Hooray! / In Dixie's Land I'll take my stand to live and die in Dixie" (S. Foster, *Minstrel* 40). Harper's labeling of her former enslaver's actions of *making* the children sing, which she repeats three times, as evidence of his having been "mean," clearly indicates a break between what she was made to do and her own desires. Her statement that she does not like the song "*now*" powerfully demonstrates the violence that made the utterance of such statement by an enslaved child impossible during slavery. What is more, the discrepancy between Harper's feelings for "Dixie" and her enslaver's shows the crucial proslavery work that minstrelsy performed. Blackface minstrel shows were not just about staging a performance of happy captives. They were also about asserting a complete control over the representation of slavery by presuming to know what the Black captives felt. As Harper's testimony indicates, what made blackface minstrelsy different from violently forcing enslaved people to sing and dance was the purposeful absenting of the enslaved, who could think or name their condition as one of subjection, and supplanting that absence with a caricatured figure who endorsed the condition as good. If, as Hazel Carby states, "the objective of stereotypes is not to reflect or represent a reality but to function as a disguise, or mystification of objective social relations" (22), the stereotype of the "happy slave" on the minstrel stage was part and parcel of the violence of slavery as well as its obfuscation.

The minstrel figure of a willing and content Black captive also extended ownership of the figure to all white people, regardless of their slaveholding status. In rendering the Black enslaved person an object of white entertainment, to be "used in any capacity that pleased the master or *whomever*" (Hartman, *Scenes* 25; emphasis added), minstrelsy made the role of property owner available to all white people. Blackface minstrelsy worked hand in glove with the legality of slavery that codified Blackness as "an object of property to be potentially used and abused by all whites" (24), as seen in the laws barring enslaved Black people from acting in self-defense or testifying against white people in court. The way minstrelsy made Blackness a fungible commodity to be consumed and enjoyed by all white people is also seen in Harper's statement, "Seems like *all* the white folks like Dixie" (Rawick 164; emphasis added). It is not surprising, therefore, that "Dixie" was adopted, albeit unofficially, as the anthem of the Confederacy that united the white South during the Civil War.

The role of minstrelsy in upholding white supremacy and producing Blackness as a fungible commodity can explain how the minstrel form, though born of slavery, did not die with it but continued to evolve within and alongside its afterlife. In fact, as the core aspect of the minstrel form was to negate Black freedom while legitimating white freedom, minstrelsy might be understood as having anticipated emancipation all along. Many of the antebellum minstrel songs already dealt with "Black" characters who were not on plantations but either traveling or pining for "home" in the South. From all the variations of the "Jim Crow" songs to the songs by Stephen Foster that were made immensely popular by blackface minstrels, such as "Camptown Races" (1850) and "Old Folks at Home" (1851; also known as "Swanee River"), the "Black" figures in the songs did not live a life of toil and misery but were in fact performing being free and roaming the country.[10] Like "Dixie," many of Foster's enduring songs—including "Oh! Susanna" (1848)—are not blatantly *about* slavery. But as the songs always cast Black mobility as fraudulent or tragic, the subtext of such songs is that Black freedom is a counterfeit performance, whereas the white performers are truly free. This subtext of the minstrel form is what circulated all across the country throughout the latter half of the nineteenth century and endured the end of slavery.

Significantly, tracking the movement of the minstrel form enables the understanding of slavery in the framework of empire and settler colonialism. The minstrel troupes were traveling performers. Foster's "Oh! Susanna" provides an example. The song became popular not only when "minstrel troupes took it up immediately and sang it all over the country" but also when "the 'forty-niners' adopted it as their special anthem and marching song as they crossed the continent to California" (John Howard, "Stephen" 79). With its lyrics, "I came from Alabama / Wid my banjo on my knee, / I'm gwyne to Louisiana / My true love for to see" (Foster, "Oh! Susanna" 3), "Oh! Susanna" was essentially a song about westward movement. On the way to Louisiana, the narrator of the song witnesses "five hundred nigger[s]" getting killed by lightning and predicts that when he does not see Susanna in Louisiana, "Dis darkie'l surely die" (5). As the song ends with the narrator imagining that he is "dead and buried" (5), the "forty-niners" sang their whiteness into being through the fantasy of a free traveling "Black" man's death as they headed toward California.

The westward movement of minstrelsy shows that the violence of slavery worked in conjunction with the violence of U.S. settler colonialism. Understanding slavery "as a colonial institution" (Byrd 138), as Jodi Byrd instructs, we can see that both violences are embedded in the structure of white supremacy. Arguing that the United States has always been an empire-state and not a nation-state, Moon-Kie Jung states that the "hierarchical differentiation of space and the hierarchical differentiation of people [are] both immanent and foundational to empire-state formation" (Jung, *Beneath* 67). Jung explains that "the construction of U.S. colonial space" as rightfully "American" "centrally turned on the racialization of their inhabitants" (67). In the colonial space of California, specifically after the Mexican-American War and the discovery of gold in 1848 that prompted a rush of migration, that racialization pivoted on the racial logic of slavery, as well as settler colonialism.

Using minstrelsy to study slavery provides a link to connect slavery and capitalism with the U.S. empire, and U.S. colonialism with U.S. imperialism. The fact that minstrel troupes were established in new U.S. territories in the West not long after the expropriation of those lands speaks to that connection, as does the travel of minstrel troupes all over the globe

in the nineteenth century. Here I am not suggesting that the overland colonialism was internal as opposed to the overseas imperialism, which was
external. Rather, minstrelsy in the West was a means through which what
was external—Native space and sovereignty (Byrd 126)—was made internal. Minstrel shows were staged as early as 1849 in California, as I show in
Chapters 2 and 3. Minstrelsy also followed the U.S. empire into the Pacific, aboard Commodore Matthew Perry's vessels sailing to Japan. In 1854,
the year following Perry's landing, Japan agreed to the Treaty of Kanagawa,
which opened up Japanese trade with the United States. In celebration of
the signing of the treaty, as recounted by Matthew Wittmann, the Americans invited the Japanese diplomats to "a banquet aboard the USS *Mississippi* at which some of the sailors staged a minstrel show" (Wittmann 5).
The show was said to have had a "marked effect even upon their sedate
Japanese listeners," and the official narrative of the event concluded that the
minstrel show's warm reception "thus confirmed the universal popularity of
'the Ethiopians'" (6). To follow the traveling minstrel form is to chart the
movement of the U.S. empire that spread the racial logic of antiblackness all
across the continental United States and beyond.

Putting such history of the minstrel form together with the history of
Chinese labor in the United States further necessitates understanding the
two in the framework of empire. Contrary to the commonplace view such
as the one claimed by Lorraine's song, the beginning of the Chinese question stretches back much before Reconstruction—even before the arrival
of Chinese workers in California in 1849 (see Tchen; Chang, *Fateful*). The
history of the Chinese labor in the United States begins not just in the context of transatlantic slavery but also in British and U.S. imperialisms, as the
Opium Wars in China and the signing of unequal treaties between Britain
and China (1842) and between the United States and China (1844) inaugurated the migration of Chinese labor. The presence of Chinese workers in
California needs to be understood in such context. Moreover, in its westward expansion, U.S. settler colonialism entailed not only the expropriation
of land from and the elimination of the Native populations but also, as
Patrick Wolfe states, the development of that land "by means of a subor-
dinated labor force (slaves, indenturees, convicts) whom [the colonizers]
import[ed] from elsewhere" ("Land" 868). The racialization of the Chinese
in California speaks to this process of the subordination of the non-Native,
non-settler labor force and exposes race to be "an organizing principle of

settler colonialism in North America," as Iyko Day argues (24). Just as the United States is an "empire born out of settler colonialism" (Byrd xviii), its mode of production can be described as, according to Day, "settler colonial capitalism" (7), which combined the racial logic of white supremacy and capitalism and the colonial logic of elimination. By studying the comparative racializations of Black captives and Chinese workers as non-Native, non-settler labor forces, we see that slavery cannot be separated from settler colonialism and the claiming of Native lands as "American."

In California in the mid- to late 1800s, Chinese workers composed the largest nonwhite population. By the end of the 1850s, there were 34,933 Chinese out of a total population of 379,994, and by the end of the 1880s, that number increased to 105,465 (Chan, *This* 43). In contrast, the Black population, in 1860, was only about four thousand (Bureau of the Census xiii).[11] From the onset, the presence of Chinese workers in the state prompted comparisons to slavery in the South. As Mae Ngai states, "By 1853 the comparison of Chinese immigration to the 'Negro slave trade' and the charge that Asiatics degraded the standard of American labor were staples of political rhetoric in the California legislature" ("Chinese" 1097). This comparison was made at the same time as when minstrel songs were getting rewritten in California to reflect the white miners' experiences. In one version of the aforementioned "Oh! Susanna," the lyrics were changed to "I came from Salem City / With my washbowl on my knee, / I'm going to California, / The gold-dust for to see" (History of Music Project, *San Francisco* 16). The popular "Camptown Races" became "Sacramento," with lyrics reflecting the title change (20). In these songs, references to Black people became fewer and were replaced with references to the Chinese. Whereas the singer of all minstrel songs were supposed to be "Black," with the assumption that white people were performing Blackness, the mining songs in California based on such songs had first-person narrators who were miners themselves. In "Prospecting Dream," set to the tune of "Oh! Susanna," the narrator sings, "Oh what a miner, / what a miner was I," and also sings, "John Chinaman he bought me out, / and pungled down the dust" (52). "The Happy Miner," set to the tune of the minstrel song "Sally Is de Gal for Me," included the lyrics, "I'm a happy miner," "but when it comes to China pay / I cannot stand the press" (54, 55). The contrast between the "I" in the mining songs and the "I" in the minstrel songs is evident in the lyrics for the original "Sally Is de Gal for Me." The narrator of that song intones, "Last year I was twenty, / Ole master set me free, / And I'se got money a plenty, / And I'se going to hav a spree" (Buckley 70). If the antebellum minstrel form delegitimized Black freedom by relying on a "Black" caricature who was going to squander away his freedom—which was granted by his "ole master"—that form was jeopardized by the Chinese figure, who held an economic advantage over the white miner.

As seen in the songs of the 1850s, the Chinese worker was cast as a co-worker, although with a lower pay, and this possibility of a nonwhite worker's freedom was violently negated in other mining songs, as well as anti-Chinese laws, in California. In "Joaquin, the Horse-Thief," for instance, the narrator sings about the heroics of the Sonoran outlaw Joaquin Murietta, stating that he "killed a Chinaman and then stole his bacon" (History of Music Project, *San Francisco* 44).[12] Set to the music of the minstrel song "Now I Warn All You Darkies Not to Love Her," the song's fantasy of killing a Chinese worker and stealing his livelihood had a parallel in the legal sanctions against the Chinese in California. These sanctions included the Foreign Miners Tax Law (1850) and the prohibition against the Chinese to testify against white people in courts as a result of *People v. Hall* (1854), which involved the murder of a Chinese worker by a white man. Both the early mining songs and the anti-Chinese laws asserted and maintained the white supremacist racial logic of the U.S. empire.

The anxiety provoked by the presence of Chinese workers in California who were nonwhite and *not enslaved* can be seen in the early mining songs that both expressed such anxiety and alleviated it through violence, reminiscent of the violence against free "Black" figures in antebellum minstrel songs. The figurative violence in such songs, as well as the physical violence against actual Chinese and Black people, paled in comparison to the violence unleashed by emancipation. As the threat of Black freedom became a reality and slavery no longer ensured that not-Black meant being free, the rhetoric of the Black captive who willingly enjoyed enslavement was replaced with an emphasis on the criminality of the free individual, against whom violence was not just necessary but also deserved (Hartman, *Scenes* 6). The fundamental dominant white belief in the illegitimacy of Black freedom did not change during Reconstruction but was reworked through the discourse of Chinese unfreedom, as I discuss in Chapter 1.

The comparison between Chinese labor and slavery became a national question during Reconstruction, particularly after the completion of the first transcontinental railroad in 1869.[13] At that point, the Chinese workers who had been working on building the railroad in California and Western states were driven out violently from the West or recruited to work in other parts of the country.[14] If the popularity of antebellum blackface minstrelsy can be explained by Black activism and practices of freedom in the rise of wage labor capitalism, the violence against the Chinese during Reconstruction can be attributed to the fact that the Chinese were not the docile workers and ideal replacement for enslaved labor that they were hoped to be, particularly at a time when the definition of free (white) labor was in flux after emancipation. Prior to the completion of the transcontinental railroad, for example, the Chinese railroad workers successfully organized a strike in 1867. As recounted by Maxine Hong Kingston, the Chinese workers asserted themselves as "indispensable labor," as "free men, not coolies, calling for fair working conditions" (140).[15] The Chinese workers also migrated to other parts of the country. Most notably, in June 1870, a month before Congress struck down Sumner's proposal for race-neutral citizenship, seventy-five Chinese workers arrived in Massachusetts, in North Adams, from California to replace striking workers at a shoe factory.[16] This eastward migration of Chinese workers touched on and exacerbated the anxiety that Chinese labor was a threat to free white labor. As during slavery, blackface minstrelsy responded to this anxiety with songs depicting violence. In "The Chinese Shoemaker," a Chinese worker is depicted as getting murdered by his neighbors. "Ching Foo" likewise portrays a Chinese cobbler in North Adams who chokes on a piece of leather and dies (Newcomb 26, 46). Both written for the famed minstrel Billy West, the songs allayed the fear of Chinese labor as a national threat through the violence of the minstrel form.

The violence against the Chinese during Reconstruction, both figurative and physical, was justified under the logic that the Chinese workers were "slave" labor. The antebellum proslavery imagination that deemed that enslavement was the natural condition of Black captives was reworked during Reconstruction through the rationale that the Chinese as a race were naturally servile and exploitable. As seen in the congressional debate on the revision to the naturalization law in 1870, this rationale sustained the legitimacy of white supremacy. It also held up race as a justification for slavery's existence in the first place—because nonwhite people were naturally unfree and incapable of freedom. Under this logic, slavery could not be seen as the process of turning human beings into property. The argument for Chinese exclusion during Reconstruction, which the lawmakers understood as an argument against slavery, continued this misrecognition of slavery. And this misrecognition could not have been possible without the work of blackface minstrelsy.

Despite its significance, the Chinese question was largely absent from dominant historical discussions of Reconstruction in the nineteenth century and for much of the twentieth century. Complicating this absence, *The Peculiar Afterlife of Slavery* looks to the literature written during Reconstruction—specifically literature associated with the West. Just months after the 1870 naturalization law debate in Congress and the migration of Chinese workers from California to Massachusetts, Bret Harte published "Plain Language from Truthful James." As I discuss in Chapter 1, the poem became an instant hit and the most popular work of literature during Reconstruction. Almost immediately rechristened as the "Heathen Chinee" poem, "Plain Language" was indeed a cultural phenomenon. Many memorized the refrain of the poem, "For ways that are dark / And for tricks that are vain, / The heathen Chinee is peculiar," which quickly became recognizable as a catchphrase (Harte, "Plain" 287). The dominant reception of the poem seized on the notion that the "heathen Chinee" figure was fresh and new, particularly linked to Harte's imagination of the West in the *Overland Monthly*, published out of San Francisco. However, Ah Sin was not exactly an original character, and the gaze that viewed him was not new. What enabled Ah Sin to be seen as a comical figure, I argue, was Harte's use of the familiar figures and form of blackface minstrelsy that pervaded every popular cultural representation invoking humor in the United States in the nineteenth century. Specifically, in Harte's "heathen Chinee," one can see the influence of one of the most iconic and enduring minstrel figures from nineteenth-century U.S. popular culture, the character of Topsy from Harriet Beecher Stowe's *Uncle Tom's Cabin* (1852).

By linking together the most popular novel and poem of the nineteenth-century United States through the form of blackface minstrelsy, I show that popular literature about the West during Reconstruction, which was read at the time as having nothing to do with slavery, relied on representational practices from slavery and was devoured readily and with delight by audiences across the country. These literary narratives about the West were central to not just the construction of a national identity and culture but also the reconstruction of the meaning of race and slavery after the Civil War.

Demonstrating Heather Cox Richardson's claim that "the nation's strongest cultural images of the postwar years came from the West" (4), this literature was part of the racial project of Reconstruction and the failed promise of emancipation in the U.S. empire. The literature of the West, or the "frontier," which actively and purposely constructed the West as a decidedly "American" space, implicitly informs the understanding of U.S. history as a developmental narrative from East to West and as having little or nothing to do with slavery.[17] But in the representations of the Chinese worker in the imagined space of the West, we see remnants of slavery through modes of representing the racialized other in the form of blackface minstrelsy.

The instant and lasting popularity of Harte's "Plain Language" during and after Reconstruction cannot be overstated. Published at the height of congressional debates on the meaning of race, labor, and citizenship after emancipation, with lawmakers voting to make the Chinese question one of exclusion based on the logic that the Chinese were voluntarily slavelike and "heathen," Harte's "Plain Language" reinforced the connection between Chinese workers and slavery. Through the repeated labels of "heathen" and "peculiar," the latter calling to mind the nineteenth-century euphemism for slavery as the "peculiar institution," the poem displaced the word "peculiar" from the *institution* of slavery to the *figure* of the Chinese worker, furthering the racial logic of slavery that it was the Black people's own incapacity for freedom that justified their dehumanization and enslavement. In this way, Harte's poem, which set a crucial precedent for representations of the Chinese worker in U.S. literature and culture for much of the late nineteenth century and beyond, exemplifies the way in which literature set the stage for the disarticulation of the history of slavery and antiblackness from the minstrel form during and beyond Reconstruction. Toward the goal of making visible the process of that disarticulation, I show how antiblack racism was recalibrated, not dismantled, through the non-Black Chinese worker figure in U.S. literature after emancipation.

. . .

The Peculiar Afterlife of Slavery is divided into two parts, each examining literature from a key historical moment that crucially defined the meaning of race and slavery in the United States. The first is the Reconstruction period (1865–1877). The most popular literary writers during this time were associated with the West, and they all wrote about the Chinese. Because of this inclusion at a time of exclusion, these writers have been read as antiracist champions of the Chinese. Rather than read for their authorial intention, however, I argue for reading their representations in the context of antiblackness born out of slavery, as well as U.S. settler colonialism. The definition of the West as a "national" space happened through these writers' literary works about the West, and the equation of the "West" with "America" happened during Reconstruction.

In addition to Harte, the first part studies the early writings of Mark Twain and Ambrose Bierce, writers who also began their literary careers in California and remain the most celebrated and remembered from the Reconstruction period. Harte, Twain, Bierce, and other white writers, such as Joaquin Miller and Ina Coolbrith, called themselves the Bohemians and believed they were forming a new literary tradition in the constructed space of the U.S. frontier. Among these early Californian writers, Harte, Twain, and Bierce stand out in their employment of the figure of the Chinese worker as they transitioned from journalistic to literary writing, particularly in the genre of the short story. In a reflective essay written toward the end of his life on his role in the formation of the "American short story," Harte named Twain, Bierce, and especially himself as the "earliest pioneers of Californian humour" ("The Rise" 6). But Harte's effort to highlight their pioneering role notwithstanding, all three writers employed the minstrel form in one way or another in their representations of the Chinese worker. Crucial to note is that these writings did not initially include Black characters. In fact, even Twain experimented with Chinese fictional characters before creating his first fictional Black character. Harte, Twain, and Bierce signaled the "newness" of the U.S. West through their inclusion of the Chinese worker and exclusion of Black characters—reversing Wong's formulation of "black inclusion/Chinese exclusion" (Wong 3). Their writings featuring the Chinese worker show the indispensable role of minstrelsy in the construction of U.S. literature, as well as an inextricable link between that literature and empire in the creation of the West.

The focus on white canonical writers in the first part of the book is meant not to reinscribe their authority but to expose the embeddedness of minstrelsy and antiblackness in U.S. literature. The first part also provides the context for the second part, which examines the crucial period at the turn of the twentieth century when the end of Reconstruction was reflected in racial violence, lynchings, and sharecropping that reduced Black people's lives to a condition of "slavery under another name" (Du Bois, *Black Reconstruction* 322). The Supreme Court decision of *Plessy v. Ferguson* (1896), which constitutionally sanctioned segregation, inaugurated the long struggle for Black civil rights in the twentieth century. In popular culture, minstrel representations of overtly antiblack images and figures abounded and spread to vaudeville shows, joke books, and literary creations by white writers such as Joel Chandler Harris and Thomas Nelson Page, who wrote nostalgically about the Old South. Whereas the focus in the first part of the book is on how white writers engaged with the minstrel form, the second part examines how writers of color employed the minstrel form in the post-Reconstruction period. These writers, Sui Sin Far and Charles Chesnutt, who were mixed-race Chinese and Black respectively, would later be hailed as "pioneers" in Asian American and African American literatures.[18] My reading of the two writers engages with Julia Lee's astute claim that the "complex relationship that the nation imposed upon African Americans and Asians heavily informed the mutual cultural representations that African American and Asian American authors produced" (J. Lee 7). While Lee's work, as well as Helen Jun's observation that "the state's racial ideologies . . . differentially define[d] U.S. blacks and Asians along the axis of citizenship" (Jun 8), focuses on how Black and Asian authors represented race in relation to U.S. citizenship, I examine Sui Sin Far's and Chesnutt's "reciprocal representations" (J. Lee 5) through the minstrel form and the figure of the Chinese worker in order to tease out the knowledge that each author produced about race and slavery.

When we read the writings of Sui Sin Far and Charles Chesnutt through the category of slavery rather than citizenship, we can clearly see a divergence in the beginnings of Asian American and African American literatures. If the Afro-Asian analogy prevalent during the latter half of the nineteenth century reveals a historical convergence of the two racialized groups, the turn-of-the-century literary "reciprocal representations" by Sui Sin Far and Chesnutt indicate the difficulty of imagining an Afro-Asian unity on the basis of that historical convergence. Rather, they reveal what Grace Hong and Roderick Ferguson name as "strange affinities" of racialized groups whose "relationality is constantly shifting" despite their seeming historical similarities (18, 10). Sui Sin Far's invocation of slavery and blackface minstrelsy was more in line with that of the white authors discussed in the first part and was categorically different from Chesnutt's, even though she personally may have identified with Black authors. Such a reading of Sui Sin Far is not to vilify her but, as Daniel Kim instructs, "to engage directly with the specific form of cultural power [that she may have believed she was] appropriating through the act of writing literature" (xxiv). Through an engagement with the minstrel form, the critical reading practice that I call for throughout the book, informed by Lisa Lowe's notion of a "past conditional temporality" (175), can open up new historical possibilities. This temporality conceives of the past not as a fixed failure but "as a configuration of multiple contingent possibilities . . . that were vanquished by liberal political reason and its promises of freedom" (175). Both Sui Sin Far and Chesnutt, and indeed Harte, Twain, and Bierce, give us a glimpse of "connections that could have been, but were lost, and are thus, not yet" (174) through their writings. In making visible their different uses of minstrelsy, I highlight the different "not yets" in their writings, ultimately advocating for seeing the incommensurability of antiblackness and anti-Chinese racism. At stake here is recognizing the specificity of enduring antiblackness as a distinct cultural form produced by slavery. In other words, at stake is the question of how we choose to remember slavery in its ongoing afterlife. The figure of the Chinese worker in U.S. literature during and after Reconstruction both hides and makes visible the legacy of slavery and blackface minstrelsy. With the understanding that a literary reading practice can be a political project, the task for us, then, is to track that legacy, even in the unlikeliest of places.

PART ONE

"Earliest Pioneers" of White Literature of the West During Reconstruction

CHAPTER ONE

The "Heathen Chinee" and Topsy in Bret Harte's Narratives of the West

In 1869, as the discriminating founding editor of San Francisco's *Overland Monthly* who would reject Walt Whitman's "Passage to India" the following year, Bret Harte wrote a less than favorable review of Harriet Beecher Stowe's novel *Oldtown Folks* (1869), about life in a post–Revolutionary War New England village.[1] He specifically panned Stowe for featuring a stock "negro bondman" character, which he hoped "we shall lose, for obvious reasons," and which "Mrs. Stowe seems to find . . . difficult to keep out of her writing" (Harte, "Current" 390). He ultimately dismissed Stowe's novel and her characters as passé and formulaic and issued a warning to "Mrs. Stowe to consider whether we may not lose her with the rest" of her characters (390). Though Harte did not specify the "obvious reasons" behind his objection to Stowe's characterization of the "negro bondman," it is not difficult for the twenty-first-century reader to guess what they might have been. Described as the narrator's grandfather's "own negro," Cæsar, Stowe's Black character in *Oldtown Folks*, is emphatically jovial—"the most joyous creature on two feet" (48)—and depicted mostly in terms of his physicality and affect: "He could sing and fiddle, and dance the double-shuffle" (63). His joy sometimes makes him a "quivering mass of giggle" (63), but in contrast to his ample laughter, he does not speak a single word throughout the novel. He patently embodies a demeaned and dehumanized "happy slave" minstrel figure. In finding fault with this characterization, Harte was thus seemingly objecting to the antiblack delineation of a literary character that borrows from blackface minstrelsy. Or was he?

Less than one year after his review of Stowe's *Oldtown Folks*, Harte published in the *Overland Monthly* the poem "Plain Language from Truthful James," which made him a household name not just in California but all across the country. It is said that he wrote the poem, did not think much of it, and asked his friend Ambrose Bierce to publish it in the *San Francisco News Letter*, a weekly paper that Bierce edited (Merwin 51; Murdock 85). When Bierce insisted that the poem deserved the bigger venue of the *Overland*, Harte decided to publish it only when he had extra space he needed to fill in the September 1870 issue. This almost accidental origin story of "Plain Language" indicates that Harte did not anticipate the poem's epic success, that it would become "one of the most popular poems ever published" in the United States (Scharnhorst, "Ways" 377). Still, the poem employs the successful formula that had worked for Stowe in her best-selling novel *Uncle Tom's Cabin* (1852) and that she reused in *Oldtown Folks*. Specifically, it replicates the form of blackface minstrelsy in the racialization of a nonwhite character as a stock comic figure for white enjoyment, notably found in the character of Topsy and recycled as Cæsar in *Oldtown Folks*. "Plain Language" employs the same figuration for which Harte had panned Stowe; but in his poem, Topsy is given a new life, not in the "obviously" outdated figure of a "negro bondman" but in the postemancipation figure of a Chinese worker. Stowe was apparently not the only one who found the representational practice of blackface minstrelsy difficult to keep out of one's writing.

Whether or not Stowe and Harte intentionally employed the antiblack form of minstrelsy is beside the point here. Of greater import is that we see an indelible trace of it in both of their works, despite the fact that "Stowe herself almost certainly never saw a minstrel show" (Meer 23), and Harte had an explicit disdain for "people who are content to go night after night to the Minstrels and listen to the pointless repetition of an inferior quality of this humor" (Harte, *Writings* 20:127).[2] The appearance of minstrel figures in their writings, therefore, points to the way in which minstrelsy had become part of the everyday, inseparable from how Blackness was imagined and antiblackness was lived in the nineteenth-century United States. In criticizing Stowe, Harte was not calling for a dismantling of the minstrel form or antiblackness. The language of antiblackness had become so ingrained that it may not have registered as consciously racist, calling to mind what literary critic Eric Lott calls the "social unconscious" of blackface minstrelsy

(Lott, *Love* 40) and what sociologist Moon-Kie Jung calls the "racial uncon-scious" of white supremacy (Moon-Kie Jung, *Beneath* 104).[3] In transfiguring Topsy into a Chinese worker in California, then, Harte did not level the minstrel form. He revamped it, and in the process, foreclosed a potential for its demise and critique.

This chapter argues that one of the ways in which antiblackness lived on after slavery was through the minstrel form in Harte's fiction set in the West featuring the Chinese worker during Reconstruction. I begin by placing the immense popularity of Harte's "Plain Language," which coined the term "heathen Chinee," in the context of the changing definitions of the word "heathen" that centered on the Chinese labor question. To show that the most popular poem written during Reconstruction was refracted through the prism of minstrel tropes, I argue that the poem evokes Stowe's Topsy.[4] Both in the 1870s and subsequently, this has not been the dominant read-ing of Harte in general or of the poem in particular. Specifically in the field of Asian American literary studies, scholars have viewed the poem mostly as a testimony of nineteenth-century anti-Chinese politics, and the general tendency has been not to engage with the poem at all.[5] Outside of Asian American literary studies, since the time of its publication, scholarship on the poem has focused on the question of whether the poem promotes, or is a biting sarcasm against, anti-Chinese racism.[6] In distinction, I read Harte's fictional writings featuring the Chinese worker through the lens of black-face minstrelsy and antiblackness as a cultural form, exposing the form in outwardly unlikely places in U.S. literature, such as the most famous anti-slavery novel written in the United States and in the figure of the Chinese worker in Harte's fictions about the West.

By showing that the figure of the Chinese worker and the minstrel form were central to the project of reconstructing the nation after the Civil War, I argue that comparative racializations motivated by antiblackness and U.S. colonialism were at the heart of the Chinese question. Harte's West and the Chinese worker were not separate from Reconstruction and representations of Blackness in the history of slavery, colonialism, and racial violence in the United States. The figure of the Chinese worker must therefore be read as signifying not only Chineseness but also Blackness during Reconstruc-tion. Ultimately, this chapter reads Harte's writings as part of a vital archive that helped to construct a national identity and culture and reconstruct the meaning of race and slavery after the Civil War. A generative figure, the

Chinese worker must be accounted for in recent studies of Reconstruction that emphasize the significance of the West as well as in studies of Western literature.[7] Harte's stories are typically read only as the genesis of the Western genre and "local color" regionalism and realism, but the nationwide fame of "Plain Language" not only broadens the scope within which we should read his works but also demands that the geographical purview of Reconstruction be extended to the West.

History of the Heathen in Harte's "Heathen Chinee"

Featuring two white miners who try to cheat Ah Sin, a Chinese worker, in a game of euchre only to get cheated themselves, "Plain Language from Truthful James" quickly became better known as the "heathen Chinee" poem. The new name reflected the fact that the lines of the poem "for ways that are dark / And for tricks that are vain, / The heathen Chinee is peculiar" (287) were widely memorized. All across the country and even abroad, the poem was reprinted countless times, making Harte the most famous writer of his time and a national—and international—literary celebrity.[8] When a pirated chapbook appeared with illustrations within a few months, a throng of people was seen "swarming about a shop window" in New York trying to get a glimpse of the characters in the poem: Truthful James, Bill Nye, and, most of all, Ah Sin, the "heathen Chinee" (G. Stewart, *Bret Harte, Argonaut* 180; see also Scharnhorst, *Bret Harte: Opening* 55). President Ulysses S. Grant supposedly refrained from talking about the "Chinese question" in his message to Congress because "the poem had made the whole matter the occasion of hilarity" (G. Stewart, *Bret Harte, Argonaut* 180). Soon after the publications of multiple illustrated chapbooks, the poem was set to music and reprinted many times as a songbook, making its varied ways into popular culture.[9] Through all these influences, "Plain Language" quickly became "one of the most popular poems ever published" (Scharnhorst, "Ways" 377), one that was "read by everybody and quoted by everybody until it became as trite as the most familiar quotation from Shakespeare" ("Bret Harte" 4).

The immense popularity of Harte's poem resulted in the wide adoption of the "heathen Chinee" in the U.S. lexicon. The label was understood not as an epithet but a factual description of a new presence of the Chinese in the West. Offering an explanation for the poem's fame, the influential

Springfield *Republican* stated that the success was partly because of the "temporary excitement of the public about the Chinese question," in addition to the poem's humor (qtd. in "Bret Harte's Books"). However, this characterization of the Chinese question as a "temporary excitement" relies on the faulty assumption that the Chinese were a new presence in the United States in 1870 and that the figure of the "heathen Chinee" reflected that newness.

The racialized category of "heathen" was not new nor was it always associated with the Chinese. Rather, it was as old as imperial conquest and slavery in the United States. As historian Sylvester Johnson writes, "The heathen as a social construct . . . was symbolically associated with Native Americans and Negroes" (12). In particular, Johnson specifies a connection between the justification of slavery and the category of "heathen," as "the public meaning of 'Negro' and 'Africa' were finely wedded to 'backward,' 'uncivilized,' and 'heathen'" (24). In the U.S. antebellum racial discourse, then, *heathen* was mostly associated with Blackness.

The meaning of the term *heathen* changed during Reconstruction, particularly owing to the racial politics in California. In a study of how various ethnic groups were racialized in California according their purported ability to assimilate and become "American," Joshua Paddison argues that religion was central to the definition of U.S. citizenship during Reconstruction. Subscription to Christianity demarcated a distinction between Christians and non-Christians. Black people, Mexican Americans, and Irish immigrants were seen as belonging in the Christian group. The Chinese and the Native population in California, derogatorily labeled as "Digger" Indians, were seen as belonging in the non-Christian group. With this demarcation, the designation of "heathen" no longer applied to Black people but to those in the non-Christian group. As Paddison writes, the racial discourse during Reconstruction deemed that "it was not 'blackness' but 'heathenism' that rendered a man unfit for suffrage, opening the door for generally Christianized African American men to become full citizens while continuing to shut out Indian and Chinese men" (12), who were seen as problems in California.

Black people also actively participated in the disaggregation of "Black" and "heathen" in the racial discourse during Reconstruction. As scholars such as Helen Jun and Dana Johnsen have shown, Black activists sought citizenship through a disidentification from the heathen category, particularly in Black newspapers in San Francisco (see also Shankman). The process of disidentification involved identifying non-Black racialized groups as "heathens," even prior to Reconstruction. In 1862, a writer in the *Pacific Appeal* downplayed the legal restrictions for Chinese and Native peoples from testifying in court by stating that they do not understand the U.S. legal institutions anyway, "they being heathens," unlike "the Negro [who] is a Christian" and feels "awe and reverence for the sanctity of an oath" (Jun 25). During Reconstruction, as the Chinese question was in the national spotlight, the word *heathen* was associated almost exclusively with the Chinese, though it was still sometimes associated with Native peoples. Black activists specifically underscored such a link between the Chinese and heathenism.[10] For instance, Philip Alexander Bell, the founding editor of the *Elevator* in San Francisco and former editor of the *Pacific Appeal*, claimed that the Chinese were "unacquainted with our system of government, adhering to their own habits and customs, and of heathen or idolatrous faith" (Johnsen 61), using the rhetoric that the Chinese were different from the Black and white "us."

This history of Black invocation of Chinese heathenism during Reconstruction is important because of its crucial difference from the dominant white practice, which linked heathenism to slavery as a justification for exclusion. The latter practice can be seen in the congressional debate on the change to the naturalization law, which took place just months before Harte's "Plain Language" was published. When the Radical Republican senator Charles Sumner proposed to revise the wording of the naturalization law to make it race-neutral, many balked in belief that it would open the floodgate for the Chinese to become U.S. citizens. The category of "heathen" was deployed as a synonym for the word "slave" as well as a marker of religious difference in the argument that the Chinese were unassimilable and could never become American. In one of his many vitriolic speeches opposing Sumner's proposal, William Stewart, a Republican senator from Nevada, branded the Chinese as being incapable of freedom because of their intrinsic "heathen faith" to their "pagan masters"; as such, he proclaimed that his "real objection [was] to naturalizing men . . . who are slaves" (*Congressional Globe* 1870, 5125).

The linking of "heathen" and "slave" in the racialization of the Chinese worker during Reconstruction was possible because of not only the former's association with the transatlantic slavery prior to the Civil War but also the existing discourse on Chinese workers as "coolies." As Moon-Ho Jung argues, the racialized Chinese coolie was a "liminal subject," "a slippery and disruptive creation between and beyond slavery and freedom, black and white" (5, 38). The debate about whether or not coolies were slaves or free workers was not only limited to Reconstruction and the United States but also, as Jung and other scholars have shown, located in the transatlantic slave trade (see Wong; Lowe; Yun). Thus, the congressional debate on Chinese coolies as heathens should be read as a discourse on slavery that reveals how lawmakers understood the institution. In declaring that the Chinese were slaves and calling for their exclusion, Congress was not denouncing the antiblack racial logic of slavery. Relying on the notion that the category of *coolie* was inherently unfree and synonymous with *slave*, the argument for the exclusion of Chinese workers replicated the logic that *slave* was a natural nonwhite, non-Christian condition that rendered one unfit for political participation in the state, reminiscent of the antebellum proslavery arguments that "Black oppression was the result of 'slavishness' rather than slavery" (Roediger, *Wages* 35). As shown by Edlie Wong, Reconstruction's "dialectical configuration of black inclusion/Chinese exclusion" did not mean that the arguments for Black inclusion razed the antiblack racial logic of slavery (3).

In addition, the common practice of labeling Chinese workers as "cheap labor" had the effect of reducing the slave to a commensurable form of "cheap labor." California Democrat James Johnson stated in May 1870 that "Chinese labor is much more degraded than our slave labor was; the laborer is a more degraded being and his labor is cheaper" (*Congressional Globe* 1870, 3879). The assertion that Chinese labor was cheaper points to what is at stake in the fallacy of the "Afro-Asian analogy" (Lye, "Afro-Asian" 1735). Analogizing the Chinese worker to the enslaved not only justified Chinese exclusion but also suggested that the Black captive was a worker who labored for cheap. However, "representing the slave through the figure of the worker (albeit unwaged and unfree)," as Saidiya Hartman argues, "obscures as much as it reveals, making it difficult to distinguish the constitutive elements of slavery as a mode of power, violence, dispossession and accumulation" ("Belly" 166). As Orlando Patterson, to whose work Hartman alludes, notes, "There is nothing in the nature of slavery which requires that the slave be a worker. Worker qua worker has no intrinsic relation to slave qua slave" (*Slavery and Social Death* 99). While enslaved people could be and, under racial capitalism, were intensively used for labor, their abject condition did not derive from their status as labor. As Moon-Kie Jung writes,

"The enslaved worked, but they were not workers" ("Enslaved" 161). The characterization of enslaved people as workers not only obfuscated their former abject condition and the violence of slavery. Through the label of "cheap labor," it also justified that violence by citing the "blameworthiness of the freed [Black] individual" during Reconstruction (Hartman, *Scenes* 6), in what might be understood as a moment of conjoined "state violence and social emancipation" that Chandan Reddy characterizes as "freedom with violence" (37). The racialized culpability of the "freed individual" was extended partly through the characterization of Chinese workers as cheap, "slave" labor. As a carry-over from slavery that ascribed agency to the enslaved, this redefinition of slavery must be noted as a part of the failure and violence of Reconstruction.

With its repeated phrase, "The heathen Chinee is peculiar," invocative of the nineteenth-century euphemism for slavery as a "peculiar institution," and the assertion, "We are ruined by Chinese cheap labor," Harte's poem provided the "plain language" through which the link could be maintained. The concluding lines of the poem, "The heathen Chinee is peculiar,— / Which the same I am free to maintain," contrast the narrator's "free" status with the "peculiar" one of the "heathen Chinee," finalizing the *un*freedom of the Chinese worker as a "plain" fact (Harte, "Plain" 288). Just four months after the poem's publication, in January 1871, a Democrat named William Mungen from Ohio employed the poem's language during a congressional debate. He referred to the Chinese multiple times as "heathen Chinee" and echoed lines resembling the poem's, such as "here I may remark" and "allow me to say in plain words," to claim that Chinese workers were "cheap labor" and "in fact, slaves, although, perhaps, voluntarily assuming the position" (*Congressional Globe* 1871, 352, 354, 355, 359). He added, "This plea of cheap labor was the foundation stone of African slavery, as it is of coolie importation and slavery now" (355). Demonstrative of the characterization of the racialized Chinese coolie as a "liminal" figure (Moon-Ho Jung, *Coolies* 5), the "coolie importation" in Mungen's statement provided a bridge between "African slavery" and "slavery now." While Harte did not single-handedly influence lawmakers such as Mungen, the language of his poem effectively supplemented the anti-Chinese rhetoric during Reconstruction that equated slavery—African or otherwise—with a system of cheap labor.

While the label of "heathen Chinee" was buttressed by the discourse of coolies, its distinct association with the American *heathen* from the "peculiar institution" of U.S. racial slavery made the category different. The transnational category of the *coolie* was never a Black figure in the way that the *heathen* was. Therefore, by studying how the latter term became inseparable from the Chinese and disconnected from Blackness, we can see the specificity of antiblackness in the United States, as the "heathen Chinee" powerfully performed the work of erasing the history of antiblackness and justifying slavery using the term. Prior to 1870, not one of the many associations linking the Chinese to "heathens" used the characterization of "heathen Chinee," suggesting that the label was originated by Harte in his poem. After 1870, "heathen Chinee" got incorporated seamlessly into the U.S. lexicon across racial lines, often without any reference to Harte's poem. In 1873, for example, the aforementioned Black activist Bell complained that "even the heathen 'Chinee' can . . . get into some business, while our people are the only class that do not develope [*sic*] their business capacity" (Johnsen 67). Illustrated here is that by 1873, the label of "heathen Chinee" helped to dissociate Blackness from the category of "heathen."

As a means of elucidating what is lost when we forget the history of the association of *heathen* with Blackness—which is to say, a history of antiblackness—I offer Harte's own use of the term in 1862, prior to the publication of "Plain Language."[11] In the California newspaper the *Golden Era*, Harte used the word to describe not a Chinese but a Black figure, specifically to express his distaste for forced conversion of non-Christians to Christianity. He wrote that he had no antipathy for the "Heathen in his unconverted state," particularly "compared with that dreadful Missionary." But he had no respect for "an imbecile black being" who claimed to be converted and groveled, "'Me so happy—bress de lor! send down him salvation berry quick,' in uncouth English," especially as Harte knew that "during this conversion his eyes were resting on the calves of that Missionary's legs with anthropophagous lust and longing" (*Writings* 20:124).

While the article in the *Golden Era* is mostly read as proof of Harte's antipathy for religious hypocrisy, it also evidences his customary technique of representing Blackness. As I explain below, Harte's characterization of a Black "heathen" speaking in "uncouth English" can be located in the white practice of representing Black speech on the minstrel stage. The practice of adding an "ee" sound at the end of a sentence, as in the long "ee" sound at the end of "Me so happy," was a common one in blackface minstrelsy. Employing the minstrel form, Harte's representation of the Black convert ascribes desire and agency to the racialized nonwhite other for the purpose of not only claiming knowledge about the lasciviousness and deviancy about that other but also putting into question the Black figure's capacity for freedom. In Harte's rendering, the Black heathen's conversion is not an exercise of free choice but an inauthentic performance that covers up the figure's natural cannibalistic desire that counters human rationality. By using minstrel speech to describe the character, Harte replicates the racial logic of the minstrel form that discounted Black freedom. Even in a satirical article that highlights the hypocrisy of white Christian missionaries, we see the antiblack racial logic of slavery at work. This racial logic cannot be wholly attributed to Harte's personal antiblack racism. Because he was a staunch Republican during the Civil War and a close friend of Thomas Starr King—a revered Unitarian minister and orator who is credited with keeping California in the Union prior to the war—Harte is often included in a "committed group of whites [who] opposed slavery" (Broussard). But in his representational strategies involving racialized others, specifically Black figures, we see an inability to represent them as anyone other than the white-mediated stereotype of the treacherous "me so happy" heathen.[12] As such, the antiblackness that we see in the *Golden Era* article reveals more than just Harte's individual racism; it also reveals the embedded antiblackness in the representational practice of depicting Black people as heathens.

When we ignore this fact, we miss the opportunity to see the racial logic of antiblackness undergirding the minstrel form in Harte's *Golden Era* article as well as "Plain Language." In the latter, Harte coupled the word *heathen* with the Chinese, and he also used the minstrel form of adding the long "ee" in the identification of the Chinese as "Chin*ee*." An even more obvious parallel between Harte's representation of the Chinese and the minstrel form can be seen in the first appearance of a Chinese character's speech in Harte's short stories, which happened in "The Iliad of Sandy Bar" (1870). In the story, a nameless Chinese worker says, "Me choppee wood, me no fightee" ("Iliad" 479), resembling the "Me so happy" speech discussed above. In noting such parallels, we can track the antiblack racial logic from slavery in the course of the Black "heathen" getting rewritten as the "heathen Chinee." As I show, Harte's borrowing from minstrelsy to construct the "heathen Chinee" reflects one of the ways in which the history of antiblackness was obfuscated after emancipation, in politics and especially in culture, specifically through literature. To further elaborate this process of obfuscation, I turn to the close resemblance between Ah Sin the "heathen Chinee" and Topsy as a minstrel figure from *Uncle Tom's Cabin*.

Ah Sin and Topsy

In Harte's "Plain Language," the racialized heathen makes the jump from the Black enslaved figure to the Chinese laborer most notably in the resemblance between the characters of Stowe's Topsy and Harte's Ah Sin. The similarity between Topsy and Ah Sin begins with each being identified with the word "heathen" to connote an otherness. In a description of Topsy, Stowe writes that there was "something odd and goblin-like about her appearance,—something, as Miss Ophelia afterward said, 'so *heathenish*'" (*Uncle* 310; emphasis added). Topsy's "heathenish" appearance is coupled with the repeated use of the word "odd," as her face is said to have "an odd mixture of shrewdness and cunning, over which was oddly drawn, like a kind of veil, an expression of the most doleful gravity and solemnity" (249). Until Topsy's conversion that saves her "heathen soul" (368), effected through the Christlike death of Eva, Ophelia cannot see past the oddness that she considers to be Topsy's unassimilable otherness, encapsulated by the word *heathenish*, that would later become synonymous with the Chinese.

The label of *heathen* tying Ah Sin and Topsy together provides an explanation for the former's name and the latter's claim to wickedness. As "Truthful James," the narrator of "Plain Language," states of the "heathen Chinee":

> Ah Sin was his name;
> And I shall not deny,
> In regard to the same,
> What that name might imply;
> But his smile it was pensive and childlike,
> As I frequent remarked to Bill Nye. (Harte, "Plain" 287)

James's nudge to the reader to guess "what that name might imply" suggests that "Ah Sin" could be read as "a sin" or "I sin."[13] Yet, despite this name, James states that Ah Sin had a "pensive and childlike" smile. This childlike Chinese male worker character, whose name is an admission of sinfulness if not sinfulness itself, bears a resemblance to Topsy, who states multiple times in *Uncle Tom's Cabin*, "I's wicked,—I is. I's mighty wicked," and "I's so wicked!" (318, 324). Topsy's self-proclaimed wickedness became a popular catchphrase, and following the publication of the novel, it was featured in many minstrel songs.

Even before such songs in which she sings proudly about her sins, however, Topsy is already a minstrel figure in Stowe's novel. Purchased for Ophelia by her brother Augustine, Topsy is dehumanized as a commodity and an object of entertainment. The introduction of Topsy in which she is described in a long, unbroken sentence of sheer performance as a "thing," makes that point clear:

> The black, glassy eyes glittered with a kind of wicked drollery, and the thing struck up, in a clear shrill voice, an odd negro melody, to which she kept time with her hands and feet, spinning round, clapping her hands, knocking her knees together, in a wild, fantastic sort of time, and producing in her throat all those odd guttural sounds which distinguish the native music of her race; and finally, turning a summerset or two, and giving a prolonged closing note, as odd and unearthly as that of a steam-whistle, she came suddenly down on the carpet, and stood with her hands folded, and a most sanctimonious expression of meekness and solemnity over her face, only broken by the cunning glances which she shot askance from the corners of her eyes. (310)

In this description, Topsy is not only performing as a minstrel figure through song and dance. Her very being is also a performance, as her "cunning glances" betray her "sanctimonious expression of meekness and solemnity." This description of Topsy as a performative minstrel figure discloses a different kind of horror of slavery than the welts on Topsy's back, seen later in the chapter about her. The limited agency Topsy is imbued with—"wicked drollery," "sanctimonious expression of meekness," "cunning glances"—reveals what Hartman calls the "terror of the mundane and quotidian" (*Scenes* 4), in which the enslaved is made to perform complicity and even enjoyment in the very ordinariness of the system of enslavement. In such technology of power, agency gets represented as duplicity, which becomes culpability. In Topsy's case, if she is dehumanized as a "thing" without agency meant solely for white people's entertainment, she is also humanized through her duplicity and "cunning glances." Her faked innocence is what humanizes her, which paradoxically negates her subject position as a child. And it is this humanity that makes Topsy effective as a figure of humor—one preferable to and more popular than Topsy as a visibly tortured body. In fact, Topsy was the reason that, as Sarah Meer writes, the early reviews of Stowe's novel highlighted the "comic aspects of the novel," focusing on the "humor in the book" as well as the sentimental aspects (Meer 21). Topsy was widely embraced as a humorous character, as a reviewer in the London *Times* found "a little black imp, by name TOPSY . . . [to be] one of the best sketches in the book" (Meer 21), and another reviewer, this time in New York, even went as far as to say, "One Topsy is worth a dozen little Evas" (Briggs 101). This impish figure is one that we see a trace of in Ah Sin, with his childlike smile and feigned ignorance, or innocence, of a game that he says "he did not understand" (Harte "Plain" 287, 288).

The introduction of Topsy as a thing that performs, which does not include any words that she speaks, reminiscent of Cæsar's characterization in *Oldtown Folks*, shows that her presence in the scene is not textual but gestural. By extension, the glimpses of Topsy that we see in Ah Sin are through a performative gesture of duplicity rather than an explicit invocation. We might think of Topsy's figuration through performance, then, as a "repertoire," or as a "set of practices such as walking, talking, laughing, and crying," per Robin Bernstein's definition (14).[14] Whereas Bernstein employs the concept of repertoire to describe Stowe's *Uncle Tom's Cabin* and its cultural significance in the nineteenth-century United States in order to show that it was always more than just a novel or even a phenomenon, I argue that Topsy's character in Stowe's novel reveals the way in which *blackface minstrelsy* was a repertoire, one that "shaped performances in everyday life" and formed a "state of vision, of feeling, and of consciousness" (Bernstein 14). That is, it was because of the ways in which minstrelsy was becoming a repertoire in the first half of the nineteenth century that *Uncle Tom's Cabin* became a repertoire in the latter half. This addendum to Bernstein's argument names blackface minstrelsy as not only the originating gestural form but also one that naturalized slavery by rendering conditions of captivity and ownership seemingly natural and normal. More than the rise in abolitionism, the prevalence of the minstrel form may have been a factor in the fanatical reception of *Uncle Tom's Cabin* that made the novel the best-selling book after the Bible in the nineteenth-century United States.

The immediate success of Stowe's novel produced a global phenomenon and a mania. In the United States, the novel was adapted and rewritten in various forms, such as popular songs, but the most enduring and substantial adaptation was on stage, particularly via blackface minstrel performances. After the Civil War, these theatrical adaptations of *Uncle Tom's Cabin*—of which there were many—experienced a powerful revival. As J. Frank Davis wrote in 1925, "In America to-day are vast numbers of middle-aged men and women who remember that 'Uncle Tom' was the first theatrical performance they ever saw" (350). The play, which came to be known simply as a "Tom Show," "travelled from the greatest theatres in the country to the shabbiest little tents on the tank circuits so small that they possessed no town halls" (360). And in the multiple theatrical adaptations, even among the most "dignified," the scene that was never left out was "Topsy's 'Golly I'se so wicked' confession," most likely with song and dance (352). As such, the glimmer of Topsy that we see in Ah Sin is not just the Topsy from the novel but also the antebellum minstrel performances of Topsy as well as the postbellum revival of the Tom Shows. In the later adaptations, the abolitionist spirit of Stowe's novel could hardly be detected (Davis 360). As a connecting link between slavery and post-slavery, minstrelsy was a crucial part of "the forces of reconciliation [that] overwhelmed the emancipationist vision in the national culture" after the Civil War (Blight 2), as white audiences in the North and South could unite around the humor offered through minstrel figures such as Topsy. In the humorous representations of the character, Topsy was never performed as a child—a little girl—who was born into the violence of slavery, and that violence was further erased by the process of separating Topsy from childhood and girlhood.

The popularity of Harte's "Plain Language" verging on hysteria might be explained by the influence of the gestural form of blackface minstrelsy present in Stowe's novel and elsewhere in popular culture, particularly through the character of Topsy. In the construction of Ah Sin, the "heathen Chinee," Harte replicates the humor and the duplicity embodied by Topsy as a minstrel figure who obfuscates the history of slavery. That is, Harte's poem evokes Topsy only as a humorous figure and not a character who is enslaved. By transforming Topsy's character, a child born into captivity, into Ah Sin, a grown man who is *not* enslaved, Harte's poem further separates the history of slavery as a system of violence and dehumanization from the minstrel form. Viewed at the height of Reconstruction without the system of slavery in place, the duplicity of a racialized nonwhite character was read as culpability, and the violence of slavery got rerouted as appropriate violence toward non-white people, whose actions could be read as challenging white supremacy.

Moreover, the transformation of Topsy into Ah Sin echoes the racial logic of Henry George, one of the most rampant anti-Chinese writers during and after Reconstruction, that Chinese workers needed to be excluded because unlike the Black worker who was like "an ignorant but docile child," the Chinese worker was like "a grown man, sharp but narrow minded, opinionated and set in character" ("Chinese Question" 2).[15] Thus a more threatening figure, and imbued with Topsy's duplicity before her conversion to Christianity, Ah Sin's character faces implied violence at the end of the poem for cheating the white characters before they can cheat him, as one of the white characters is said to have "went for that heathen Chinee" (Harte, "Plain" 288). In the many pirated illustrated versions of the poem that circulated immediately after the original publication, the implied violence was made into a full spectacle, as seen in Joseph Hull's illustration suggesting a festive atmosphere of white enjoyment (see Figure 1.1).[16] Hull's illustration

FIGURE 1.1 Illustration of violence against Ah Sin, by Joseph Hull. From F. Bret Harte, *The Heathen Chinee* (Chicago: Western News, 1870). Courtesy of the Clifton Waller Barrett Library of American Literature, Special Collections, University of Virginia.

turned the two white characters in the poem into a mob that joyfully terrorizes Ah Sin. This multiplication of whiteness evinces the original minstrel form's extension of enjoyment of Black captivity to all white people. Hull's drawing anticipates gleeful white crowds gathered at lynchings in the latter nineteenth century, demonstrating the unleashing of violence directed at racialized freedom during and after Reconstruction. While Harte would not have endorsed such violence against the Chinese or Black people in real life, the narrator of "Plain Language"—"Truthful James"—justifies the white characters' violence by citing the evidence of Ah Sin's cheating and underscoring Ah Sin's agency and blameworthiness. The figurative violence of the minstrel form in Harte's poem operated alongside the physical violence against the Chinese among increased calls for their exclusion, as well as rising violence against Black people after emancipation.[17]

Antiblackness in Harte's Stories in the Overland Monthly

In his journalistic writings immediately after the Civil War, Harte criticized those who held a "sentiment that excluded the negro or Chinese" (Harte, *Bret Harte's California* 52), implying that anti-Chinese racism was a remnant of antiblack racism. He specifically maligned the Irish immigrants in California in 1866 for viewing the Chinese "with a jealousy and malevolence only equal to their old intolerance of the negro" and "put[ting] the Mongolians on the level of the African, and abus[ing] them on theological grounds" (114). His appellation of "heathen Chinee" in "Plain Language from Truthful James" was therefore meant to satirize such racism, though the epithet ended up giving life and vocabulary to the anti-Chinese movement. What Harte failed to realize is that the physical exclusion of and violence against the Chinese and Black people were tied to a deeply embedded representational practice of race from slavery, which he himself employed. Even before "Plain Language," Harte's stories written for the *Overland Monthly* impart a gestural presence of minstrelsy and the form of antiblackness that together exhibit traces of the white supremacist racial logic of slavery. These traces can be seen in "The Outcasts of Poker Flat," published in the *Overland Monthly* in January 1869. Set in 1850, the story is about a group of outcasts—who are all white—exiled from a town called Poker Flat. In it, Harte expands on John Oakhurst, one of the minor characters from his first acclaimed short story, "The Luck of Roaring Camp" (1868). A gambler with a conscience and penchant for justice, Oakhurst is a stoic, imperturbable Western hero. As fresh and endemic to the West as characters such as Oakhurst were thought to be, they betray the way in which antiblackness of slavery structured the everyday speech in the literary imagination. The story describes Oakhurst as having returned the money to a younger white man after winning it all from him, "and so made a devoted slave of Tom Simson" (Harte, "Outcasts" 43). This "slave" named Tom plays music to pass the time while being snowed in and is accompanied by his fiancée who plays the "bones" (46), a musical instrument used in blackface minstrel performances.

The gestural presence of blackface minstrelsy in "The Outcasts" works hand in glove with covert antiblackness in the story, seen when the Western hero Oakhurst tells Simson, "when a man gets a streak of luck—nigger luck—he don't get tired" (45). The *Oxford English Dictionary* (*OED*) and the *Dictionary of American Regional English* (*DARE*) both indicate that the first time "nigger luck" appeared in print was in Rodney Glisan's memoir, *Journal of Army Life*. Glisan's book describes his nine-year military experience in the Pacific Northwest beginning in 1850, which coincided with the Washington and Oregon territorial Indian wars from 1855 to 1858. In a chapter that takes place in 1851, Glisan describes a lieutenant from Kentucky who is competitive about hunting and gets envious of "my nigger-luck, as he is pleased to term it" (91). The *OED* and *DARE* cite this 1851 entry as the first recorded use of the term. However, the two dictionaries also designate correctly that Glisan's book was not published until 1874. Therefore, "The Outcasts," which the *DARE* lists as second to *Journal of Army Life*, may actually be the first text to have used the antiblack slang in print. But more important than the publication chronology are the similarities in Harte's and Glisan's writings. Though Harte's is a work of fiction, both take place in the early 1850s and in spaces that are being actively contested as American, specifically the U.S. West under U.S. settler colonialism. In Glisan's book, the term takes on a proprietary ownership and the colonialist right to name, as Glisan and the young lieutenant are in a battle with "lurking savages" (91). The term likewise functions as a colonizing gesture in Harte's story, as Oakhurst affirms his unquestioned authority over his "devoted slave" in Tom Simson. Particularly when read alongside the "bones" musical instrument, the term "nigger-luck" demonstrates the way in which antiblackness was a part of the everyday repertoire for Harte's white characters in the U.S. empire, including the Western hero.

To reiterate, the argument here is not that Harte intentionally employed antiblackness in constructing John Oakhurst's character in "The Outcasts of Poker Flat." Rather, the traces of antiblack literary figures and form from slavery seen in Harte bring to light the racial unconscious of blackface minstrelsy and white supremacy, which reveals how integral antiblackness was to U.S. literature and culture, particularly in the moment of nation-building cum empire-building during Reconstruction and the popularization of the stories about the West. For example, in "Brown of Calaveras," a story published in the *Overland Monthly* in March 1870, Harte introduced another recurrent Western hero in the name of Jack Hamlin. While riding in the woods alone, Hamlin begins singing, and "the subject of his song was some sentimental lunacy borrowed from the Negro minstrels" (Harte, "Brown" 285). The story does not state that Hamlin is singing a minstrel song. Rather, the song he sings is described as "borrowed from the Negro minstrels," and perhaps not even recognized by Hamlin as such. The song serves no purpose in the main plot of the story, yet Hamlin's mindless action acutely displays what counts as everyday performance, what Ju Yon Kim describes as the "racial mundane" (8). This fact, that the pioneering figures of the white Western hero in John Oakhurst and Jack Hamlin are so intertwined with antiblackness, is never noted in readings of Harte's stories, which shows the degree to which antiblackness continues to be a part of the everyday repertoire through the reading practice of U.S. literature.

Reconstructing Ah Sin: The "Heathen Chinee" and the "American" Short Story Form

In addition to "The Outcasts of the Poker Flat," Harte's stories in the *Overland Monthly*, such as "The Luck of the Roaring Camp" and "Tennessee's Partner" (1869), had already put Harte and the magazine on the cultural map in the United States, but that early acclaim was nothing compared to what came after "Plain Language from Truthful James." Most notably, the poem bought Harte a ticket to the East to write for the *Atlantic Monthly*, the most prestigious literary magazine in the country at the time. The $10,000 contract to write exclusively for the *Atlantic* for one year made

Harte the highest-paid writer in the United States to date, and Harte clearly understood the source of his newfound wealth. In the four issues of the *Overland Monthly* that he edited before his departure for the East in 1871, Harte contributed two short stories—"The Iliad of Sandy Bar" (1870) and "The Christmas Gift That Came to Rupert" (1871)—which did not include his stock white Western heroes such as John Oakhurst or Jack Hamlin but instead each featured a Chinese character, albeit a minor one, described using the word "heathen" (Harte, "Iliad," 479; "Christmas" 89). In these two stories, we can see Harte experimenting with how to incorporate the successful "heathen Chinee" figure into the Western short story form, which he considered uniquely American and claimed to have founded ("Rise" 1). In both cases, the worker figure, along with the minstrel form, performs the labor of providing the backdrop for the main narrative. The two stories prove to be a testing ground for "Wan Lee, the Pagan," the first of Harte's short stories titled after a Chinese character who is also a protagonist, in which Harte tries his hand at creating a Chinese Western hero. The question of how Harte employs the minstrel form in the three stories, all set in California, is the focus of the following discussion.

"THE ILIAD OF SANDY BAR" (1870)

The first Chinese worker appears in "The Iliad of Sandy Bar," published in November 1870, two months after the publication of "Plain Language." Though he is not "*the* first Chinese character in American fiction" in prose, as Axel Nissen claims (111; emphasis in original), the character's unprecedented appearance in a short story in the two-year history of the *Overland Monthly*, particularly following the success of Harte's most famous poem, warrants our close look.[18] "The Iliad of Sandy Bar," like "The Luck of Roaring Camp" and "Tennessee's Partner," blends together humor and pathos to recount the mostly homosocial space of the frontier in a mining town in California.[19] In the story, two partners, Scott and York, who used to be "singularly devoted to each other," get into a big fight that becomes a life-long feud (479). They do not reveal the source of their discord to anyone, but "a serious Chinaman, cutting wood before [their] cabin, had witnessed part of the quarrel" (479). In contrast to the "heathen Chinee" Ah Sin, an international figure of hilarity, the nameless Chinese worker in "The Iliad" is repeatedly described as "serious," "stolid, indifferent, and reticent" (479).

Initially reminiscent of Herman Melville's recalcitrant Bartleby, the Chinese worker merely repeats, "Me choppee wood, me no fightee," to all the eager queries about what caused the quarrel (479).

The nameless Chinese worker's words are not at all like Bartleby's stoic phrase, "I'd prefer not to" (Melville 48), however. Despite the description of the nameless Chinese worker as serious, the character ends up being not too different from Ah Sin, as the words that he speaks—"Me choppee wood, me no fightee"—belie that seriousness. The practice of adding "ee" at the end of a word to describe "Chinese English" is usually believed to be applicable uniquely to the Chinese, but, as previously stated, it was also used to mock "Black" English in early minstrel songs. For example, in every one of the verses from the popular song from 1853 called "Sambo's 'Dress to He Bredren," also known as "Ching-a-Ring Chaw," "ee" or "e" was added to the end of certain words:

> No more wid black an brush, make boot an shoe to shin-e,
> But hab all good tings flush, an all ob dem sublim-e;

and

> Dar too, we sure to make our dortars de fine la-dee,
> An wen dey husban take, dey bove de common gra-dee.

The poem, about an enslaved Black man who dreams of taking a boat to Haiti to flee his bondage, also included this refrain:

> Chinger ring, ringer, ching, ching,
> Ho ah ding, ding, ah kum darkee;
> Chinger ring, ringer, ching, chaw,
> Ho ah ding, kum darkee.

The line "Chinger ring, ringer, ching, chaw," imitating a steamboat engine sound, was incorporated into other popular songs, including the "Oh, I'se So Wicked" song (1854) that was inspired by Stowe's Topsy, wherein Topsy sings, "Ching a ring a ring a ricked," with "ricked" rhyming with "wicked" (G. Howard). Here my argument expanding on Bernstein's claim that *Uncle Tom's Cabin* should be thought of as a repertoire applies as well. The reiteration of the minstrel song, "Sambo's 'Dress to He Bredren," as Topsy's song and the Chinese worker's dialogue in Harte's short story demonstrates the degree to which the *minstrel form*—not Stowe's novel or the performances of it—worked as a repertoire. Bernstein's definition of repertoire as that which is "in constant flux, always being re-made" (14) is particularly applicable here. Three years after Topsy's song, "Ching Ring Chaw" was easily adapted to make fun of "Chinese" English in an 1857 song called "A Chinaman's Tail" with the lines, "Ching ring wow, ricken chicken, a chew. Chinaman loves big bow wow and little puppies too" ("A Chinaman's" 66). In the 1870s, after the success of Harte's poem, the refrain appeared again in the song "Artful Chinee" by Frank Curtis, as a more faithful rendition of Topsy's song: "Chingaring chi, and chingaring chee, / Chingaring chi for the young Chinee" (Moon 42). As I discuss below, Harte would also take up the refrain, "Ching a ring a ring chaw," in his future representations of the Chinese.

The words of the nameless Chinese worker in "The Iliad" underscore the powerful pull of blackface minstrelsy in representations of the racialized other in the nineteenth century, even in literature that is not customarily read as having anything to do with minstrelsy and associated only with the West. Harte himself had a disdainful attitude toward the minstrel form even though his characters and stories are undeniably influenced by it. He characterized minstrel humor as "pointless" and "inferior" (Harte, *Writings* 20:127), but despite this class disdain, he was not free from the influence of minstrel shows, much as one of his most beloved characters, Jack Hamlin, who mindlessly sings a song "borrowed from the Negro minstrels," was not. Harte's application of the minstrel form for a non-Black character more effectively illustrates the power of that form—and indeed, its racial unconscious—than the obvious inclusion of a caricatured Black character, who is actually absent in all of Harte's short stories published in the *Overland Monthly*.

If *how* Harte represents the Chinese worker's words in "The Iliad" can be traced to the cultural imagination rooted in racial slavery, then *what* the worker is made to say bolsters that connection. Even though the Chinese worker figure has the potential to be a key character in the plot, he never actually occupies the role. Instead, the entire story depends on the Chinese worker's self-exclusion from the main plot through the words, "me no fightee," and his proclamation of his work *as* his identity: "Me choppee wood." Such a link between identity and work calls to mind how the category of the "heathen" in "Plain Language" and in larger U.S. culture justified Chinese exclusion and anti-Chinese violence by associating the word to cheap or enslaved labor. "The Iliad" highlights and extends that analogy. In the most vocal response to the Chinese worker's words, a character named Colonel Starbottle, a Southerner and a "Gentleman of the Old School" (481), yells, "And this yer's the cattle . . . that some thinks oughter be allowed to testify agin a White Man! Git—you *heathen*!" (479; emphasis added). Starbottle's remark about Chinese testimony is a clear reference to the 1854 *People v. Hall* ruling in California. The courts ruled that in accordance with the existing 1850 law, which stated that "no black or mulatto person, or Indian, shall be allowed to give evidence in favor of, or against a white man," the testimony of a Chinese witness was not valid. The ruling was justified using the logic that "Indians originally migrated from Asia, and so all Asians were conversely also Indian, and that, at any rate, 'Black' was a generic term encompassing all nonwhites, and thus included Chinese persons" (Haney López 51–52). Starbottle takes the racial logic of equating Black and Chinese one step further by coupling the nonhuman "cattle" with "heathen." This coupling, as well as his anti-Chinese politics in the West that erases the presence of the "Indian" in the 1850 law, exposes Starbottle's unstated antiblackness constitutive of chattel slavery in U.S. settler colonialism.

However, neither Starbottle's antiblackness nor his anti-Chineseness is critiqued in the story. Rather, Starbottle is given rein to shape the lives of the story's Chinese characters, as his dismissal of the single worker using the word "heathen" becomes a material reality for *all* the Chinese workers in the story, when "Scott . . . in conjunction with Colonel Starbottle, first organized that active opposition to the Chinamen which resulted in the driving off of York's Mongolian laborers" (481–82). Though the expulsion may be "dramatiz[ing] the social consequences of *People v. Hall*" (Hsu, *Sitting* 39), as Hsuan Hsu argues, and Starbottle's character may be Harte's way of saying that this is the kind of reader who would take his "Plain Language" literally, "The Iliad" is certainly not a scathing criticism of anti-Chinese politics. The workers themselves are not imagined as having any capability or desire to negate their ostensibly servile, passive positions. With the "driving off," we never hear from the nameless Chinese worker or any other Chinese worker again. Starbottle has the last word in the story of the Chinese workers in "The Iliad," since no one negates the use of the word "heathen" that justifies their disappearance.

Ultimately, the Chinese worker as a minstrel figure functions as a sideshow to the main story and the question of why Scott and York, the two partners, quarreled. The figure acts as a deferral of a punch line and is there-fore not privy to the story's resolution. After decades of estrangement, the partners Scott and York are reunited at Scott's deathbed. In this poignant scene full of pathos, Scott reflects on their quarrel and utters his last words: "Old man, that *was* too much saleratus in that bread!" (485; emphasis in original). These words are only heard by York, and so the joke—that the fight that drove them to nearly kill each other was over Scott's observa-tion that York had used too much baking soda in his bread—remains an inside one. By refusing to disclose what he knows, or through his inability to know to begin with, the Chinese worker maintains "The Iliad" as a tale of frontier homosocial domesticity and bond between two white men told with Harte's characteristically caustic humor. And the key is that it does not matter whether the worker knew and refused to disclose that knowledge, or that he really did not know. Cast as a heathen, the worker is limited to a fate of violent expulsion from that tale of the West and humor either way.

"THE CHRISTMAS GIFT THAT CAME TO RUPERT" (1871)

In January 1871, two months before his final issue as the editor of the *Over-land Monthly*, Harte published a Civil War story called "The Christmas Gift That Came to Rupert," which ended up being the last story he wrote for the magazine. The story can be read as a prosification of a poem, "The Rev-eille" (1863), that Harte wrote at the request of the respected California Re-publican Thomas Starr King during the Civil War. Paralleling the drum in the poem that beckons the soldiers to "come!" and fight to save the Union (Harte, "Reveille" 86), a drum comes to a young boy named Rupert in the story—with his name written on it—as a mysterious Christmas present. No one knows where the drum came from, and only the boy hears its beat. Always a sickly child, Rupert falls gravely ill soon after but manages to run away from home and goes to serve the army, where he plays the drum—which everyone can now hear—bringing joy and honor to the Union army for a short while until his death. This story about a patriotic white boy mar-tyr during the Civil War is an unlikely venue for a Chinese worker figure, but the figure does make a fleeting and ultimately generative appearance.

While most of the story takes place during the war away from California, its present is set during Reconstruction inside a Californian home that has all the trappings of a domestic space around Christmastime. An omniscient narrator begins the story, but the rest is told by a traveling doctor who recounts Rupert's story to a group of white children with "flaxen heads" (89). Into this group, the doctor/narrator attempts to mix in a Chinese boy servant by stating, "Bob, put your feet down. . . . Flora shall sit by my side. . . . Fung Tang shall stay, too, if he likes" (89). Coming at the end of his order for the other children on how they should behave, what the doctor says to Fung Tang is not exactly an order but an invitation that Fung Tang is given the choice to accept. The story extends this invitation with the description, "Fung Tang, the little heathen page, who was permitted, on this rare occasion, to share the Christian revels in the drawing-room, surveyed the group with a smile that was at once sweet and philosophical" (89). As this description is the final mention of Fung Tang in the story, we do not know if Fung Tang decides to stay. What we *can* see, however, is that Fung Tang does not operate in the story as a minstrel figure. He is given a choice, and the story does not make the choice for him. He is not called a racial epithet, his clothing is not described as a racializing marker, he is not made to speak words such as "me choppee wood," and he is not meant to serve as a punch line. Even the appellation "heathen page" is modified by "little."

In fact, the word "little" is crucial to the characterization of Fung Tang and his brief inclusion in the story, because it also modifies his "smile that was at once sweet and philosophical." That smile may call to mind not only the "heathen Chinee" Ah Sin's "pensive and childlike" smile but also the multiple descriptions of Topsy's grin in *Uncle Tom's Cabin* (Stowe, *Uncle* 313). However, Fung Tang's "sweet and philosophical" smile does not exactly imply a cunning duplicity seen in Ah Sin's. It is equally distinguishable from Topsy's grin—and never a smile—which is described as "so goblin-like" (Stowe, *Uncle* 314), mirroring the previous description of Topsy as "so heathenish" (310). In the delineation of Fung Tang, the "little heathen page," we see an active dissociation from Ah Sin and Topsy.

Unlike Ah Sin and Topsy, Fung Tang is not a comical character. "The Christmas Gift" overall is a rare Harte story that does not have much humor in it—save for the doctor's sardonic threat of amputation for misbehaving children. Most important to my argument, "The Christmas Gift" is an attempt at rewriting the "heathen Chinee" into a Chinese boy. And this rewriting happens through Fung Tang's "sweet and philosophical" smile, which has a precedent in Harte's Western hero Jack Hamlin's, described as a "smile of cynical philosophy" (Harte, "Brown" 284). The cynically philosophical smile of Hamlin's is rewritten as the less jaded "sweet" one of Fung

Tang's. Associated with a character who sings a song borrowed from minstrelsy, Fung Tang's act of surveying and smiling can also be read to be in
line with the privileged white subject of enjoyment, distinct from the object
position of being the source of that enjoyment or having the prescribed
agency of enjoying one's own objectification.

In the process of transforming the childlike "heathen Chinee" into a
"little heathen page" and an actual child, Harte aligns the Chinese child in
the West with whiteness, not Blackness. This aligning of a Chinese worker
figure with a white Western hero can only happen through the figuration
of Fung Tang as a child. Though Fung Tang's character does not get further
developed in "The Christmas Gift," in the story that establishes the seat
of storytelling that reconstructs the nation squarely in California, we see
the beginning of how Harte would address the possibility of constructing
a Chinese boy character into a Western hero. This construction happens in
"Wan Lee, the Pagan," as the Chinese boy character is not only in alignment with Jack Hamlin but, more crucially, in contradistinction to Topsy
and consciously dissociated from the minstrel form.

"AMERICAN HUMOR" AND "WAN LEE, THE PAGAN" (1874)

In 1874, his $10,000 long gone and the lucrative contract with the *Atlantic
Monthly* not renewed, Harte turned to the Chinese character again in his
first short story with a Chinese worker as a major character: "Wan Lee,
the Pagan" (1874). Ridden with debt, he was also traveling and delivering
lectures for money, and writing his first novel, *Gabriel Conroy*, which was
widely panned.[20] During this challenging time, he developed a lecture on
"American humor," which he began delivering in January 1874. The prox-
imity in date of the lecture and "Wan Lee" suggests that the one informed
the other. Through an examination of Harte's lecture, we can see how Harte
attempted to replicate the success of the "heathen Chinee" by creating a
new Western hero in Wan Lee's character and moving away from Topsy and
the minstrel form in the process.

In his lecture, Harte notably cited Topsy from *Uncle Tom's Cabin* as an
emblematic figure of American humor. However, rather than crediting the
New England writer Stowe for her creation, Harte characterized Topsy—
and American humor—as having originated in the South: "It was in the
South, and among conditions of servitude and the habits of an inferior race,

that there sprang up a humor and pathos as distinct, as original, as perfect and rare as any that ever flowered under the most beneficent circumstances of race and culture" (Harte, *Lectures* 22). Without naming slavery or black-face minstrelsy directly, Harte implied that the "original" American humor that birthed Topsy was inspired by the "conditions" and "habits" of enslaved Black people in the South. However, he claimed that this humor derived from the South "has no place in enduring American literature" (22–23). He declared, quite dramatically, that "Topsy and Uncle Tom are dead," because "they were too much imbued with a political purpose to retain their place as a humorist creation" (23). In place of these passé characters, calling to mind his review of Stowe's *Oldtown Folks*, Harte said that one should turn to the West for American humor, particularly the "Californian wit" and the "humorous but irreverent style in which California newspaper men described events of the most serious nature" (24). A former California newspaperman himself, Harte credited the local sketches of the West for carrying on the American humor founded in the South. Though he claimed that "it is to the South and West that we really owe the creation and expression of that humor which is perhaps most characteristic of our lives and habits as a people" (22), for Harte, it was the West that was truly responsible for engendering "a condition of romantic and dramatic possibilities . . . unrivalled in history," as he would write in an essay called "The Rise of the 'Short Story'" toward the end of his life in 1899 ("Rise" 6).

This move of connecting the South and the West and declaring the latter to be the seat of "American humor" and the birthplace of the "American short story" during Reconstruction can be seen in Harte's stories in the *Overland Monthly*, which are heralded as some of the best of his fiction writing. The story that put Harte's name on the map—the first one that he published in the *Overland Monthly*, in its second issue in August 1868—is a prime example. "The Luck of Roaring Camp" is about the eponymous all-male mining camp that experiences a "regeneration" (186) after the birth of an "Ingin baby" (189) and the death of the baby's mother, "Cherokee Sal" (183), but ends with the sentimentalized deaths of the baby and a character named "Kentuck" (189). The repeated use of the word "regeneration" in the story moves the question of Reconstruction in the South and expropriation of Native lands—emblematized by the name Kentuck[21]—to a deracialized, white mining camp in the Sierra foothills. The unceremonious death of Cherokee Sal caused by the birth of the mixed-race baby, unironically named by the miners as "Luck," exemplifies the strategy of erasure and elimination in settler colonialism that Native and settler colonial studies scholars such as Lisa Kahaleole Hall and Patrick Wolfe discuss (see L. Hall; Wolfe, "Settler Colonialism").

In Harte's lecture on American humor, then, we see two goals: first, to locate the seat of American humor in the West, especially in narratives about the West; and second, to call for a new figure to replace the outdated characters of humor such as Topsy. "Wan Lee, the Pagan" is Harte's attempt to achieve these two goals, particularly by using a "humorous but irreverent style" to describe "events of the most serious nature" (Harte, *Lectures* 24).

In "Wan Lee," Harte develops the supposedly unique Western style, distinct from humor founded in the South, by actually expressing a desire to move away from the minstrel form. In describing one of the Chinese characters in the story named Hop Sing, the story's white male narrator states:

> Before I describe him, I want the average reader to discharge from his mind any idea of a Chinaman that he may have gathered from the pantomime. He did not wear beautifully scalloped drawers fringed with little bells (I never met a Chinaman who did); he did not habitually carry his forefinger extended before him at right angles with his body; nor did I ever hear him utter the mysterious sentence, "Ching a ring a ring chaw," nor dance, under any provocation. (552)

Here, Harte underscores the difference between Hop Sing and a minstrel figure who says, "Ching a ring a ring chaw." In announcing that Hop Sing is not a minstrel figure, Harte implicitly makes a distinction between Hop Sing and Ah Sin, the "heathen Chinee." Hop Sing is wealthy and friends with the most powerful white men in San Francisco, including the narrator. He is a fully assimilated figure, who does not speak "pidgin" English. A "Pagan shopkeeper," he is described as a "handsome gentleman" who speaks fluent French as well as English (553, 552). Eschewing the words "heathen" and "heathen Chinee" completely, the story defines "Pagan" not as a synonym for "heathen" and an overdetermined marker of unassimilability associated with the history of blackface minstrel representations but as a category of assimilability, not antithetical to whiteness.[22] The story divorces "pagan" from "heathen" by explicitly declaring Hop Sing to be a nonminstrel, nonworker figure in the West. But as discussed previously, the line "Ching a ring a ring chaw," originally from a minstrel song and eventually adapted to make fun of the Chinese, became even more closely associated with the Chinese because of the success of Harte's "Plain Language from Truthful James." Demonstrating the nature of a repertoire that is "in constant flux [and] always being re-made" (Bernstein 14), the minstrel form that Harte disavows through a negation of the "pantomime" was in fact remade and given further life by his own "heathen Chinee" creation.

The disavowal of the minstrel form in the characterization of Hop Sing serves as a model for reading Wan Lee's character—as a permanently deferred possibility for what Wan Lee could have become. "Wan Lee, the Pagan" deals with the eponymous protagonist as a boy who is placed in the charge of a newspaper editor in northern California and lives an idyllic life until his premature death at the hands of a racist mob in San Francisco. Labeling Wan Lee's life story as "veracious history" (553), the narrator spends some time in the beginning in what amounts to an instruction of how the "average [U.S.] reader" should read Hop Sing's character and, by extension, the story as a whole. The instruction takes the form of the narrator reading Hop Sing's letter inviting the narrator for a visit, which has three layers of meaning. When the narrator opens Hop Sing's letter, he states that, first, "there fluttered to the ground a square strip of yellow paper covered with hieroglyphics which at first glance I innocently took to be the label from a pack of Chinese firecrackers" (552). Disparagingly characterizing Chinese characters as "hieroglyphics," the narrator not so "innocently" misreads the outermost layer of Hop Sing's invitation as a label for "Chinese firecrackers." But next, he sees "a smaller strip of rice paper . . . that I at once knew to be Hop Sing's visiting card" despite the fact that it was in Chinese, which the narrator cannot read (552). This strip of paper contains "two Chinese characters," which the narrator says he later translated (552). The translation of two characters comes out to be an entire paragraph of caricatured "ancient Chinese" aphorisms (552). While the narrator's immediate recognition of Hop Sing's visiting card suggests that friendship and familiarity may trump cultural difference, his confession that "I was at a loss to make any immediate application of the message" of the translated Chinese characters implies otherwise. It is only through the "third enclosure in the shape of a little note *in English*," which spells out the invitation to Hop Sing's warehouse for tea and "explain[s] all," that the narrator fully understands the meaning of the missive (552; emphasis added). If this opening scene of the story is a lesson in not relying on stereotypical impulses on matters of racial and cultural difference, it is also a display of ethnocentrism that puts forth Hop Sing's adoption of the English language as a condition for him to be recognized and understood. The story implies that as much as the act of interpreting meaning from a text depends on the reader, the text itself, in plain English, is also crucial. Simply put, the text has to be American. The beginning of "Wan Lee, the Pagan" intimates that just as the "two Chinese characters" were translated into English and made sense of, the rest of the story will make legible Hop Sing and Wan Lee—the story's two Chinese characters— and thereby ensure that the overall story is American despite its characters' Chineseness. The question for the story, then, is whether or not the Chinese characters themselves can become American and how.

Harte answers the question by moving away from the minstrel form to the literary by setting up Wan Lee's birth as a textual one, which also happens in three stages. The narrator gets invited to Hop Sing's warehouse for an evening of entertainment and is joined by other prominent white men of San Francisco. There, he and the guests are treated to a performance of Wang, the court juggler. After several magic tricks that delight the men, Wang places three pieces of cloth on the floor, one of which is the narrator's handkerchief, and starts chanting over them. The white guests all sit and wait in dread and anticipation, until Hop Sing gets up and points his finger at the center of the shawl, and the narrator observes, "There was something beneath the shawl. Surely—and something that was not there before" (Harte, "Wan Lee" 553). As Wang's chant continues, that "something" begins to take "the outline of a small but perfect human figure, with extended arms and legs" (554). In this scene of disquietude, we are told that one of the men "broke the silence by a gibe that, poor as it was, was received with a spontaneous enthusiasm" (554). This ability to make a joke at a time when a "human figure" starts to take shape where it "was not . . . before" is in line with Harte's characterization of "California wit"—the ability to find humor in "events of the most serious nature." The humor in the scene is reserved only for the white men, as Hop Sing, who is consistently described as "quite serious," "imperturbable," and "grave," has no such capacity (553, 554). It is also at this moment, when the white men break into laughter, that the chanting stops and Wang strips away two of the pieces of cloth to reveal "a tiny Chinese baby," "sleeping peacefully upon [the narrator's] handkerchief" (554), who turns out to be the title character, Wan Lee. Wan Lee is born in the midst of the "irreverent" white U.S. masculinist humor that counters the unknown and the other by laughing it off—the humor in which Hop Sing, Wang, and certainly Wan Lee take no part for now. By not disclosing what the man's "gibe" was, Harte maintains the humor in this scene as an exclusive one, much like the joke in "The Iliad of Sandy Bar."

Wan Lee comes into being in the story not through a natural childbirth but through the chanting and the joking—meaning, he is conceived and birthed discursively. In this "birth," the narrator's handkerchief plays a key role in the stage of three cloths. It is out of the narrator's handkerchief that "something that was not there before" (Harte, "Wan Lee" 554) emerges, which turns out to be the baby Wan Lee. More so than the chanting of the conjurer, the narrator's handkerchief plays a vital role in Wan Lee's birth. Though given to Hop Sing by happenstance, it is what cradles Wan Lee or, one might even say, the womb that carries the fully formed baby. This handkerchief has a counterpart in "The Luck of Roaring Camp." In it, John Oakhurst, not quite yet an established Western hero and only as a minor character, places "a very beautifully embroidered lady's handkerchief" (Harte, "Luck" 185) in a collection box for the mixed-race baby Luck in a mining camp with only men. In "Wan Lee," the handkerchief itself becomes the collection box, as the narrator folds it into a bag and passes it around for funds for the baby. This similarity between "Wan Lee" and "The Luck" is not merely superficial. In his 1899 essay "The Rise of the 'Short Story,'" Harte locates the birth of the American short story in the West and specifically in the publication of "The Luck" (7). If, in Harte's mind, the genesis of the American short story was "The Luck," his invocation of it in Wan Lee's birth scene is an attempt to assimilate the latter into the genre through the figure of a racialized child whitewashed and raised by white men. And this whitening of Wan Lee happens through writing against Topsy.

As a textual "crowning performance," Wan Lee's birth scene is both seemingly similar to and crucially different from the reference to Topsy's absent parentage in *Uncle Tom's Cabin.* In Stowe's novel, in response to Ophelia's questioning of her age and parents, Topsy states that she does not know, avowing, "Never was born . . . never had no father nor mother, nor nothin'" (314).[23] This absurd claim that she was "never born" suggests that Topsy had always and already been enslaved. The claim also denies "the process by which a child was made into a slave," which Walter Johnson states was "often quite brutal," as "enslaved children were taught to experience their bodies twice at once, to move through the world as both child and slave, person and property" (*Soul* 21, 22). The humor of the scene attempts to vacate that brutal process, a part of which comes right before the scene when Ophelia sees on Topsy's back "great welts and calloused spots, ineffaceable marks of the system under which she had grown up thus far" (Stowe, *Uncle* 313). Topsy's relating that she does not know her origins "with a grin" (313) makes light of both the physical and epistemological violence of slavery, as captives often did not have access to such information, calling to mind Orlando Patterson's theorizations of "natal alienation" and the "social death" of slavery (*Slavery* 7, 39).

Through the birth scene of Wan Lee, Harte revises Topsy's "never was born" into a textual birth, distinguishing Wan Lee from Topsy as a noncaptive figure. By providing him with a traceable literary lineage, Harte creates a divergent path for the racialized Chinese boy character that is ultimately antithetical to Topsy's path, and, in the process, separates him from minstrelsy and slavery. Countering the seeming similarity that both Wan Lee and Topsy have no knowledge of their parents and are raised from around the same age by white people, Harte provides Wan Lee with a literary lineage in the West. As far as the story is concerned, Wan Lee's birthdate is when he is introduced in the narrative, notwithstanding the description that he is "a pretty little boy about a year old" (Harte, "Wan Lee" 554) when he is "born." The story announces, "And thus was Wan Lee, on the night of Friday, the 5th of March, 1856, born into this veracious chronicle" (554), and with this birth, Wan Lee is cast as a free character.

With an exact textual birthdate, Wan Lee is not only distinguished from Topsy's claim of "never was born" and slavery but also aligned with whiteness. After Wan Lee's "birth," the white men, appointed as the baby's "godfathers" by Hop Sing, debate what they should name him (Harte, "Wan Lee" 554), resembling a similar scene involving a baby's naming in "The Luck." In "Wan Lee," of all the names that are suggested, three are related to color—Erebux, Nox, and Terra Cotta—and one, Antæus, is linked to Africa. According to Greek mythology, Erebux—"Nether Darkness"—and Nox (Latin for Nyx, identified as "black") were formed from Chaos (Graf 80), and "Antæus" was a giant whose birthplace was said to be in Africa (E. Robinson 103). Faced with these suggested names, Hop Sing quietly reminds the men that the baby already has a name, which is Wan Lee, and the men agree to keep it. If we read the name as a play on "wan-ly," we uncover an interesting etymology of "wan" used as an adjective. According to the *OED*, the original meaning of the word as "lacking light, or lustre; dark-hued, dusky, gloomy, dark" had gone obsolete by the sixteenth century. In the seventeenth century and beyond, the word was understood to mean "pallid, faded, sickly; unusually or unhealthily pale," and this later definition would have been the common understanding during Harte's time. What we see in the white men's initial attempt to name Wan Lee is an impulse to racialize him as nonwhite, aligned specifically with Blackness. Against this impulse, the story settles on a name that, while still Chinese, drains it of color. Like the etymology of the word "wan" itself, the Chinese baby goes from dark to pale, and this color designation assimilates him into whiteness, apart from Blackness and Topsy.

After Wan Lee's "birth," the next time he appears in the story is as a nine-year-old in 1865, when the narrator is acting as an editor of a newspaper in a town some distance away from San Francisco. Wan Lee had been living in San Francisco with Wang the conjurer as his "reputed son" but is harassed by white boys (Harte, "Wan Lee" 554). To save Wan Lee, Hop Sing asks the narrator to take in the boy. The narrator agrees to hire him as the "printer's devil," a name for an apprenticeship for young boys at a newspaper, and Wan Lee begins working for and living with the narrator. From the time that the narrator meets him as a boy, Wan Lee is described as being full of mischief yet good will, in whom we can glean perhaps a combination of Mark Twain's famous future creations, Tom Sawyer and Huckleberry Finn. In fact, after Wan Lee plays a practical joke at the narrator's newspaper, the narrator describes Wan Lee as having "happiness beaming from every tooth, and satisfaction in his *huckleberry* eyes" (556; emphasis added).[24] The characterization of Huckleberry Finn as the "romantic outcast" in *The Adventures of Tom Sawyer* (1876), in particular, published two years after "Wan Lee, the Pagan," closely resembles that of Wan Lee. Harte and Twain scholar Margaret Duckett has even noted of Wan Lee that "his pranks might be considered Oriental prototype of Tom Sawyer's" (*Mark* 108).

As Huckleberry Finn did not make an appearance until two years after the publication of "Wan Lee," Harte's Wan Lee could not have been based on Twain's most famous character, though the reverse may have been case. Given Harte and Twain's on-again, off-again friendship—they were close friends in California beginning in 1864, not on speaking terms from around 1870 to 1871, then permanently estranged from 1877 onward—and Twain's bitter sense of rivalry against Harte, which I discuss in the next chapter, it is entirely possible that Twain may have borrowed from Wan Lee's character when he created Tom Sawyer and Huckleberry Finn, his two boy heroes. But proving Wan Lee's potential influence on Twain's characters is not the point here. What is noteworthy is that the characterization of Wan Lee's boyhood is reminiscent of the characterization of white boyhood by Harte and Twain, seen through not only their shared word of "huckleberry" in their fictional writings but also their similar life experiences. In his autobiography, for instance, Twain narrated an incident that Harte had relayed to him from the time that Harte himself had been a printer's devil and played a prank that was very similar to the one pulled by Wan Lee (Twain, *Autobiography* 2:510–11). Twain had also been a printer's devil prone to mischief.[25] Though Tom Sawyer and Huckleberry Finn are not printer's devils, their antics in *The Adventures of Tom Sawyer* are quite similar to Wan Lee's. These similarities between Wan Lee's boy character and Harte's own biography suggest that though Wan Lee is outwardly cast as Chinese, he is essentially meant to be read as white.

Even more than the preceding factors that whiten him, Wan Lee's refusal to convert to Christianity makes him a free and worthy American/Western hero in the story's estimation. After working and living with the narrator for two years, Wan Lee is forced to move to San Francisco because of the narrator's new job. The transition does not delight Wan Lee, who, like Huckleberry Finn, has a "fondness for the free, vagrant life" (Harte, "Wan Lee" 558).[26] Still, some of Wan Lee's happiest days occur there, especially after he is placed in a Chinese missionary house and lives with a widowed Christian woman and her cherubic daughter, who tries to convert him to Christianity in an attempted "civilizing" process. The scenes describing the friendship between the white girl and Wan Lee closely resemble the scenes depicting Eva and Topsy in *Uncle Tom's Cabin*. Harte describes the two children as the "little Christian girl with her shining cross hanging around her plump, white little neck; and this dark little Pagan, with his hideous porcelain god hidden away in his blouse" ("Wan Lee" 558). Stowe describes the two children as "representatives of the two extremes of society. The fair, high-bred child, with her golden head, her deep eyes, her spiritual, noble brow, and prince-like movements; and her black, keen, subtle cringing, yet acute neighbor" (*Uncle* 319). However, unlike Eva, who tells Topsy, "I love you, and I want you to be good" (367) and wants Topsy to convert to Christianity, the little white girl in Harte's story "show[s] [Wan Lee] wherein he [is] original and valuable" and "fill[s] him with her own Christian goodness" but does not "effect his conversion" (Harte, "Wan Lee" 558). Unlike Topsy or the lecherous "heathen" in Harte's 1863 *Golden Era* article, Wan Lee never converts to Christianity or takes off his porcelain Buddha, which he carries inside his shirt. His beliefs are genuine and his own, as he openly adores the white girl without accepting her religion and forsaking his.

Wan Lee's practice of carrying a porcelain Buddha also crucially distinguishes him from Topsy. In Stowe's novel, Topsy carries a lock of Eva's hair inside her shirt, and this symbolizes Topsy's conversion to Christianity and her commitment to be "good." In Harte's story, the porcelain Buddha acts as proof of Wan Lee's individual a priori moral compass, not based on societal pressure and norms but strictly based on his own sense of what is right. In such manner, Wan Lee, like Fung Tang, is like Harte's white Western heroes, particularly Jack Hamlin, emblematized by his "smile of cynical philosophy." Responding to Wan Lee's tale of the hard life that he has lived so far, the editor states, "If he had thought at all, he would have been a skeptic, if he had been a little older, he would have been a cynic, if he had been older still, he would have been a philosopher" (Harte, "Wan Lee" 557). Unencumbered by obligation or the need to feel accepted—much like Jack Hamlin's character in many of Harte's stories[27]—Wan Lee is truly free, as a "little imp" "willing to try virtue [only] as a diversion" (557).

Wan Lee's abiding faith in his pagan religion therefore separates him from the servile *heathen* and whitens him, which is pivotal to making the story one of American humor. Wan Lee dies in a fictionalized race riot in San Francisco, which is a possible allusion to the Los Angeles Chinatown massacre in 1871 and presciently predicts the 1877 San Francisco race riot.[28] As the editor condemns the white riot in moral outrage, he is asked by Hop Sing to come to his warehouse, the same place of Wan Lee's "birth." The story comes full circle, as the narrator enters the basement where Wang the Chinese conjurer's performance had taken place. There, he sees "something lying on the floor covered by a shawl" (Harte, "Wan Lee" 558). Just as Wang drew away the shawl and revealed the baby Wan Lee at the beginning of the story, Hop Sing lifts the shawl "with a sudden gesture, and revealed Wan Lee, the Pagan, lying there dead!" (559). The overuse of the exclamation point in the scene continues to underscore the outrage over Wan Lee's demise: "Dead, my reverend friends, dead! stoned to death in the streets of San Francisco, in the year of grace 1869, by a mob of half-grown boys and Christian school-children!" (559).[29] Were the repeated use of the word "dead" and how Wan Lee died not enough of a climax, the story ends with the final line describing what Hop Sing and the narrator find inside Wan Lee's shirt: "It was Wan Lee's porcelain god, crushed by a stone from the hands of those Christian iconoclasts!" (559). In this moment of forced pathos punctuating every sentence with an exclamation point, Hop Sing smiles, and the narrator states that it was "the first bitter smile I had ever seen on the face of that pagan gentleman" (559). If, as Harold H. Kolb argues, Harte's humor is defined by the use of irony and juxtaposition, in Hop Sing's smile we see effected in "Wan Lee" an assimilation of the Chinese immigrant Hop Sing into what Kolb describes as the "narrative commentary that is refined, cynical, and aloof" (56). Such is the narrative of American humor, and that humor is usually limited to the narrator or white male characters like Jack Hamlin in Harte's stories. In Hop Sing's smile, however, we see what Wan Lee could have been—a participant in American humor unique to the West, who finds "humor" in the "events of the most serious nature," not unlike a white man.

In "Wan Lee, the Pagan," the ability to appreciate the irony of a pagan boy with the qualities of a white Western hero getting stoned to death by "Christian iconoclasts" is what ultimately emerges as a quality worthy of being called "American," which is predicated on Wan Lee's refusal to convert to Christianity and a distinction from Topsy. As such, even though it is Wan Lee who dies, it is Topsy's redemption in *Uncle Tom's Cabin*, effected through her conversion that saves her "heathen soul" (368), that gets annihilated by the story. Through "Wan Lee, the Pagan," Harte seems to say that Topsy's conversion is what kills her as a humorous figure, whereas Wan Lee's refusal to convert preserves him as a humorous character as well as a tragic and innocent Western hero. But maybe Topsy was always and already dead for Harte because he never saw her as an innocent child. He evidently thought much about Topsy's character, bringing her up again in the aforementioned essay on the American short story form and calling her a "purely American character" (Harte, "Rise" 4). This American character had no place in his fictions of the West, however. In his extensive oeuvre of short stories and other writings, Harte to my knowledge never included a Black child character—only Black grown-up characters who, like Ah Sin, were "childlike."[30]

. . .

"Wan Lee, the Pagan" and other writings by Bret Harte featuring the Chinese worker character ought to be read as part of his long contradictory engagement with antiblackness as a cultural form before and during Reconstruction. "Wan Lee" is particularly noteworthy in its stated desire to separate depictions of the Chinese from the minstrel form. But that literary experimentation did not prove successful. If the connection to the minstrel form and the figure of Topsy made Ah Sin, the "heathen Chinee," a wild success, the self-conscious dissociation from Topsy and the minstrel form might explain why Wan Lee—or Hop Sing as an assimilated "gentleman"—did not become one of Harte's better-known characters. In his subsequent delineations of the Chinese character after "Wan Lee," Harte seems to have oscillated between the two modes of representation, often opting for the former that was more aligned with financial success. He named a character resembling the "heathen Chinee" minstrel figure "Hop Sing" in his play, *Two Men of Sandy Bar* (1876), rewriting the character from "Wan Lee" and setting the precedence for numerous future caricatured Chinese worker characters in Westerns named Hop Sing. Based on the positive response to the character in *Two Men of Sandy Bar*, Harte wrote a yellowface play called *Ah Sin* (1877) with Twain, in what Scharnhorst calls was "arguably the most disastrous collaboration in the history of American letters" (*Opening* xiv). The play went through an extensive revision, according to Twain, and it is not clear which of the two authors wrote the part for the Ah Sin character in the only written version that survives. Though the "heathen Chinee" figure would proliferate on the minstrel stage and other aspects of U.S. popular culture, Harte's own staged version did not bring him the wealth and fame that "Plain Language" did.

After the disappointment of *Ah Sin*, we see a noticeable change in Harte's employment of the minstrel form in relation to his representation of the Chinese worker figure. This change can be seen in the poem "The Latest Chinese Outrage" (1878) and the short story "The Queen of Pirate Isle" (1886). At first glance, "The Latest Chinese Outrage" appears to be yet another effort to cash in on the "heathen Chinee," as it features a Chinese worker named Ah Sin, whom the speaker of the poem refers to as "that heathen" (Harte, "Latest" 705). One of the characters even attributes to the Chinese the speech of "ching a ring chow" (705), adopting almost exactly the description of "Ching a ring a ring chaw" that the narrator of "Wan Lee" dismissed as a "mysterious sentence" that he never heard Hop Sing utter. However, it is not only the Chinese worker who functions as a minstrel figure in the poem. As the poem is about a feud between white miners and Chinese workers—not all of whom work in the mines—it describes a white miner in particular who boasts of his white bravery and masculinity as he heads to fight the Chinese alone. When he is later found by his fellow miners, he is tied up in a tree and mistaken for Chinese. The entire stanza about the recovered miner deserves to be quoted here:

> In his mouth was an opium pipe—which was why
> He leered at us so with a drunken-like eye!
> They had shaved off his eyebrows, and tacked on a cue,
> They had painted his face of a coppery hue,
> And rigged him all up in a heathenish suit,
> Then softly departed, each man with his "loot."
> > Yes, every galoot,
> > And Ah Sin, to boot,
> > Had left him there hanging
> > Like ripening fruit. (705)

Through a poem in which a white man is made to take on the part of a Chinese worker in a "heathenish suit," Harte exposes minstrelsy as a form expressing whiteness more so than nonwhiteness. As the possible coercion for the performance of Chinese identity happens "off-stage," the reader is not privy to what made the white miner surrender so completely to the identity change—opium? The sheer number of the Chinese? But while the transformation could be read as a satirical poke at the bravado of the white miner, the imagery of him "hanging like a ripening fruit" makes light of the fact that lynching of nonwhite people was a regular occurrence during and after Reconstruction. In the aforementioned 1871 massacre in Los Angeles, for example, fourteen Chinese men were hanged and three were shot (Zesch 150). In the South and elsewhere, lynchings of Black men and women numbering in the thousands amounted to what the Equal Justice Initiative calls "terrorism" ("Equal"). Abel Meeropol would write a poem called "Strange Fruit"

FIGURE 1.2   "Each Other's Hands," by Kate Greenaway. From Bret Harte, *The Queen of the Pirate Isle* (London: Chatto and Windus, 1886), p. 28.

in 1937 describing the hanging body of a Black lynched victim (Blair). With the description of the white miner as a "ripening fruit" hanging in a tree, Harte's poem betrays a connection between the minstrel form and racial violence, even as it attempts to cover up the violence with a humorous tone.

Harte thus ultimately leaves it up to the reader to make the connection between the minstrel form, antiblackness, and representations of Chineseness and race. In "The Queen of Pirate Isle," an illustrated children's tale first published in England, Harte resurrected Wan Lee as a side character. As a servant boy in a white household in California, Wan Lee operates more or less as a white child in the story (see Figure 1.2). He engages in make-believe adventures with Polly, the daughter of his employers, until they come upon a real-life adventure when they fall down an abandoned mine. There, they encounter "pirates," who are white miners performing the part to amuse the children. Remarkably, the story describes the men as "strangers [who] bore a singular resemblance to 'Christy Minstrels' in their blackened faces and attitudes that somehow made them seem less awful" (Harte, "Queen" 44). The repeated description of the men's "dark resemblances to Christy Minstrels" (46) underscores lightheartedness and joviality of the scene as the men begin to dance (46). The minstrel form thus performs the function of the familiar, as the men become "less awful" "strangers." Performing through their "Blackness," the men announce Polly as their queen and accept Wan Lee as her "faithful Chinese henchman" (54) (see Figure 1.3). The pairing of the minstrel form and Wan Lee diffuses the tension in the story and results in the children being carried safely home. Any possible hint of antiblack violence associated with the minstrel form is dissipated, as the men's actions are described by Polly's mother as "dressing themselves up to play with children" (57), just as innocently as Polly and Wan Lee play make-believe. But while the form serves an inclusive function for Wan Lee and other characters, it also makes glaring the aforementioned absence of Black child characters in Harte's stories as well as the contrast between depictions of the happily assimilated Wan Lee and the violence unleashed by figure of the "heathen Chinee" that Harte's poem popularized.

FIGURE 1.3   "Wan Lee," by Kate Greenaway. From Bret Harte, *The Queen of the Pirate Isle* (London: Chatto and Windus, 1886), p. 52.

The connection between the minstrel form, his Chinese characters, and antiblackness is something that Harte himself never fully recognized. Two years before he died of throat cancer, Harte published a short story called "The Three Vagabonds of Trinidad" (1900), set in Trinidad County in California. The three vagabonds in the title refer to a Chinese boy, a Native man, and a white boy. The story, about the three characters who find themselves on the run, with a tragic outcome for all except the white boy, is a sort of a rewrite of "Wan Lee," with an overt message of anti-imperialism. In it, a white character named Skinner makes a speech in which he exclaims, "I kin tell you, gentlemen, that this is a white man's country! Yes, sir, you can't get over it! The nigger of every description—yeller, brown, or black, call him 'Chinese,' 'Injin,' or 'Kanaka,' or what you like—hez to clar off of God's footstool when the Anglo-Saxon gets started! . . . . It's our manifest destiny to clar them out!" (Harte, "Three" 412). Suggesting that Skinner's antiblackness is foundational to his racism toward other nonwhite groups, the story links that racism to U.S. imperialism, both overseas and, in a later statement, overland in the U.S. West. But Harte does not seem to have registered a connection between Skinner's racism and his own literary practice that either depicted Black characters as dehumanized stereotypes or avoided them altogether. He also most likely did not recognize the antiblackness in having the Chinese boy character, Li Tee, speak in minstrel English, as Li Tee describes himself as "me no changee. Me no ollee China boy" (411). In fact, antiblackness as a formal quality born out of slavery in Harte's stories of the West would never be owned by Harte, and it would take his future readers well over a century to make the connection through his various "heathen Chinee" characters.

CHAPTER TWO

Mark Twain's Chinese Characters and the Fungibility of Blackness

One year before his death in 1909, William Stewart, one of the most vocal anti-Chinese politicians of his time, published a memoir documenting his experience in U.S. politics as the first senator of the new state of Nevada. In the preface, George Rothwell Brown wrote that Stewart was a true pioneer in the "Golden West," and that it was not until "many years after" when "Mark Twain and Bret Harte, called 'pioneers,' appeared upon the scene, and wrote the stories this blue-eyed, iron-fisted, fearless giant helped enact" (W. Stewart 18). Brown's mention of Twain and Harte not only valorizes Stewart as the true pioneer who "fought Indians" (18)—a valorization that discounts the history of displacement and genocide of Native peoples from "U.S. territory." It also evidences the cachet associated with the two writers' names by the early 1900s and the fact that their fame was owed to their ostensibly pioneering literature of the West.

Stewart himself also engages in this kind of literary name-dropping in the body of his memoir in order to establish himself as a forerunner. In describing his days of practicing law in Nevada and California, he refers to his role in *People v. Hall* (1854), which declared Chinese testimony against white people to be inadmissible in court.[1] He calls the trial a "murder case" involving the "heathen Chinee" (76), which makes it seem as if the trial was against the Chinese and not George W. Hall, who had killed Ling Sing, a Chinese worker. Using the label from Harte's poem that would not become popular for more than fifteen years after the trial, Stewart anachronistically locates the "heathen Chinee" in an earlier time in the West before Harte showed up on the scene. In line with what would become the dominant understanding of Harte's poem, Stewart's memoir employs the "heathen Chinee" as a figure of racial, class, and religious difference deserving of exclusion. The shorthand performs the work of deindividualizing and racializing Chinese workers as "Chinamen" (78) indistinguishable from one another, which justifies the ruling that Stewart had argued *against* in *People v. Hall*, as he tried to preserve the murder conviction of Hall. Though Stewart had argued for the individuality of the Chinese witnesses in 1854, fighting for their testimony against Hall to be legally binding, he would not see them as anything but a pack of exclusion-worthy "heathen Chinee" during Reconstruction, when he fervently campaigned for their exclusion. As if to underscore his later anti-Chinese attitude, the section on Reconstruction in Stewart's memoir excludes any mention of the Chinese. The label of the "heathen Chinee" relegates the Chinese workers to the past of the "frontier" and justifies their exclusion in the latter part of the memoir as a foregone conclusion and a closed matter.

In place of the missing Chinese workers in Stewart's remembrance of Reconstruction, we see an unexpected insertion in the form of another literary appearance. In a chapter wedged in between the discussions of the Civil Rights Act of 1866 and the passage of the Fourteenth Amendment of the U.S. Constitution in 1868, Stewart recounts a meeting with "a very disreputable-looking person" with a "very sinister appearance," who came to see him in Washington, D.C., in the winter of 1867 (219, 220). Stewart adds, "He was a man I had known around the Nevada mining camps several years before, and his name was Samuel L. Clemens . . . . He wrote his book in my room, and named it 'The Innocents Abroad.' I was confident that he would come to no good end, but I have heard of him from time to time since then, and I understand that he has settled down and become respectable" (220, 224).[2]

By the time Stewart published his memoir, Clemens, almost exclusively known by his pen name, Mark Twain, was the most famous writer in the United States and abroad. He received honorary doctorate degrees from Yale and Oxford universities in 1901 and 1907, respectively, and his name had become synonymous with American literature, if not the very identity of American.[3] Stewart's statement that Twain had "settled down" and "become respectable" is therefore a humorous understatement speaking to the stature associated with Twain's name.[4] More important, the seemingly out-of-place insertion of Twain in this particular moment in the memoir emblematizes how literature can provide a way to examine what is excluded in historical narratives of Reconstruction and the West.

The production of "American literature" through writers such as Harte and Twain happened during Reconstruction, simultaneously with the construction of the Chinese worker figure in their writings. Stewart's remembrance illustrates that while the fame of the two writers survived in the collective memory in the United States—though not necessarily in connection with Reconstruction politics but tangentially—the history of the Chinese worker character during the 1870s in literary or political memory did not, except as the epithet "heathen Chinee." Where the previous chapter discussed the construction of the "heathen Chinee" and its significance in Reconstruction and post-Reconstruction politics in relation to representational practices from slavery in popular culture, this chapter studies the role that the Chinese worker figure played in the construction of "Mark Twain" as a distinctly U.S. literary brand in the early 1870s. Precisely during the time of the Chinese workers' absence in Stewart's memoir, Twain, like Harte, was experimenting with Chinese characters as he began his literary career. While the inclusions of the Chinese in his writings have been read as proof of his liberal, and even antiracist, politics (see Kanellakou; Ou; Lai-Henderson; Foner; Zehr), they are not widely remembered as a part of Twain's signature oeuvre. Against the temptation to pit Stewart and his vociferous anti-Chinese racism against Twain, whose writings on the Chinese are read as "exposing 'the brutally outrageous treatment' of the Chinese" (Foner 187), this chapter takes a different approach. I read both Stewart's and Twain's writings as revealing the racial logic of antiblackness undergirding the construction of the settler colonial space of the West, specifically through the racialization of the Chinese. In his discussion of *People v. Hall*, for instance, Stewart writes that the court ruled that "the statute prohibiting Indians from testifying [against white people] applied to Chinamen, they being of the same race" (79). He focuses exclusively on the racialization of the Chinese in comparison to Native peoples, explicitly excluding Black people from his mention of a precedent in the 1850 California law, which had stated, "No black or mulatto person, or Indian, shall be permitted to give evidence in favor of, or against, a white person."[5] Based on the 1850 law, *People v. Hall* ruled that "black" was a generic racial category that applied to all nonwhite people. The interdiction against Black testimony was rooted in slavery in the United States and the barring of the enslaved from testifying in court. California passed a law promulgating the same bar on Black testimony in the founding year of its statehood, which shows that even though it entered the Union as a "free" state, California was far from being free for all. Stewart's expulsion of this history of antiblackness and slavery in the "new" space of the West is what ties him to Twain.

As Twain engaged in an effort to develop a uniquely American voice through his literary writing during Reconstruction, he experimented with Native and Chinese but not Black characters. These writings can be found in a literary magazine called the *Galaxy*, in which Twain saw an opportunity to move away from journalism to become a respectable literary writer (see Twain, *Mark Twain to Mrs. Fairbanks* 127–28). There is not a single major Black character in Twain's writings in the *Galaxy*. This absence is noteworthy because, like Harte's "heathen Chinee," Twain's Chinese characters are constructed using the minstrel form. Unlike Harte, who outwardly expressed a disdain, Twain was an avid fan of minstrel shows. In 1906, four years before his death, Twain raved in his narrated autobiography that blackface minstrelsy—what he unironically called a "genuine nigger show"—was "delightfully and satisfyingly funny" (*Autobiography* 2:294). Twain's love of minstrelsy is not commonly known or remembered by the average U.S. reader of Twain, even though many scholars have noted the connection between that love and his literary writings, characterizing in particular the influence of the minstrel dialogue and the development of his Black characters as revealing what Eric Lott calls "love and theft" (*Love* 6). Building on such scholarship, this chapter examines Twain's writings at the start of his fiction-writing career for how he attempted to incorporate the minstrel form in his development of the Chinese character. In Twain's early writings, we see minstrelsy as not only functioning as a repertoire, discussed in Chapter 1 as that which is part of the everyday, prereflexive performance, but also revealing a belief in the fungibility of Blackness and the minstrel form rooted in slavery. While Twain's employment of the minstrel form did not rely on a wholesale disavowal of the history and material conditions of slavery, it did not challenge the fundamental racial logic of slavery that turned humans into property. In fact, Twain's use of the form shows an unintentional complicity with the logic of slavery, and his Chinese characters in the *Galaxy* contributed to and enabled that complicity. I chart Twain's development of his Chinese characters during Reconstruction and argue for reading that development alongside his eventual turn to Black characters, attributing the reason behind the shift to his understanding of literary proprietorship as well as his belief in the fungibility of Blackness.

The West in the Reconstruction of Mark Twain

To understand the significance of the *Galaxy* writings in the construction of Mark Twain as a writer, it is helpful to consider his biography prior to 1870, particularly his time in the West and the shifts in his politics. At the start of the Civil War, the twenty-six-year-old Samuel (Sam) Langhorne Clemens, who was born in Hannibal, Missouri, to a family that owned enslaved people—a rarity in Missouri—served in the Missouri State Guard fighting on the side of the Confederacy. When his older brother Orion was assigned to be the Secretary of the new territory of Nevada during the war, Sam Clemens also decided to try his luck out West. The two brothers landed in the predominantly Republican Virginia City in 1862, and Sam Clemens began writing for the Virginia City *Territorial Enterprise.* He started to sign his bylines as Mark Twain in 1863. Though a steamboat term that Sam Clemens learned while a cub pilot on the Mississippi, the name Mark Twain was an invention that originated in the West.

Twain's adoption of his pen name and the start of his journalistic career coincided with a shift in his politics. According to Arthur Pettit, Twain was initially known for his anti-Union politics in Nevada and was called a "damned secessionist" by James Nye, the territorial governor (Pettit 26). But, "unhinged by the rapid growth of Union sentiment in the territory, he first hedged about his Southern convictions, then threw them away altogether" (26–27). It would appear that the space of the West had a crucial hand in what Joe Fulton calls the "reconstruction of Mark Twain," so that by the time of Twain's death in 1910, the "damned secessionist" was lauded by William Dean Howells as not just "the most desouthernized southerner I ever met" (Fulton 40) but also the "Lincoln of our literature" (Fulton x).[6] In this characterization of Twain as a reformed Southerner, the West is seen as having had a liberalizing influence. As Bernard Bell writes, "When Twain went West in 1861, his experiences as a reporter, silver prospector, gold miner, and, later, world traveler certainly helped to democratize and deepen his humanity" (11). These depictions cast the West as a place of democracy and liberalism, one embodying the ideals of the United States and setting into motion Twain's shift from someone who "detested Yankees, free African Americans, and abolitionists with equal vehemence" (Fulton x) to the "Lincoln of our literature."

The West, however, was also a space of uninterrupted racial logics of settler colonialism and slavery. The ease with which white men such as Twain could begin a new life and form a new identity in the territory of Nevada—and shortly thereafter San Francisco—bespeaks the intricate connection between the westward expansion and the construction of a national identity during and after the Civil War through the claiming of Native lands as "American." Simply put, the westward expansion of U.S. settler colonialism mirrored the development of Mark Twain the writer. In 1864, Twain moved to San Francisco, where he wrote for the *Morning Call* and met Bret Harte. The two men became close friends, and Twain became a part of Harte's literary circle, the Bohemians. It was around this time that Twain first received national attention after publishing, with Harte's encouragement and editing help, a short story called "The Celebrated Jumping Frog of Calaveras County" (1865). The success of the story, featuring a naïve narrator and deadpan humor, won him the sobriquet "Wild Humorist of the Pacific Slope," and his Western sketches, along with "The Celebrated Jumping Frog," were published as a book—his first—in 1867. Also included in the book were Twain's writings from Hawai'i—then called the Sandwich Islands and a sovereign kingdom—when he was sent there in March 1866 by the *Sacramento Union* to write local sketches. One such sketch made an appearance in the first issue of Harte's *Overland Monthly*, attesting to Harte's continued assistance in Twain's writing career as well as the seamless, undramatic way in which the U.S. empire and settler colonialism structured the literary careers of both men. When Twain returned to San Francisco after his four-month trip to Hawai'i, he decided to give a lecture in October 1866 based on the visit, which was a raging success and began his lecturing fame.[7] The colonial space of the West—California, Nevada, and Hawai'i—where Twain traveled laid the foundations for what came after, as Twain's early success as a journalistic writer and lecturer depended on his narration of the U.S. empire using a naïve voice narrating that empire. But that narrative voice was not a new invention in the West. Like the name Mark Twain and Harte's "American humor," this narration had a Southern origin, specifically in blackface minstrelsy, to which Twain was first introduced in the early 1840s in Hannibal, Missouri. Both the form of minstrelsy and its history in San Francisco would have an indelible influence on Twain's literary writings, including his representations of the Chinese.

Minstrelsy and Twain in San Francisco

The construction of Mark Twain in the West was enabled by and existed alongside blackface minstrelsy as a thriving industry in San Francisco. After the initial success of his first lecture in San Francisco in 1866, Twain often went on the road to speak, which was more lucrative than newspaper writing. Twain scholar Stephen Railton has shown that newspaper announcements for Twain's lectures often appeared alongside advertisements for minstrel shows.[8] But there was an even more direct invocation of blackface minstrelsy in the announcements themselves. The poster advertising Twain's 1866 lecture in San Francisco had the tagline "The Trouble to begin at 8 o'clock" (see Figure 2.1), a familiar phrasing of minstrel show advertisements. Moreover, the venue for the San Francisco lecture was Maguire's Academy of Music, a theater house built by Thomas Maguire. Maguire was known as the "Napoleon of San Francisco's theatrical world" (Estavan, *Tom* 1), and his contribution to the proliferation of minstrel shows in San Francisco was unparalleled. A transplant from New York City—the "birthplace of the minstrel show" (Toll 32)—who arrived in San Francisco in 1849, Maguire had an affinity for blackface minstrelsy matching Twain's. From the time that he engaged the Sable Harmonists, advertised to be "direct from the East," to perform at his Jenny Lind Theatre in January 1851 (Estavan, *Minstrelsy* 15), Maguire almost single-handedly established the minstrelsy industry in San Francisco. He also expanded minstrelsy outside San Francisco in the 1860s, sending troupes to the mining camps in the Sierras and "into the new fortune-earning camps of the Washoe, which had opened with discovery of large silver and gold deposits across the Nevada line" (Estavan, *Minstrelsy* 70). Maguire therefore may have had a hand in the minstrel performances that Twain had attended in Nevada. By the time Twain arrived in San Francisco, blackface minstrelsy was a booming cultural industry, with at least four or five permanent minstrel companies at a given time (Estavan, *Minstrelsy* 65). The theater district in San Francisco was part of Twain's beat as a journalist at the *Morning Call*, so it is very likely that

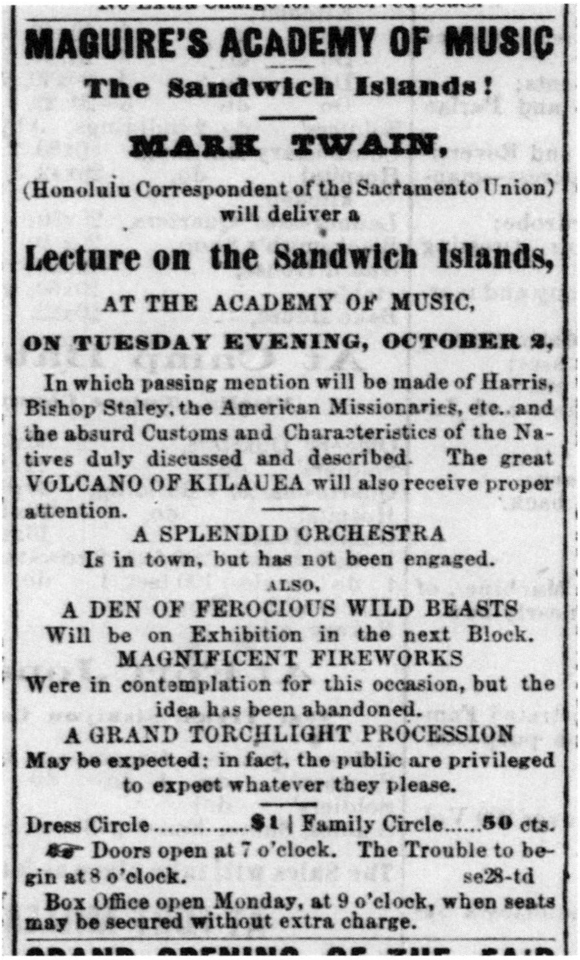

MAGUIRE'S ACADEMY OF MUSIC

The Sandwich Islands!

MARK TWAIN,

(Honolulu Correspondent of the Sacramento Union)
will deliver a

Lecture on the Sandwich Islands,

AT THE ACADEMY OF MUSIC,

ON TUESDAY EVENING, OCTOBER 2,

In which passing mention will be made of Harris,
Bishop Staley, the American Missionaries, etc., and
the absurd Customs and Characteristics of the Natives duly discussed and described. The great
VOLCANO OF KILAUEA will also receive proper
attention.

A SPLENDID ORCHESTRA

Is in town, but has not been engaged.

ALSO,

A DEN OF FEROCIOUS WILD BEASTS

Will be on Exhibition in the next Block.

MAGNIFICENT FIREWORKS

Were in contemplation for this occasion, but the
idea has been abandoned.

A GRAND TORCHLIGHT PROCESSION

May be expected: in fact, the public are privileged
to expect whatever they please.

Dress Circle................$1 | Family Circle......50 cts.
☞ Doors open at 7 o'clock. The Trouble to be-
gin at 8 o'clock.   se28-td
Box Office open Monday, at 9 o'clock, when seats
may be secured without extra charge.

FIGURE 2.1
Advertisement for Mark
Twain's lecture. From
Daily Alta California,
October 1, 1866, p. 4,
California Digital
Newspaper Collection,
Center for Bibliographic
Studies and Research,
University of California,
Riverside, http://cdnc
.ucr.edu.

Twain attended a blackface minstrel show "virtually every night" (Scharnhorst, *Life* 268) and knew just how much it was in demand. The "Trouble to
begin at 8 o'clock" tagline therefore speaks to Twain's and Maguire's shared
enthusiasm for blackface minstrelsy as well as the belief that the reference
would sell more tickets for the lecture.[9]

If the tagline in Twain's lecture poster exemplifies his strategic use of aspects of the minstrel show to construct his identity as Mark Twain, it also
illustrates that he was most influenced by one minstrel troupe in particu-

lar—the San Francisco Minstrels, who were specifically associated with the tagline, according to Sharon McCoy ("Trouble" 245). McCoy points out that when Twain was reminiscing nostalgically about the "real nigger show" in his dictated autobiography in 1906, he was describing the San Francisco Minstrels, as he stated that "Birch, Wambold, and Backus are gone years ago; and with them departed to return no more forever, I suppose, the real nigger show" (*Autobiography* 2:294). Formed by Charles Backus, Billy Birch, and David Wambold in San Francisco in 1864, the troupe was indeed immensely influential—for the development of not just Twain as a writer but also the industry of minstrel shows in the United States during and after the war. Their greatest contribution to minstrelsy was in breathing new life into the formal qualities of a minstrel performance. From the first staged performance of minstrelsy as its own show in the United States in 1843, the structure of a minstrel show remained constant. A typical production was divided into three parts. The first opened with blackfaced performers sitting in a semicircle, in the middle of which was the interlocutor, or the middleman, who acted as the emcee to a series of jokes told by the other men. The second part was the "olio," showcasing the given talents of the performers such as playing musical instruments or singing. The third, concluding part was a short skit. "Minstrel shows were formulaic in nature," Gary Engle writes; and, "like most mass arts, they were popular because they were familiar" (xxi).

As the formal aspects of a minstrel show would have become common knowledge by the time Twain began his writing career, Twain must have seen something new and worth imitating in the San Francisco Minstrels. Indeed, that something new was *how* the troupe performed old, familiar roles. Rather than change up the format that was already working, the San Francisco Minstrels perfected the existing roles of the interlocutor and the joke-telling "end men," and this, more than the tagline, is where we see the troupe's greatest influence on Twain. Acting as comical sidekicks to the serious interlocutor, the two end men were named Tambo and Bones for the instruments they played. Though these roles had been in place for decades, the San Francisco Minstrels, particularly with Backus and Birch playing Tambo and Bones, set a new standard. More than ever before, the roles emphasized jocularity, setting the tone for other minstrel shows, which had incorporated elements of sentimentalism and melodrama. Though they still incorporated jokes depicting a happy former plantation life, the San

Francisco Minstrels also integrated contemporary political satire into their shows and ended a typical performance with a parody of a popular play of the time. In short, they took an antebellum form of minstrelsy and made it *current*. Thanks to their success, the cultural form of blackface minstrelsy enjoyed renewed currency and popularity in the dominant white U.S. culture during and beyond the Civil War. In 1865, the San Francisco Minstrels relocated to New York City and remained there until they disbanded in 1883, enjoying a lasting popularity that cut through class lines. Proudly writing about the troupe in New York before leaving on the European excursion that would become the basis for *The Innocents Abroad* (1869), Twain wrote in 1867, "Our old San Francisco Minstrels have made their mark here, most unquestionably. . . . Every night of their lives they play to packed houses—every single seat full and dozens of people standing up" (*Travels* 176). As a lecturer who also wanted to "play to packed houses" and a writer who wanted to sell books, Twain would incorporate the formal elements of the San Francisco Minstrels into his writings, particularly in the figures of the interlocutor and end men.

While McCoy states that Twain seems to have been particularly influenced by the interlocutor figure from the San Francisco Minstrels' performances, and it is true that the narrators that he developed in his early fiction writings look to have been modeled on the figure, what Twain took from the troupe is that there needs to be a mixture of the interlocutor and end men, combining a straitlaced observer as well as a teller of punch lines. One of Twain's favorite minstrels was Billy Birch, who frequently appeared in Nevada (Twain, *Early* 1:490) before joining the San Francisco Minstrels and playing his iconic role as an end man. As Randall Knoper states, Twain "compared some of his own efforts at 'uncouth burlesques' to the 'incomprehensible' and 'conflicting' tale telling of Billy Birch . . . who slowly drawled his stage monologues and dialogues in a quiet, lazy, lumbering way" (59). William Bernard, who played the interlocutor part in the San Francisco Minstrels, was considered "the greatest interlocutor, or middle-man, that minstrelsy has ever known" (Rice 71), as he was thought to have had "no living equal as an interlocutor or middle man" (Slout 3). On the basis of Anthony Berrett's argument that Twain's most famous narrator, Huckleberry Finn, shifts from the role of an end man to an interlocutor depending on who he is with, we can surmise that Twain seems to have adapted both Birch's and Bernard's performances in his writings.

Twain's borrowing from both the end men and interlocutor figures reflects his assumption of the fungibility of the minstrel form. He apparently felt no compunction about the flexibility with which he adopted aspects of the San Francisco Minstrels' shows as his own, starting with but going beyond their tagline. After mentioning the San Francisco Minstrels in his autobiography, Twain describes the interlocutor and end men without crediting the troupe for their innovations on the figures. He discusses in particular the interlocutor, also called the middleman, as a "dainty gentleman" (*Autobiography* 2:294) who sat between Bones and Tambo, whom he mistakenly calls "Banjo." Twain states, "This middleman was the spokesman of the show. The neatness and elegance of his dress, the studied courtliness of his manners and speech, and the shapeliness of his *undoctored* features made him a contrast to the rest of the troupe and particularly to 'Bones' and 'Banjo'" (294–95; emphasis added). Twain's description of the interlocutor's "undoctored features" correctly implies that the interlocutor was not always in blackface and was sometimes the only one on stage who was "white." The fact that this interlocutor, with his class pretensions, was often the butt of jokes has been cited to argue that minstrelsy was not really about antiblackness but the enactment of white working-class men's frustrations and anxieties amid the rise of wage labor capitalism (see McCoy, "Trouble"). However, in the interlocutor's interchangeability as a white or Black character, we see the masking of slavery's racial logic that deemed the enslaved Black person to be a commodity marked by exchangeability. That is, regardless of the interlocutor's performance as a white or Black man, at work in a minstrel show was the logic of slavery in which Blackness and "blacks were envisioned fundamentally as vehicles for white enjoyment," not just for enslavers but all white people (Hartman, *Scenes* 23). As Saidiya Hartman argues, the belief in "the fungibility of the commodity, specifically its abstractness and immateriality, enabled the black body or blackface mask to serve as the vehicle of white self-exploration, renunciation, and enjoyment" (26). Hartman insists that the performance of Blackness, even as it belies a desire for that Blackness, is ultimately founded on the material relations of chattel slavery, and the "amazing popularity of the 'darkies' of the minstrel stage must be considered in this light" (23). The unequivocal popularity of minstrelsy in San Francisco and Twain's love of it should therefore be seen as part of the afterlife of slavery, as a reminder that "slavery had established a measure of man and a ranking of life and worth that has yet to be undone"

(Hartman, *Lose* 6). That Twain's interlocutor figure could have been white in his mind does not change the fact that the figure was an integral part of an entertainment form born out of slavery. As much as minstrelsy was about the construction of a white masculine identity, it was, "in and of itself, a defense of slavery," with the "myth of the benign plantation" as its main content (Saxton, "Blackface" 79). The interlocutor's whiteness, as well as the San Francisco Minstrels' innovations, masks this fact. Twain's adoption of the minstrel form similarly disaggregates minstrelsy from slavery.

Minstrelsy and slavery went hand in hand in San Francisco, however, as the popularity of minstrelsy in the city corresponded with the proslavery ideology and the antiblack racial logic seen in the 1850 California law that nullified Black testimony against white people in court. As Alexander Saxton states, "Several 'founding' minstrels as well as two or three of the nation's best-known minstrel companies can be placed in a scattered but consistent pattern of pro-Southern expression and innate contact with Democratic party leaders in New York and San Francisco" ("Blackface" 77). These antebellum antiblack policies and everyday practices in San Francisco did not disappear after emancipation. Lynn Hudson writes that Black people were banned from many public places such as the theater in San Francisco during Reconstruction, and as a result, "many African Americans believed, according to San Francisco's black newspaper, *The Pacific Appeal*, that 'prejudice against color is now as bitter among proprietors of public places' as it was before the passage of the Civil Rights Act of 1866 and the Fifteenth Amendment" (174). Specifically, Hudson recounts the experience of Charles Green, a Black man who tried to attend the performance of the Tennessee Jubilee Singers—who were billed by the aforementioned Tom Maguire as "most superb colored company in America"—at Maguire's New Theater in January 1876 (188). Green was denied a seat, demonstrating that the mind-set that saw Black people primarily as "purveyors of pleasure" (Hartman, *Scenes* 23) and entertainment was incapable of seeing them as equal agents of enjoyment. With the help of other Black San Franciscans, Green took Maguire to court under the Civil Rights Act of 1875. Green lost but took his case all the way to the Supreme Court, which also ruled that there was "insufficient evidence" of the violation of Green's civil rights (Hudson 188–89).[10] The strictly segregated space of the minstrel theater from which Black people were excluded is therefore a prime site to locate the ongoing inequalities after emancipation and the inextricable connection between minstrelsy and the racial logic of slavery and its afterlife.[11]

This inseparable tie between minstrelsy and slavery was reinforced in San Francisco through the popularity of minstrelsy and the birth of the San Francisco Minstrels there, but that tie was also obfuscated by the notion that minstrel figures such as the interlocutor and end men could be dissociated from slavery and Blackness. And that same notion can be seen in Twain's experimentation with the Chinese character in his early fiction writings. Here I am not arguing that Twain intentionally disavowed slavery in his writings about the Chinese. Rather, by employing the minstrel form to construct his Chinese character, he unwittingly exposed minstrelsy's extrapolation of an abstract form of the "slave," supported by the belief in the fungibility of Blackness. We see this logic at play in Twain's description of a minstrel show:

> The minstrels appeared with coal-black hands and faces, and their clothing was a loud and extravagant burlesque of the clothing worn by the plantation slave of the time; not that the rags of the poor slave were burlesqued, for that would not have been possible; burlesque could have added nothing in the way of extravagance to the sorrowful accumulation of rags and patches which constituted his costume; it was the *form* and color of his dress that was burlesqued. (*Autobiography* 2:294; emphasis added)

Revealingly, Twain implies that minstrelsy did not make fun of slavery itself. Instead, from the "rags" of the enslaved person, minstrelsy abstracted a "form" of his dress, and in that process, turned something "sorrowful" into a comical "extravagance." Understanding blackface minstrelsy as a performance of a form, which he thought was "a most competent laughter-compeller" (*Autobiography* 2:296), Twain used that form to make his debut as a writer in San Francisco.

Reconstructing Redface in "John Chinaman in New York"

When Twain moved to San Francisco from Nevada, his reputation as a humorist preceded him. That may have been the reason why Mark Twain was chosen to give a speech celebrating the military heroics of Major Edward C. Perry of New York in June 1864, not long after Twain's arrival in San Francisco in late May. The written version of the speech appeared on the first page of the San Francisco *Alta California* on June 13, 1864, and it was Twain's first publication in his new city (Twain, *Early* 2:5). In the speech,

Twain employed the minstrel form but spoke in redface. The speech is signed, "Mark Twain, High-you-muck-a-muck" (8), and is from the vantage point of someone who speaks on behalf of one of the "red men whom I represent" (7). It contains the themes that Twain would take up in his other writings about Native peoples, one of which was their aversion to cleanliness. Twain characterized this aversion as a result of "the absence of soap and their natural indifference to water," which made the Native peoples "visibly black" (7). In his public debut in performance—which he would repeat in two years in a lecture on Hawai'i—and writing, we see the construction of Mark Twain as a humorist whose humor is founded on performing a racialized other, a practice borrowed from minstrelsy. Demonstrating that indebtedness, even when—or because—that performance embodies Indigeneity, Twain has to mark the Native peoples as "visibly black."

Despite Twain's linking together Indigeneity and Blackness, there is an important distinction between the white performances of the two. As Philip Deloria has shown, "playing Indian" has been a central part in the construction of an American identity and a "persistent tradition in American culture" (7), beginning with the Boston Tea Party. But the tradition of playing Indian or "going native" cannot be subsumed under the tradition of minstrelsy. Instead, as Shari Huhndorf posits, the former must be understood through "the historical relations between European America and Native America, particularly the nature of the conquest," which has played a "determining role in the forms that going native has taken" in the nineteenth-century United States (8). This specificity means that the way we read performances and constructions of "Indianness" through redface such as Twain's must keep in mind settler colonialism's logic of elimination, noting that the performances function as "an act of symbolic genocide" (Richards 37). If, as Jodi Byrd argues, Indianness functions as a "transit," "a site through which U.S. empire orients and replicates itself by transforming those to be colonized into 'Indians' through continual re-iterations of pioneer logics" (xiii), the fact that there were sometimes—though not frequent—redface actors on the minstrel stage speaks to the way in which minstrelsy was in service of the colonial narrative that the U.S. empire tells itself. The practices of playing Indian and blackface minstrelsy, then, should not be "hierarchize[d] . . . into coeval or causal order" but rather be read as what Byrd calls "cacophonies of colonialism" (xxvii). Twain's debut as a writer in San Francisco demonstrates such cacophonies.

If Twain relied on a performance in redface when he first began his journalistic writing in San Francisco, he would turn to yellowface at a time most formative to the construction of his identity as an American literary writer. This moment was immediately following the success of *The Innocents Abroad*, which would be the best-selling book that Twain would write, and just before the respectable sales of *Roughing It* (1872). Between May 1870 and April 1871, Twain was given his own column called "Memoranda" in the *Galaxy*, a well-regarded monthly magazine. In his new position, Twain began to think of himself as a literary writer and not just a journalist. He also wanted to become a nationally recognized writer, not just one associated with the West. The figure of the Chinese worker was an important component in this transition. Five out of the eleven "Memoranda" columns contain stories featuring a Chinese worker, three of which were one story serialized. In these stories, more than any others in "Memoranda," we see Twain's attempt to develop a distinctive voice and hone the literary device of a narrator, whose naïve and earnest voice resembles the interlocutor in a minstrel show. Of the three stories about the Chinese, two featured a fictional narrator. The first, "John Chinaman in New York," was published in September 1870, the same month when Harte's most famous poem was published in the *Overland Monthly*. Just as we see traces of minstrelsy in Harte's poem, we also see the same in Twain's story, as the "John Chinaman" in the story is not a Chinese man at all but an Irishman who is dressed to play the part.

Like "Disgraceful Persecution of a Boy," a satirical essay condemning anti-Chinese racism in San Francisco that Twain published in the inaugural installment of "Memoranda" in May 1870, "John Chinaman in New York" employs the format of journalistic writing, only to distance itself from it. It begins with a note stating, "A correspondent (whose signature, 'Lang Bemis,' is more or less familiar to the public) contributes the following" (Twain, *Contributions* 70). Despite this note purporting veracity, however, Twain most likely made up the figure of Lang Bemis. Bruce McElderry Jr. writes that "long search has failed to identify the 'Lang Bemis' to whom Twain refers as familiar to the public" (Twain, *Contributions* 146n2), so Twain was not exactly lying about Bemis's being "more or *less* familiar to the public." Bemis is one of the earliest first-person fictional narrators in Twain's writings, making "John Chinaman" a short story by genre, even though it is rarely read as such.

Despite the title, "John Chinaman" is a character study of Lang Bemis and an exercise in the development of a fictional first-person narrative voice, distinct from Twain's own voice, using the minstrel figure of the interlocutor. Through Bemis, the story explores the technique of disguise and performance in the process of narrating fiction. A story about false fronts, it centers on the experience of Bemis as he comes across a Chinese worker who is "acting in the capacity of a sign" outside a teashop (Twain, *Contributions* 70). On one level, the story is premised on the disguise of the narrator who is not Mark Twain but Lang Bemis, a supposed correspondent of the *Galaxy*. On another level, there is the eponymous "John Chinaman," whose personhood is reduced to a literal sign, as he is alienated from not only the fruits of his labor but also the normative space of work as he is made to sit *outside* the shop (70). On yet another level, the Chinese worker is not Chinese at all but Irish. Ignorant of the last point, Bemis focuses only on the treatment of the Chinese worker as a sign and implicitly blames white supremacist racism for the mistreatment, criticizing not only the worker's situation but also those who, in the process of gawking at the worker, objectify him:

> Men calling themselves the superior race, the race of culture and of gentle blood, scanned his quaint Chinese hat, with peaked roof and ball on top; and his long queue dangling down his back; his short silken blouse, curiously frogged and figured (and, like the rest of his raiment, rusty, dilapidated, and awkwardly put on); his blue cotton, tight-legged pants tied close around the ankles, and his clumsy, blunt-toed shoes with thick cork soles; and having so scanned him from head to foot, cracked some unseemly joke about his outlandish attire or his melancholy face, and passed on. (70)

Bemis implies here that the gaze of the white passersby inevitably resulted in "some unseemly joke" at the expense of the Chinese, as the mere appearance of the Chinese was enough to produce a racist reaction.[12] He draws a connection between "some unseemly joke" and the "outlandish attire," reminiscent of the "form" of the enslaved people's clothing in Twain's discussion of minstrelsy. Though Bemis himself does not burlesque the Chinese worker's clothing or repeat the joke, at hand is the point that if not outright funny, the Chinese worker's appearance is at least curious and entertaining, a point that Bemis also gives in to when he provides a detailed description of his appearance. Meaning, Bemis is implicated in the white supremacist mode of seeing, or reading, the Chinese worker. As if in anticipation of this criticism, in the next sentence, Bemis differentiates himself from the other "men calling themselves the superior race" by stating, "In my heart *I* pitied the friendless Mongol" (70; emphasis added).

Bemis's pity not only exempts him from the dominant racism of other New Yorkers but also ends up being self-serving in multiple ways.[13] It enables him to imagine the Chinese worker's interiority, as he wonders condescendingly "what distant scene his vacant eye was dreaming of" (70), and it gives him a sense of moral superiority.[14] Most of all, Bemis's pity endows him with an authoritative if not an authorial voice. After rhapsodizing about the romanticized "by-gone time" that he imagines "this bronzed wanderer" to be thinking about, Bemis decides to do something about the situation by talking to the worker. He thinks his approach will elicit sympathy in the passersby, as they "might be touched at least by the words of the poor fellow, since the appeal of his pauper dress and his dreary exile was lost upon them" (70). In this manner, Bemis assumes the role of the interlocutor, as he assigns himself to be the conduit that brings forth the words of the Chinese worker to the masses that do not have the sensitivity and compassion to be moved as he is. Bemis's lofty goal backfires, however, as often happens for the interlocutor in minstrel shows. When Bemis asks the worker how much he is getting paid for his job, the worker responds, "Divil a cint but four dollars a week and find meself; but it's aisy, barrin' the bloody furrin clothes that's so expinsive" (70). Here is the climax of the story and the punch line of the joke, as the heavily accented response reveals the worker to be Irish. It turns out that the "John Chinaman" in New York was only a performance as well as the imagination of Bemis. The story ends without a revelation or recognition of error on the part of Bemis, with his commenting noncommittally that the "New York tea merchants who need picturesque signs are not likely to run out of Chinamen" (70). The joke is on Bemis, as he has misread the sign, or the "Chinese" worker acting as one.

This short sketch by Twain lampoons not only the Irish "Chinese worker" but also, and mostly, the naïve and self-righteous narrator-interlocutor who believes that he alone feels compassion for the persecuted Chinese and wants to use the words of the Chinese to move the indifferent white people. What is made fun of in the story is the antiracism of the narrator and possibly the reader who may have also felt sympathy for the Chinese worker. The point of the story is not to speak out on behalf of the Chinese worker or to criticize the minstrel form of performing the racial nonwhite other. Quite the contrary; the story underscores Twain's characterization of minstrelsy as "a most competent laughter-compeller" (*Autobiography* 2:296), as he tries to use the wildly popular minstrel form in the construction of a new non-Black character in literature, such as an Irish worker performing the role of a Chinese worker.

By locating "John Chinaman" not in San Francisco but in New York, Twain also plays with the transposability of the minstrel form and his exploration of it through redface. This practice speaks to the capacious appeal and use of the minstrel form, according to Tavia Nyong'o—"its facility for inverting, burlesquing, and blackening anything" (108). "John Chinaman" is virtually a replica of Twain's "Day at Niagara," which was published in the *Buffalo Express* in the previous year in August 1869. In that story, the narrator, who is not characterized as anyone other than Twain, has various encounters with workers in Niagara whom the narrator thinks are Native but also turn out to be Irish. The story recounts his visit to the famous falls in New York, and contains a section under the subheading, "The Noble Red Man." The section opens this way:

> The noble Red Man has always been a darling of mine. I love to read about him in tales and legends and romances. I love to read of his inspired sagacity; and his love of the wild free life of mountain and forest; and his grand truthfulness, his hatred of treachery, and his general nobility of character; and his stately metaphorical manner of speech; and his chivalrous love for his dusky maiden; and the picturesque pomp of his dress and accouterment. Especially the picturesque pomp of his dress and accouterment. (Twain, "Mark Twain's 'Day'" 3)

The narrator's satirical "love" of the "noble Red Man," particularly the repeated fascination with the "picturesque pomp of his dress and accouterment," calls to mind again the burlesquing of the form of the the the enslaved people's clothing. It also parallels the fetishization of the exotic Chinese costume that so impressed and duped Bemis in "John Chinaman." The naïveté of the narrator in "Day at Niagara" is further accentuated by his excitement upon seeing "a noble Son of the Forest sitting under a tree, diligently at work on a bead reticule" (3). Similar to Bemis in "John Chinaman" who exoticizes the "Chinese" worker, the narrator in "Day at Niagara" addresses the worker by stating, "Is the Wawhoo-Wang-Wang of the Wack-a-Whack happy? Does the great Speckled Thunder sigh for the war-path, or is his heart contented with dreaming of his dusky maiden, the Pride of the Forest? Does the mighty sachem yearn to drink the blood of his enemies, or is he satisfied to make bead reticules for the papooses of the pale face? Speak, sublime relic of by-gone grandeur—venerable ruin, speak!" (3). The narrator's speech, in the highfalutin fashion of the interlocutor, is a catalog of racist stereotypical images of Native peoples. Furthermore, the repeated demand to speak is reminiscent of Bemis in "John Chinaman" who does not realize that the racialized other's speech will reduce him to a joke. And sure enough, as in "John Chinaman," the words of the supposedly blighted racialized worker end up undoing the narrative and lampooning the narrator. The worker responds, "An is it mesilf, Dinnis Hooligan, that ye'd be taking for a bloody Injin, ye drawlin' lantern-jawed, spider-legged divil!" (3). Like the "Chinese worker," the "Indian worker" turns out to be Irish. The ultimate joke in "Day at Niagara" is that despite the corrections by multiple Irish workers around Niagara, the narrator persists in viewing them as Native people, until "the entire tribe" goes after him as an angry mob and throws him down the falls (3).

As with "John Chinaman in New York," what is being made fun of in "Day at Niagara" is first and foremost the narrator's naïveté. But this naïveté must be read in conjunction with Twain's not so innocent anti-Native racism. By rewriting "Day at Niagara" as "John Chinaman," Twain transposed the naïveté of the former narrator onto a fictional narrator, Bemis, and changed the misidentified racialized group from Natives to the Chinese. At the same time, Twain separated out the anti-Native racism from "Day at Niagara" and gave it its own space in the *Galaxy*. Immediately following "John Chinaman" in the "Memoranda" column, Twain included an essay called "The Noble Red Man," whose title replicates the aforementioned subheading from "Day at Niagara." In "The Noble Red Man" in "Memoranda," Twain—not a fictional narrator—goes on a diatribe against Native peoples and their romanticized representations that have distorted the "truth" about them. Twain corrects the supposed distortion by explaining that Native peoples are "ignoble—base and treacherous, and hateful in every way. Not even imminent death can startle [them] into a spasm of virtue" (Twain, *Contributions* 71) and that the "red man's" "heart is a cesspool of falsehood, of treachery, and of low and devilish instincts" (72), and he is "the scum of the earth!" (72).[15]

In his venomous anti-Native rant, Twain employs the language of antiblackness. Similar to his earlier description of Native people as "visibly black" (Twain, *Early* 2:7), he represents them in "The Noble Red Man" as "black, and dirty" (71). What we can glean here is the expansive work that the word *black* performs in the racial logic of U.S. empire, as seen in the 1850 California law that proclaimed "black" to be a generic category applicable to all nonwhite people. Twain relies on such utility when writing about Native peoples. Writing without irony—except in the title—or humor, Twain unleashes his unmitigated anti-Native racism in "The Noble Red Men," which he would go on to repeat in portions of *Roughing It*. In describing the Goshute Shoshones in *Roughing It*, Twain employs the derogatory term "digger," which Ned Blackhawk explains was a "debasement of Shoshone gathering practices with strong homophonic resonance with America's most powerful racial epithet, 'nigger'" (275). Making this resonance explicit, Twain compares the Shoshone to the "Bosjesmans (Bushmen) of South Africa," stating that their complexion was a "dull black like the ordinary American negro" (*Roughing It* 131). The intertwined working of antiblackness and anti-Native racism is incontestable here.

Twain's racist representations of Native peoples have been characterized by mostly non-Native scholars as a paradox (see Harris; McNutt; Coulombe; Foner). Philip Foner, for example, cites Twain's racism against Native peoples as contradicting his otherwise liberal stance on race. But if we read Twain's anti-Native invective in "The Noble Red Man" alongside "John Chinaman in New York," we can see that the avowed antiracism in the latter is a *work of fiction*, in which the fictional Bemis states, "America has a broader hospitality for the exiled and oppressed. America and Americans are always ready to help the unfortunate" (*Contributions* 70). While meant to be satirical, Bemis's words reveal a fundamental hypocrisy in the self-identification of the United States as a land of the free. Even though Twain is often read as exposing that hypocrisy, his part in it is undeniable. This contradiction is seen in the violence at the core of his writings about Native peoples, characterized by Blackhawk as revealing "distant pity and proximate revulsion" (275; see also Byrd; Driscoll; Kaplan). When that revulsion is articulated using the existing vocabulary of antiblackness, we can read the anti-Native racism in "The Noble Red Man" as neither anomalous nor surprising but revealing of the violent racial logic of U.S. settler colonialism.

Twain's anti-Native racism is part and parcel of the narrative of empire, particularly the narrative strategy that saddles humor with vicious hate speech to justify white supremacy and the expropriation of Native resources and land in the United States. For Twain, the authority to narrate that empire comes not from "books, but from personal observation," as he blames both the tendency in the "Atlantic seaboard" to side with the "poor abused Indian" and the white literary writers whose writings romanticize the Native peoples (*Contributions* 73). As this liberal attitude sounds similar to the naïve Lang Bemis's in "John Chinaman in New York," we might read the authorial and authoritative voice in "The Noble Red Man" as criticizing Bemis in the previous story. In other words, while "John Chinaman" uses humor to explore the fictional voice of Lang Bemis, the narrator of "The Noble Red Man," who is understood to be Twain, stands in contrast to the liberal and inclusive Bemis who imagines the Chinese to be a downtrodden race. The romanticized view of the Chinese on the part of Bemis is criticized indirectly through the narrator in "The Noble Red Man," who cautions against fictionalized representations of the racialized other by labeling them as untrustworthy. If all of this makes it difficult to be conclusive about the consistency of Twain's antiracism, perhaps that is because antiracism was not the goal of his writings. The main objective, instead, was to develop a narrative voice with authority while still being able to tell a joke, to model a minstrel show and its ability to be "delightfully and satisfyingly funny" (Twain, *Autobiography* 2:294).

"The History of a Chinaman's Sojourn in America"

In the month following the publication of "John Chinaman in New York" and "The Noble Red Man," Twain published another story in his "Memoranda" column featuring the Chinese worker and called it "Goldsmith's Friend Abroad Again" (1870). As it was also the month after the fanatical reception of Harte's "heathen Chinee" poem, the timing was just right. Twain used the Chinese worker as the narrator of the story, beating out even Harte in writing the first fictional short story in U.S. literature to feature a Chinese first-person narrator. For the story, Twain drew on established literature and took inspiration from the eighteenth-century Irish novelist Oliver Goldsmith's creation of a series of fictionalized letters written by a traveling Chinese philosopher named Lien Chi Altangi. In Lien's letters, which were eventually compiled into a novel called *The Citizen of the World* (1762), Goldsmith developed the highly opinionated voice of the Chinese philosopher, who became the novel's protagonist. Alluding to Goldsmith's novel in the title, Twain's serialized stories consist of letters all written by a Chinese worker named Ah Song Hi to Ching-Foo, Ah Song Hi's friend whose location is unspecified and whose receipt of the letters is never acknowledged. Based on the fact that the Ah Song Hi letters were the only items in the *Galaxy* that were serialized, appearing in October and November 1870 and January 1871, we can surmise that perhaps they were also meant to be collected later into a novel, as Goldsmith's fictional letters had been. In other words, Twain may have been developing a novelistic fictional narrator in Ah Song Hi.

Scholars of "Goldsmith's Friend Abroad Again" have not focused on *how* Twain developed the Chinese character's voice in the serialized stories. Instead, as with "Disgraceful Persecution of a Boy," many have read the story as demonstrating Twain's antiracism or pro-Chinese attitude through the character of Ah Song Hi (see, most notably, Ou; Lai-Henderson; Foner; Zehr). When Twain's formal strategies *are* noted, they are read as proof that that Twain was using sarcasm to launch a critique of anti-Chinese racism. While it is true that "Goldsmith's Friend" does expose the hypocrisy of anti-Chinese racism, the main point of the story, again, is not social critique. In particular, despite McElderry Jr.'s claim that they are "notable examples of serious invective" (McElderry xx) against the mistreatment of the Chinese, I argue that the main function of Ah Song Hi's letters is to explore the limits of the interlocutor figure in an attempt to create serious literature that does not rely just on humor. This reading intervenes in the propensity to read the story not only as historical evidence of Twain's liberalism but also, during Twain's time, as authentic representation of a Chinese worker and his history. And that reading rarely involves a critical engagement with the mode of representation using the minstrel form, which can reveal the work that the Chinese character performs in the construction of Mark Twain and American literature.

If the serialized "Goldsmith's Friend Abroad Again" has not been read as fictional literature, this is partly because Twain himself presented the story as nonfiction. Twain began each publication of "Goldsmith's Friend" with a disclaimer that read, "Note. No experience is set down in the following letters which had to be invented. Fancy is not needed to give variety to the history of a Chinaman's sojourn in America. Plain fact is amply sufficient" (*Contributions* 79).[16] In announcing itself as "Note," the short preface blurs the boundary between "fancy" and "history." But while it seems to be saying that what follows will be "plain fact," the note does not assert that the letters are such. The "experience" and "history of a Chinaman's sojourn in America" are called factual, but the note does not say that the letters themselves are. In this move, the unsigned note establishes the authority of Twain as the author of the fictional letters.

The claim about "plain fact" in the note could be seen as a reference to Harte's "Plain Language from Truthful James." While it is not known that Twain had read Harte's poem prior to writing Ah Song Hi's letters, there are points of parallel as well as important, perhaps knowing, divergences. Though both Ah Sin and Ah Song Hi are cast as workers in California, the serialized depiction of Ah Song Hi is in sharp contrast to the cartoonish caricature of Ah Sin as a Topsy-like figure and a naïve yet duplicitous mining worker who meets a violent end at the hand of white miners. Whether or not Ah Song Hi was intentionally created to complicate the character of Ah Sin, Ah Song Hi was a much more developed characterization of the Chinese worker than Ah Sin was.

Twain's multiple inclusions of the Chinese worker figure in the "Memoranda" columns, around the same time as when Harte thought that a poem about a Chinese worker would be a suitable fill-in for an empty space in the *Overland Monthly*, indicate that both Harte and Twain were mining the figure for literary gold during this time. Anticipating Twain's own claim during the curtain speech to *Ah Sin*—a yellowface play cowritten with Harte—in 1877 that "the Chinaman is going to become a frequent spectacle all over America by and by, and a difficult political problem, too" (Fatout 104), "Goldsmith's Friend" explores the "difficult political problem" by fictionalizing how a Chinese worker might narrate his own story. In the process, Twain casts Ah Song Hi in the role of the interlocutor.

Ah Song Hi speaks in highly formal English, reminiscent of the interlocutor's "stilted, courtly, artificial, and painfully grammatical form of speech" (Twain, *Autobiography* 2:294). The letters in "Goldsmith's Friend" follow the narrative arc from an excited Ah Song Hi in Shanghai set to sail to the United States as a laborer to a beaten-up and jailed Ah Song Hi who receives an unfair trial and is sent back to jail. The use of the epistolary structure allows Twain to imagine Ah Song Hi speaking in standard instead of pidgin

English. What Ah Song Hi writes and how he writes it are both marked by exuberant enthusiasm and optimism: "Congratulate me, Ching-Foo! In ten days more I shall step upon the shore of America, and be received by her great-hearted people" (Twain, *Contributions* 80). Ah Song Hi's naïve and trusting faith in the United States expressed through flowery language in this particular instance communicates to the reader not only his excitement but also a gross misunderstanding of his situation and the history of racial violence in the United States, particularly the history of slavery. For instance, immediately before his ebullient exclamation to Ching-Foo, Ah Song Hi describes a fight among the Chinese workers onboard the ship that was sailing for the United States from Shanghai. He states that the white captain "turned a volume of hot steam upon a mass of them and scalded eighty or ninety of them more or less severely. Flakes and ribbons of skin came off some of them . . . [while] some who were not scalded got trampled upon and hurt" (80). Ah Song Hi merely describes this situation without providing any commentary, adding, "We do not complain, for my employer says *this is the usual way of quieting disturbances on board the ship*, and that it is done in the cabins among the Americans every day or two" (80; emphasis added). Ah Song Hi's description of violence on a ship calls to mind the history of the Middle Passage and mutiny and violence on ships used for captivity. It also recalls the fact that, as Evelyn Hu-Dehart writes, "many of the same ships and captains used in the African slave trade now transported Chinese coolies" (45). Ah Song Hi himself does not make this connection, however. Ah Song Hi does not notice the specter of slavery in the treatment of racialized labor in U.S. capitalism, which is seen throughout the first installment of the story. Before leaving China, Ah Song Hi states, "For a mere form, I have turned over my wife, my boy, and my two daughters to my employer's partner for security for the payment of the ship fare" (Twain, *Contributions* 79). Ah Song Hi's decision to work abroad in the United States transforms his family into not just currency but commodity that can be bought and sold, and yet Ah Song Hi is optimistic and naïvely believes his employer who states, "They are in no danger of being sold" (79).

The idea of using his wife and children as collateral for his stay in the United States shows not just his naïve trust in the contractor but also calls to mind the practice of slavery, so that when Ah Song Hi states that his employer has arranged jobs for the Chinese workers at "*plantations* in the far eastern portion of this continent" (80; emphasis added), the reader is prompted to make an explicit connection between slavery and Chinese labor. However, this connection might not entail a remembrance of Black suffering under chattel slavery but rather enable a forgetting of that suffering in light of the condition of Chinese workers as the new slavelike workers. In this manner, the story's invocation of the language of slavery to describe Chinese suffering actually mirrors the practice of using the language of slavery to discuss Chinese labor by lawmakers during Reconstruction.

While most lawmakers used such language to align the Chinese with slavery to justify their exclusion, there was an important exception: Anton Burlingame, diplomatic minister to China (1861–1867) and the man behind the Burlingame Treaty (1868), which amended the previous unequal treaty between China and the United States.[17] In a speech delivered at the signing of the treaty, Burlingame argued against unequal treaties between the Western powers and China, stating that such treaties engender the mind-set that "these people [the Chinese] have no rights which we are bound to respect" (Speer 675). Burlingame's speech references the most well-known line from the most well-known court case from slavery, *Dred Scott v. Sandford* (1857): "They [the Black captives] had no rights which the white man was bound to respect" (*Dred Scott* 407). In denying citizenship to all Black people, "free" and enslaved, *Dred Scott* affirmed the justification of slavery, that it was natural for Black people to be "bought and sold, and treated as an ordinary article of merchandise and traffic whenever a profit could be made by it" (407). The case codified into law not only that *all* Black people could not be free but also that *any* "white man" was. By alluding to *Dred Scott* as an example of an injustice against (Chinese) humanity without taking into account the specificity of its antiblackness that reduced Black people to the nonhuman category of "merchandise," Burlingame's speech falls short of recognizing the actual violence behind the case.[18]

We see Burlingame's failed recognition of slavery as a process of dehumanization repeated in the Ah Song Hi stories as well as "The Disgraceful Persecution of a Boy," which is most often cited as an evidence for Twain's advocacy for the Chinese. Twain's views toward the Chinese were greatly influenced by his friendship with Burlingame, who fought for cooperative policies with China and was a champion of the Chinese in the United States (Duckett). The unequivocally pro-Chinese essay "The Disgraceful Persecution of a Boy," published three months after Burlingame's death in 1870, may have been Twain's homage to the ambassador. As Martin Zehr points out, Twain replicates Burlingame's reference to *Dred Scott* in the story, stating that all the legal and cultural institutions of the United States have conspired to promote the notion that "a Chinaman had no rights that any man was bound to respect" (*Contributions* 43). Both Twain and Burlingame remove Blackness *and* whiteness from the original line in the *Dred Scott* ruling, obfuscating the violence of defining whiteness in association with freedom and Blackness with unfreedom. Twain's calling attention to anti-Chinese violence at the expense of erasing the continued violence against Black people reflects the way in which such violence still defined the reality of Black people in the United States after emancipation. His Ah Song Hi's stories, which were clearly meant to elicit sympathy for the Chinese worker's plight, function in a similar way, by imbuing Ah Song Hi with a historical ignorance of slavery in the United States. When Ah Song Hi states after experiencing abuse on the ship on the way to San Francisco, "I shall straighten myself up and feel that I am a free man among freemen" (80), he shows ignorance of the historical fact that not everyone living in the United States had been free just five years ago. The use of the word *freemen* indicates Ah Song Hi's unawareness about the practice of referring to the formerly enslaved people as "freedmen," highlighting his naïve thinking that he would be seen as free when in fact a different fate awaited him.[19] The story implies that the injustice of Ah Song Hi's subsequent situation in the United States is that he is treated as if he is Black when in fact he is not. The logic that Blackness is antithetical to freedom goes unchallenged.

Moreover, "Goldsmith's Friend" never explicitly states that Ah Song Hi is indeed free, but only that he "feels" as such. In fact, as Ah Song Hi's chief trait is his naïveté, he is not portrayed as an active agent in his own story. Ah Song Hi's trusting assessment of "America" and unfeigned innocence, which may be described as "childlike," to echo Harte's poem, are reminiscent of Lang Bemis's speech to the "Chinese" worker in "John Chinaman in New York." But a key distinction for "Goldsmith's Friend" is that unlike in "John Chinaman in New York," the narrator's naïveté has no humorous function. There is irony in "Goldsmith's Friend" but no humor. Without the humorous function, the irony of Ah Song Hi's situation as an innocent "free" worker who is vilified has nowhere to go. At every turn, Ah Song Hi's hopes and expectations for the United Sates are thwarted. The biggest irony is that all Ah Song Hi wants to do is to work but he is prevented from doing so—first by his employer, who loses the contract for Ah Song Hi and other

Chinese laborers and abandons the workers, then by the Irishmen who harass him on the street in San Francisco, then by the police who lock him up, and finally by the judge who orders him back to jail because he cannot pay the five-dollar fine for disturbing the peace. All throughout, there is no humor—just Ah Song Hi's abject suffering and mistreatment. So even though Ah Song Hi is given the voice to narrate his own story, he is more like Jim than Huck Finn in *Adventures of Huckleberry Finn*, but without the unintended humor prompted by Jim's gullibility.

In Ah Song Hi's character, then, Twain may have been exploring the question of whether or not the Chinese worker figure can be a viable character as an interlocutor figure in U.S. literature, distinct from the cartoonish rendering of the "heathen Chinee" seen in Harte's poem. Could the Chinese worker both be a serious character and fit the interlocutor form? Without a racialized other to act as his foil and end man, where was Ah Song Hi to draw from for humor? Most of all, "Goldsmith's Friend" seems to ask whether a nonwhite character could be the protagonist of his own story without being burdened by racist stereotypes and mockery. For Twain, the answer ultimately seems to be no, and the reasoning behind that answer can be seen in his peripheral use of Black figures by the second installment of "Goldsmith's Friend."

There are just three mentions of Black people in Twain's "Memoranda" columns. They are all placed near two of his three Chinese stories. The first mention, in "About Smells," occurs right before "Disgraceful Persecution of a Boy" in May 1870, in an allusion to the distinctive body odor of Black people, which was a pet topic for Twain (see Pettit 41). The next two occur in the November 1870 issue: one in "Riley—Newspaper Correspondent," placed right before the second installment of "Goldsmith's Friend," and the other one in the short story itself. In the third mention, Twain compares the Chinese directly with Black people, as he describes that punishment was meted out to different groups in the criminal justice system based on their nationality and race. He states, "Negroes were promptly punished, when there was the slightest preponderance of testimony against them; but Chinamen were punished *always*, apparently" (Twain, *Contributions* 94; emphasis in original). This relational depiction of Black people and the Chinese could be read as an example of how "[Twain's] works register and critique the structural inequalities that ground racial comparisons," according to Hsuan Hsu (*Sitting* 26). However, while Twain points out the antiblack bias in the legal system, he ultimately concludes that the anti-Chinese bias is worse. In his rendering, the Chinese are the most abjectly treated race in the United States. The practice of erasing Black suffering through Chinese suffering persists here. But even as he wrote about the latter, Twain seems to have struggled with painting that abjection without indulging in humor and his own enjoyment. Given that Twain's understanding of humor was structured by his love of blackface minstrelsy, which was predicated on the "economy of [white] enjoyment" (Hartman, *Scenes* 26), we see this struggle and its resolution in his essay, "Riley—Newspaper Correspondent," in the form of a joke about a Black character.

In "Riley—Newspaper Correspondent," we are told that Riley, "one of the best men in Washington—or elsewhere," is "full of humor" (Twain, *Contributions* 90). Twain's description of Riley's deadpan humor borders on self-description, as he writes, "Riley has a ready wit, a quickness and aptness at selecting and applying quotations, and a countenance that is as solemn and as blank as the back side of a tombstone when he is delivering a particularly exasperating joke" (91). In fact, the entire story blurs a clear-cut distinction between Twain and Riley, who was a real person and not Twain's creation like Lang Bemis. We are told that Riley is a correspondent for California newspapers currently living in Washington, D.C., and that the two men lived together from 1866 to 1867 while Twain was also working in the same capacity. In the present moment, in spite of his keen sense of humor, Riley is forced to write letters that "display a more than earthly solemnity, and like an unimaginative devotion to petrified facts, which surprise and distress all men who know him in his unofficial character" (90). Riley tells those surprised friends that he was hired to "write facts, not fancy," and that when he did try to insert humor, it was misunderstood and excoriated (90). The repetition of the word "facts," particularly when placed in opposition to "fancy," calls to mind the note that appears in the beginning of the "Goldsmith" stories: "Fancy is not needed to give variety to the history of a Chinaman's sojourn in America. Plain fact is amply sufficient" (*Contributions* 79). Riley's forced position of reporting on facts makes him so unhappy that sometimes he sneaks into his den to scribble down furiously a "sparkling and absorbing readable letter," but "with suffering such as only a mother can know, he destroys the pretty children of his fancy" (90). It cannot have been mere coincidence that Riley's wretchedness in having to write humorless letters is placed alongside Twain's own humorless letters in

"Goldsmith's Friend." In the essay on Riley, Twain states that Riley led an exciting life before he was tied down by his current boring job, particularly as he traveled to and lived in Alaska, the Sandwich Islands, Mexico, and, most of all, California, where he worked as a courtroom interpreter for the Chinese. Of all the places, Riley's stay in California is highlighted and cited to showcase both Riley's and Twain's deadpan humor, as Twain states that Riley worked as a court interpreter for the Chinese, even though he "did not know a word of the Chinese tongue and only adopted interpreting as a means of gaining an honest livelihood," but that he was eventually removed from his position, perhaps for being too free with his translations (90). In writing about how Riley was full of humor, Twain vicariously exhibits his own aptitude for humor—the humor that has been withheld in the writing of his Ah Song Hi letters.

Twain's eulogistic paean to his humorous friend achieves the following: first, it provides space to showcase Riley's "sparkling" humor, one that has been suppressed by newspaper writing. Second, Twain gets a reprieve of his own from his story's commitment to "plain fact[s]" by writing about the Chinese in an irreverent way through Riley's experience in California. And third, Twain gets to publish a racist joke without being its teller. The essay on Riley ends with a climax, which is a joke told with deadpan humor about a Black woman servant who dies next door to the house where Twain and Riley were boarding. Their white landlady is absolutely heartbroken by the death of the Black woman, who worked for her. She tells them how faithful and loyal the woman was and that she literally worked herself to death by falling asleep over a stove and getting "roasted to a crisp" (91). She says that she wants to scrimp together whatever funds she can to buy a tombstone for the dead woman, and she asks Riley for an apt epitaph. Riley, without a smile, tells her to put, "*Well done*, good and faithful servant!" (91; emphasis in original). In telling a joke that relies on the absurd obtuseness and dehumanization of a Black character—a familiar sight on the minstrel stage—Twain may have been doing something similar to Riley's sneaking into his den to write humorous letters full of "fancy."

There is yet another calculating function served by the Riley piece and its reliance on a Black figure for humor. In December 1870, one month after the publication of "Riley—Newspaper Correspondent," Twain drafted a long, 2,500-word letter to Riley in private. In it, he proposed a business venture in South Africa that would make both men rich. With the diamond rush in South Africa after the 1869 discovery of an 83.5-carat diamond—later named the Star of South Africa—Twain saw an opportunity similar to the silver rush in Nevada that he was writing about at the time in *Roughing It*. Twain wanted to have a part in the diamond rush, but he also wanted *stories* from the mines, perhaps rivaling Harte's California stories. For reasons that are not explicitly stated, however, Twain could not or did not want to go to Africa himself, so he enlisted Riley to go on his behalf. Riley would keep a journal that he would never share with anyone else, and after his visit to Africa, he would live at Twain's house for up to a year, during which time he would tell Twain about his trip for at least an hour a day. Unfortunately for Riley, Twain's outrageous plan was agreed upon, and Riley promptly sailed for Africa. Riley held up his end of the bargain, but on his return journey back to the United States, he accidentally stabbed the inside of his cheek with a fork, which caused blood poisoning and ultimately led to his death in 1872. By that point, Twain would be referring to his friend as the "Riley debt" for the $2,000 he was advanced from his publisher for Riley's travels (Hill 112). Without Riley and his funny anecdotes explaining the notes taken in the mines, Twain abandoned his South African book project. The Riley essay in "Memoranda," then, could have been an advertisement for what Twain envisioned as his next big literary break.

The strange tale of Twain's proposal for Riley to act as his double, as well as the climactic joke in the essay about Riley, reveals how Twain understood the fungibility and availability of Blackness to suit his given purpose. His belief that Africa was going to be his new West and make him rich and famous was shaped by his current understanding of Black people in the United States, as he supposedly told Riley before the latter's departure, "give my love to the niggers" (qtd. in Pettit 49). Though his South African venture did not work out, he still used "South Africa" in his anti-Native and antiblack language in *Roughing It*, as seen in the previous example in which he compares the Shoshone and South African "Bosjesmans" to the "American negro" (Twain, *Roughing It* 131). Moreover, that he found an escape from the drudgery that had become his monthly installment in the *Galaxy* in a Black caricature and Africa suggests that his Chinese character in Ah Song Hi was not panning out as he had hoped. Even though Ah Song Hi's earnestness and naïveté align him with Twain's other characters and narrators, Ah Song Hi was ultimately not a bankable narrator, one realistic enough to elicit identification, and definitely not funny enough. Besides,

Twain would soon realize that the Chinese worker figure is a proprietary one in the U.S. literary market, and his reason for abandoning the figure would be compounded all the more by the accusation that he plagiarized Harte.

"Three Aces": A "Feeble Echo of Bret Harte"?

In the late 1870s and early 1871, the Chinese character in popular culture that most people in the United States were talking about was not Ah Song Hi but Ah Sin, simply known as the "heathen Chinee." As discussed in Chapter 1, Harte's poem "Plain Language from Truthful James" was memorized and reprinted countless times, and, according to Gary Scharnhorst, "During the first months the poem was parodied at least fourteen times" (*Opening* 57). The *New York World* claimed that "some of Mr. Harte's Poems are known to every reader of American newspapers, for there is hardly a journal in the country which has not reproduced his quaint ballads" (qtd. in "Mr. Francis" 42). The "heathen Chinee" mania had also reached the *Buffalo Express*, which Twain was editing at the same time that he was writing his "Memoranda." On December 3, 1870, "Three Aces," a poem about a game of euchre clearly written in the style of "Plain Language" (though not featuring a Chinese worker), was published in the *Express* under the authorship of "Carl Byng."

Exactly who Carl Byng was, and whether or not this name was yet another pseudonym of Twain's, has been something of a literary mystery for much of the twentieth century. This mystery is not a minor one, because it concerns the question of whether or not Twain was imitating Harte and attempting to profit from the fame of Harte's poem. If Twain *was* trying to capitalize on Harte's fame, then his writing of "Goldsmith's Friend Abroad Again" featuring a Chinese worker takes on a more mercenary note than otherwise might be imagined. At the very least, Twain permitted the publication of a poem that clearly attempted to ride on the coattail of the success of Harte's poem. Also, curiously, the word *huckleberry*, which is used to describe Harte's boy character Wan Lee in "Wan Lee, the Pagan" (1874) and is the name of Twain's most famous literary creation, appears in "Three Aces," suggesting the possibility that *huckleberry* could have become a meaningful signifier for the two writers in establishing their literary originality following the publication of "Three Aces." At the time, Twain and Harte's once close friendship was on hiatus, and the two men were not speaking to each other. Still, it is difficult to establish conclusively that Twain plagiarized Harte, though Twain was accused of just that by Thomas Aldrich, the august editor of *Every Saturday*. Aldrich wrote in the January 7, 1871, issue of his magazine, "Twain's versified story of the 'Three Aces' seems to be a feeble echo of Bret Harte. The 'Truthful James' vein is one that can be worked successfully only by the owner of the 'claim'" (Aldrich 19). Aldrich was calling out Twain not only for copying Harte but also for doing a "feeble" job of it.

Such criticism from Aldrich would have been already hurtful to a writer such as Twain, who seems to have been particularly sensitive to slights and was desirous of impressing himself upon the literary elite of the East. But if Aldrich was incorrect, and it was indeed a writer named "Carl Byng" and not Twain who wrote "Three Aces," the criticism would have been doubly infuriating. However, surprisingly, Twain did not immediately refute Aldrich's accusation. Twain instead waited until after the publication of the January 14, 1871, issue of Aldrich's *Every Saturday*, which just happened to be devoted almost entirely to Harte, to complain and demand a retraction. The January 14 issue had a portrait of Harte on the cover—the first artistic rendering of the author's face to be printed on the East Coast—and the entire issue was nothing short of a hagiography of the man. It reprinted Harte's story, "Tennessee's Partner," which is ironic, as many future scholars would come to believe that the story was inspired by Harte's friendship with Twain and was meant as a peace offering, as well as a full-page biography of Harte. The issue was also replete with ads for Harte's books, including his collections of poems (which was the best-selling book that Harte would write) and stories. The issue included an anecdote of a U.S. writer who supposedly said of Harte, "Well, he's about the only literary man we've got that amounts to anything, ain't he?" ("Mr. Francis" 42). For Twain, who was aspiring to become a "literary man" himself, the claim that his former friend was the only one of its kind in the United States "that amounts to anything" must have been unbearable. At any rate, it was not the issue of *Every Saturday* accusing him of plagiarism that prompted Twain to write a letter of protestation. It was the following issue on Harte that did.

In a letter dated January 15, Twain wrote to demand that Aldrich "correct [his] mis-statement" that Twain was the author of "Three Aces." He wrote that the verse was written by "a writer who has for years signed himself 'Hy

Slocum,'" and added that Twain had many offers from "responsible publishing houses" to write poems in the fashion of Harte's "Plain Language,"
but that he "burned the letters without answering them, for [he is] not
in the imitation business" (Greenslet 95). Twain's mistake of confusing Hy
Slocum with Carl Byng, the credited author of "Three Aces" in the *Buffalo
Express*, did not help his cause with future critics who believed that Twain
was not being entirely honest in his letter to Aldrich. Digging his hole even
deeper when he got no response from Aldrich, Twain wrote another letter,
on January 22, stating, "Please do not publish the note I sent you the other
day about 'Hy. Slocum's' plagiarism entitled 'Three Aces'" (Greenslet 95).
Instead, Twain suggested the following: "If you would simply state, in *a line
and a half* under 'Literary Notes,' that you mistook one 'Hy. Slocum' (no,
it was one 'Carl Byng,' I perceive) 'Carl Byng' for Mark Twain, and that it
was the former who wrote the plagiarism entitled 'Three Aces,' I think that
would do a fair justice without any unseemly display" (Greenslet 96; emphasis and strikethrough in original). Twain's persistent confusion with the
names Carl Byng and Hy Slocum, particularly in his role as the editor of a
paper that regularly published writings attributed to both names, is one of
the reasons that made future scholars suspicious about Twain's protestation
that he did not author "Three Aces" (see McCullough; Schmidt). Regardless, in the January 22 letter to Aldrich, Twain explained that "it *is* hard
to be accused of plagiarism—a crime I never have committed in my life"
(Greenslet 96; emphasis in original).

Later, Twain implied that what he found particularly hurtful was that he
was accused of plagiarizing Harte. In a different letter to Aldrich, Twain confessed, "I did hate to be accused of plagiarizing Bret Harte who trimmed and
trained and schooled me patiently until he changed me from an awkward
utterer of coarse grotesquenesses to a writer of paragraphs and chapters that
have found a certain favor in the eyes of even some of the very decentest people in the land" (Greenslet 97–98). Without any solicitation, he added the
explanation that "Bret broke our long friendship a year ago without any cause
of provocation that I am aware of" (98). In a book devoted to the relationship between Mark Twain and Bret Harte, Margaret Duckett concludes that
the fallout between the two men around 1869 was mainly the fault of Twain,
mostly because he was highly competitive, manipulative, and "so shrewd a
schemer" (106). After Harte became an overnight sensation for his "heathen
Chinee" poem, Twain wrote to his friends and his brother Orion complain-

ing about Harte's undeserved success (Twain, *Mark Twain's Letters* 62, 249). Specifically, six months after the publication of "Plain Language," and two months after the humiliating accusation of plagiarism in *Every Saturday*, in March 1871, Twain, who was experiencing some family tragedies and resenting his post at the *Galaxy*, wrote the following to his brother Orion: "I must & will keep shady & quiet till Bret Harte simmers down a little & then I mean to go up head again & *stay* there. . . . I will 'top' Bret Harte again or bust" (Twain, *Mark Twain's Letters to His Publishers* 58; emphasis in original). This rivalry that Twain seems to have felt for Harte can be attributed to the fact that in the public's mind, Harte and Twain were often associated together as writers of the West, as seen in George Rothwell Brown's introduction to Stewart's memoir. Twain often received letters addressed to him asking about stories that Harte had written, and a cartoonist even drew Twain as the "new heathen Chinee" in 1873, which must have vexed Twain ("Mark Twain as 'Heathen Chinee'"; see Figure 2.2). In the illustration, Twain is depicted as teaching Nasred-Din, the Shah of Persia, how to play American draw poker, when both were in England and Twain was covering the Shah's visit for the *New York Herald*. The practice of labeling *anyone* who might be scheming in a card game the "heathen Chinee" demonstrates the reach of Harte's poem, as well as the transferability of the minstrel form embodied by it. For Twain, the illustration would also have been a painful reminder of the accusation of plagiarism in *Every Saturday* and how wide-reaching it might have been.

After the *Every Saturday* episode, Twain never wrote another single-authored literary piece with the Chinese worker as a protagonist, much less a narrator. And no other Chinese character resembling Ah Song Hi, particularly one who does not speak in pidgin English, can be found in Twain's writings. As Duckett observes, "Goldsmith's Friend," the only one out of the three Chinese *Galaxy* stories that was published after "Plain Language," is also "the only one not republished in the authorized edition of Mark Twain's writings" (55), indicating the possibility that Twain wanted to distance himself from it. It cannot be proven conclusively that the *Every Saturday* episode was the reason why that was so—especially since "Goldsmith's Friend" in the January 1871 issue of the *Galaxy* does not have the usual "Not Yet Concluded" note at the end of the story, signaling that by December 1870, Twain had already decided that Ah Song Hi's story was at an end. However, it is not too much of a stretch to speculate that in writing a story featuring a Chinese worker, Twain must have known that he was doing so under the shadow of the phenomenal success of Harte's poem.

FRANK LESLIE'S ILLUSTRATED NEWSPAPER.

THE NEW HEATHEN CHINEE.
MARK TWAIN TEACHES THE SHAH THE AMERICAN GAME OF DRAW POKER.

FIGURE 2.2 Mark Twain as "the New Heathen Chinee." From *Frank Leslie's Illustrated Newspaper*, July 26, 1873. Courtesy of Martin Zehr.

For Twain, the Chinese worker as a literary figure, particularly after the accusation of plagiarism, seems to have become a proprietary one. He never tried to do anything innovative with Chinese characters again. Twain's later writings featuring the Chinese worker were all in the model of the "heathen Chinee" caricature and as a peripheral figure, never anything resembling Ah Song Hi. In *Roughing It*, published a year after Twain stopped his "Memoranda" column in the *Galaxy*, Twain describes a Chinese character named Tom, who is said to speak "faultless English," explaining the Chinese lottery thus: "Sometime Chinaman buy ticket one dollar hap, ketch um two tree hundred, sometime no ketch um anyting; lottery like one man fight um seventy—may-be he whip, may be he get whip heself, welly good" (396). Tom's "faultless" English resembles the pidgin English spoken by most of

Harte's Chinese characters as well as the character of Ah Sin in Harte and Twain's cowritten play, *Ah Sin* (1877). The possibility of a Chinese worker narrating his own story without the denigrating designation of an imagined dialect got buried forever in Twain's writings after "Goldsmith's Friend Abroad Again."

Ah Sin, *Yellowface Minstrelsy, and the End of Reconstruction*

Further demonstrating that he ceded the subject of writing about the Chinese to Harte, Twain's only notable writing featuring a Chinese character after *Roughing It* was in collaboration with Harte. Harte's play *Two Men of Sandy Bar* had been produced in 1876, and while the play itself was critically panned, the character of Hop Sing, played by the minstrel actor Charles Parsloe, drew considerable praise even from the harshest critics.[20] Twain, who had reconciled with Harte in late 1871, the same year as the "Three Aces" incident, also watched the play. He remarked that it had "entertained [him] hugely" and that the Chinese character of Hop Sing was a "wonderfully funny creature, as Bret presents him" (Twain and Howells 157). Inspired by the acclaim for Parsloe and the character of Hop Sing, Harte decided to write *Ah Sin*, using the same name as the "heathen Chinee" character in his famous poem, specifically as a vehicle for Parsloe. Twain, who was not new to the lucrative business of writing plays after the success of a theatrical production of *The Gilded Age*, readily agreed to Harte's request for coauthorship. And so, in the fall of 1876, Twain and Harte began their work on *Ah Sin*, in what Scharnhorst states was "the most ill-fated collaboration in the history of American letters" that "doomed their friendship" ("Bret Harte–Mark Twain" 29).

Though the parts describing Ah Sin's character were supposed to be written by Harte, it is not clear which author wrote which parts in the only surviving copy of the play. Twain claimed to have overhauled the play after Harte abandoned it, and left "hardly a foot-print of Harte in it anywhere" (Twain and Howells 192). *Ah Sin* has elements that are familiar from both Twain's and Harte's writings. About mistaken identities of various white characters in a mining camp on the Stanislaus River that ultimately get sorted out through the title character's cagey shrewdness, the play surprisingly does not end with racial violence against Ah Sin but instead with his celebration. Nonetheless, the play depicts Ah Sin speaking in a caricatured language reminiscent of the minstrel speech discussed in Chapter 1—"you wantee washee-washee" (Twain and Harte, *Ah Sin* 11)—or characterizes his speech as "shrieking and gibbering Chinese" (45). One of the characters exclaims with exasperation that Ah Sin is a "poor dumb animal" with "the monkey faculty of imitating" (52). Such depictions confirm James Moy's reading of the play that "while provided with a presence on the stage, the Ah Sin character existed as an absence made complete by the addition of aspects which validated the Chinese character's marginality and foreignness" (Moy 191). This absence is similar to that of the missing Black captive in minstrel shows about slavery. In fact, in addition to the blackface minstrel actor Parsloe, the portrayal of Ah Sin draws from common jokes from the minstrel stage about the end men who take everything literally. One of the white characters in the play asks Ah Sin to sing, stating, "My Chinaman is always meddling around the shows and picking up something or other" (Twain and Harte 67). In response, Ah Sin empties his bag and displays the things that he has literally picked up. When corrected, he sings a song from the "theatres in San Francisco" (68), which could very well have been a minstrel tune, though this is not specified.

Twain and Harte worked on their play featuring the caricatured figure of a Chinese worker redolent of blackface minstrelsy during a crucial moment in U.S. history. The presidential election in 1876 made Rutherford Hayes the nineteenth president after a backdoor negotiation that gave Republicans the presidency in exchange for the reassignment of the federal troops from the South. The election effectively ended Reconstruction. Policies and laws passed by Southern state governments both immediately after the Civil War and post-Reconstruction produced conditions of living for Black people similar to the condition of slavery, namely through the promotion of convict leasing, sharecropping, and the permissive official stance on lynching. In this moment, Harte and Twain—the writers that many today consider progressive, antiracist, and quintessentially American—were affirming and reproducing a racist vision of the Chinese character that would persist for much of the twentieth century and beyond using the antiblack theatrical form of minstrelsy.[21]

As previously stated, for Twain, the "real nigger show," the "genuine nigger show" (*Autobiography* 2:294), disappeared with the disbanding of the San Francisco Minstrels in 1883. The fact that Twain provides no explanation for what made them "real" and "genuine" shows the degree to which blackface performances had become naturalized in his mind in the postbellum United States. Twain does not seem to align the minstrel form with antiblackness necessarily, just as he does not draw an explicit connection to the prevalent practice of blackface minstrelsy in his telling of "John China-man in New York" or "A Day at Niagara" and *Ah Sin*. When his collabora-tion with Harte on the play *Ah Sin* did not fare as well as both had hoped, Twain blamed everything on Harte and permanently ruined the two men's friendship. Twain suggested to William Dean Howells that Harte shirked his responsibilities and left all the necessary revisions to Twain. He wrote, "It is full of incurable defects: to-wit, Harte's deliberate thefts & plagia-risms, & my own unconscious ones. I don't believe Harte ever had an idea that he came by honestly. He is the most abandoned thief that defiles the earth" (Twain and Howells 192). Twain's charge of Harte's deliberate plagia-rism and the description of his own unconscious plagiarism are curious and ironic, particularly considering the history of the *Every Saturday* episode and Twain's mocking of "unconscious sarcasm" of journalistic writing in "Disgraceful Persecution of a Boy" (Twain, *Contributions* 44).

What is important to note here is that the "real" and "genuine" quali-ties that made the blackface performers like the San Francisco Minstrels so great in Twain's mind seemed to be missing in the yellowface performance of *Ah Sin*. Echoing Moy's characterization of Ah Sin as an absence, Sean Metzger states of the titular character, "The Chinaman character serves as a vessel, encapsulating a range of anxieties produced by white concerns over the presence of Chinese people in the United States social and economic order" ("Charles Parsloe's Chinese Fetish" 643). Even a contemporary review panned *Ah Sin* for perpetuating a white stereotype of what it means to be Chinese, by stating that the play "fails to give us any illustration of Chinese character whatever, and presents us with an American burlesque" (qtd. in Metzger, "Charles Parsloe's Chinese Fetish" 643). Though Twain claimed that he was satisfied with the parts for the Chinese character that he wrote, which he said were "killingly funny" (Twain and Howells 193),[22] after the disappointment of the play and the breakup of his friendship with Harte, he never attempted another fictional representation of the Chinese.

Back to Black: *"A True Story"*

In his valedictory note in the *Galaxy*, in April 1871, Twain wrote that he was ending his "Memoranda" and instead would be putting all of his time to "pleasant and diligent use in writing a book" (*Contributions* 131). If he had believed that a literary magazine, as opposed to newspapers, would further his ambitions, he was now leaving the magazine writing behind for grander forms of writing. The result was *Roughing It*, a humorous narration of settler colonialism writ large. Following *Roughing It*, Twain cowrote *The Gilded Age* (1873) with Charles Dudley Warner, beginning his career as a novelist. Twain's turn to Reconstruction politics in *The Gilded Ages* roughly coincided with what historian William Gillette calls a "retreat from Reconstruction" (xi), which Gillette claims began in 1869 with Ulysses S. Grant's presidency. For Twain, the period after 1871 was sort of a turn away from the West and a renewed interest and focus on the South and Reconstruction. This turn happened particularly after Twain's move to Hartford, Connecticut, in 1871. There, he became acquaintances with the New England elite. Many of these new friends and neighbors had house servants who were Black, and by 1874, so did Twain.

In that same year, he published "A True Story," which was told to him by Mary Ann Cord, a Black woman who worked for his sister-in-law in Elmira, New York, where Twain wrote many of his writings at this time.[23] The publication was not a small deal, as it was the first time that Twain's writing was featured in the venerable *Atlantic Monthly*. Given this occasion, it is noteworthy that Twain chose this particular story, especially with its subtitle, "Repeated Word for Word as I Heard It." He stated in a letter to his friend William Dean Howells, the editor of the *Atlantic Monthly*, that he "changed the middle, etc." (Twain and Howells 23), but the subtitle does not make any pretense about whose story this is. Despite the claim for truth, Cord's name is changed to "Aunt Rachel" in the story, while the narrator's name is left unambiguously close to Twain's real name as "Misto C——," as it is called by Rachel. Rachel personifies the popular "black mammy" figure in Reconstruction writings. She is described as "a cheerful, hearty soul, and it was no more trouble for her to laugh than it is for a bird to sing. . . . She would let off peal after peal of laughter, and then sit with her face in her hands and shake with throes of enjoyment which she could no longer get breath enough to express" (Twain, "True Story" 591).[24] Rachel is given the opportunity to tell her own story, however. Also remarkable is the depiction of the white man's failure to recognize Black suffering in the story's beginning. The white man asks, "Aunt Rachel, how is it that you've lived sixty years and never had any trouble?" to which Rachel responds by stopping her laughter, and "without even a smile in her voice," saying, "Misto C——, is you in 'arnest?" (591).

Rachel tells her story about her life during slavery and of having to watch her husband and children get sold to different plantations. She cooks for her white enslaver's family, and after the war, she cooks for the Union army. All throughout, she desperately searches for her favorite child, a son who was sold when he was a young boy. It just so happens that he also decided to search for her after the war, and the two are happily reunited after an initial lighthearted and humorous misrecognition. In this narrative, the white men are the listeners. First, the narrator listens to her. Second, after cooking for the Union soldiers, she tells the soldiers her story, and she states, "dey a-listenin' to my troubles jist de same as if I was white folks" (592).

The story seems to suggest that the act of storytelling neutralizes the socially constructed racial hierarchy. In the beginning of the story, the narrator establishes a naturalized hierarchy of races in his mind: "We were sitting on the porch of the farm-house, on the summit of the hill, and 'Aunt Rachel' was sitting respectfully below our level, on the steps,—for she was our servant, and colored" (591). This positioning changes as the story progresses. The last time we hear from the narrator before he completely disappears from the story is when he states, "Aunt Rachel had gradually risen, while she warmed to her subject, and now she towered above us, black against the stars" (592). In this position, Aunt Rachel is the one who is in full command of the story, as she narrates and performs it for the narrator as if he were also a bodily presence in the story. However, the complete incorporation of the narrator in the story also works in reverse as Rachel's story becomes the narrator's, and, by extension, Mark Twain's. If the goal of the story is to neutralize a racial hierarchy that has been naturalized, the most obvious beneficiary of that is the author Mark Twain, as Rachel's story becomes Twain's "true story."

The acclaim Twain received for "A True Story," as well as his decision to write it to begin with, might be read as Twain's realization that as much as Blackness and the minstrel form were fungible and portable, which explains why he employed the form in his depiction of Native and Chinese characters, the "real" performance of that minstrel form required actual Blackness. Returning to his idea that it was the *form* of the clothing that the enslaved people wore that was burlesqued, we see that crucial to that form is the belief in the transferability of Blackness *in the enslaved themselves* wearing the costume. Without the "coal-black hands and faces" (*Autobiography* 2:294) performing the part of the enslaved, the form could not be burlesqued. In other words, the white imagination of Blackness was inseparable from that form. We see Twain's subscription to this belief in another one of his reveal-ing statements in his autobiography, worth quoting at length:

> We had a faithful and affectionate good friend, ally and advisor, in "Uncle Dan'l," a middle-aged slave whose head was the best one in the Negro quarter, whose sympathies were wide and warm and whose heart was hon-est and simple and knew no guile. He has served me well these many, many years. I have not seen him for more than half a century and yet spiritu-ally I have had his welcome company a good part of that time and *have staged him in books* under his own name and as "Jim" and carted him all around—to Hannibal, down the Mississippi on a raft and even across the desert of Sahara in a balloon—and he has endured it all with the *patience and friendliness and loyalty which were his birthright*. It was on the farm that I got my strong liking for his race and my appreciation of certain of its fine qualities. This feeling and this estimate have stood the test of sixty years and more and have suffered no impairment. The *black face* is as welcome to me now as it was then. (Twain, "Chapters" 454; emphasis added)

Along with Twain's estimation that being patient and loyal is the "birth-right" of an enslaved Black person, what is remarkable here is the porta-bility of "Uncle Dan'l" for Twain to have "carted . . . all around," which Twain justifies through a "strong liking for his race." While a stretch to say that Twain's reference to "black face" bespeaks the subconsciously intended meaning of "blackface," his admission that he has "staged [Dan'l] in books" suggests that minstrelsy and Twain's "liking for [Dan'l's] race and [Twain's] appreciation of certain of its fine qualities" were closely wedded together.

This indelible connection between the white-imagined Blackness and the minstrel form can be seen in Twain's writings featuring Black characters that came after his experimentation with Chinese characters. True to his word, Twain did use the name of his "good friend" for one of his Black characters in his first novel, *The Gilded Age* (1873). In the novel, "Uncle Dan'l" has lines that could have been taken straight from a minstrel joke book. He states, for instance, that the children in the Bible were all boys because they were "*he*-brew chil'en" (Twain and Warner 39; emphasis in original). In *The Adventures of Tom Sawyer* (1876), Jim, a "small colored boy" who is enslaved, is described as "skipping out at the gate with a tin pail, and singing 'Buffalo

Gals'" (27). Twain mentions the song "Buffalo Gals," made popular on the minstrel stage, in his discussion of minstrelsy in his autobiography (2:296).[25] In *Adventures of Huckleberry Finn* (1885), the little boy Jim gets reincarnated as the adult Jim, who tells Huck Finn that he speculated in stock. In one of their exchanges that has been noted for resembling a minstrel dialogue, Huck asks Jim, "What kind of stock?" and Jim replies, "Why, live stock—cattle, you know. I put ten dollars in a cow" (71). That Twain admitted to having in mind an actual Black person behind all these character more than showcases the genuineness of his "strong liking" for Black people, as some scholars would argue (see Fishkin). Rather, the admission reveals the racial logic of slavery and its afterlife that saw Blackness, and by extension the minstrel form, as fungible—the logic that Twain would embrace whole-heartedly during his brief experimentation with the Native and Chinese characters until he turned to his Black characters for good.

Twain's dependence on the notion of Blackness as a fungible commodity tied inseparably to minstrelsy did not preclude him from writing against antiblack racism. But even in his writings that are clearly intended to criticize the condition of being Black in the United States both during and after slavery, we see his fundamental failure to recognize that condition as well as his positionality of writing as a white man about that condition. For example, the novel *Pudd'nhead Wilson* (1894), featuring two babies who are switched at birth by an enslaved Black woman who wants to save one of those babies—her son—from slavery, is typically read as Twain's trenchant criticism of the legality of slavery, particularly as the novel proclaims that race is "a fiction of law and custom" (15). Yet, even in a clearly antislavery novel, as in *Adventures of Huckleberry Finn*, Twain cannot imagine Blackness "outside of the vocabulary already provided by nineteenth-century racism," as Sandra Gunning writes (52). In the Black characters in *Pudd'nhead Wilson*, we see iterations of the mammy figure—specifically in the character Roxy, who is repeatedly referred to by one of the characters as a "nigger-wench" (40, 82), "wench" being a term describing white performances of "Black women" in minstrelsy—and "Uncle Dan'l," as they are made to perform caricatures that were familiar and popular on and off the minstrel stage. When a Black character is called out for his dishonorable actions by Roxy, he is told, "It's the nigger in you" (149).

Twain's inability to truly understand antiblackness can be seen most demonstratively in his essay "The United States of Lyncherdom" (1901), the trump card for anyone wanting to make the argument that Twain is truly the "Lincoln of our literature." Writing in moral outrage in response to the reports of mass lynchings in his home state of Missouri, Twain sets out to expose the reality of lynchings in the United States. Noteworthy in this report is what he says about the white participants and viewers at the lynching. He states repeatedly that contrary to what has been said, "people at a lynching" do not "enjoy the spectacle" (*Complete Essays* 675, 676). He states, "It cannot be true," and "It is certainly not true" (675, 676). The reason for the crowds at lynchings, he reasons, is not enjoyment but peer pressure of the mob mentality. The documented photographs of gleeful crowds at lynchings disprove Twain's reasoning (see Allen).

We must understand Twain's vehement denial of white enjoyment of violence against Black people in conjunction with his love of blackface minstrelsy. Such understanding of Twain reveals the true nature of what it means that he is viewed as the quintessential American writer, as it unveils the many faces of U.S. empire. To highlight what a focus on Twain's liberal, antiracist, and anti-imperialist politics at the end of his life may miss, I conclude with a contemporary novel by a Black writer that can be read as a rejoinder to Twain's defense of the white lynching mob.[26] In *The Underground Railroad* (2016), set during slavery, Colson Whitehead depicts a scene of white enjoyment at a park in North Carolina, as viewed by a fugitive enslaved Black woman named Cora, who is watching from the window of her place of hiding. On a particularly festive night with the entire town gathered for the occasion, Cora sees

> two white men, their faces blackened by burned cork, caper[ing] through a series of skits that brought the park to exuberant laughter. Dressed in mismatched, gaudy clothes and chimney-pot hats, they molded their voices to exaggerate colored speech; this seemed to be the source of the humor. (Whitehead 159)

The description of a minstrel show mirrors almost exactly Twain's description in his autobiography, specifically regarding the minstrels' dress. Different, however, is that in Whitehead's novel, the scene ends with the lynching of a captured fugitive enslaved woman named Louisa, with "people of all ages rush[ing] to . . . the platform" (163) when asked for volunteers to help with her hanging. The lynching of Louisa seamlessly serves as the climax of the minstrel performance in *The Underground Railroad*, with no change in the white enjoyment at the park, a space that Cora comes to realize as "the miserable thumping heart of the town" (163). Instead of presenting the white townspeople as mere spectators, Whitehead's novel underscores the "participatory, infectious spirit of carnival" (Nyong'o 108) that pervades both blackface minstrelsy and lynching, which affords the participants the collective ownership of whiteness.[27] The racial logic of slavery that makes possible the condition of the lynching at the park cannot be separated from the minstrel performance that precedes it. In contrast, for Twain, writing in 1906, the "negro show" was a "thoroughly delightful thing" and he was "sorry it [was] gone" (*Autobiography* 2:296). What Cora sees from her small opening to freedom Twain never did see.

CHAPTER THREE

Ambrose Bierce's Critique of Blackface Minstrelsy and Anti-Chinese Racism

In the conclusion of Colson Whitehead's *The Underground Railroad* (2016), set in the 1850s, Cora, who liberates herself from slavery in Georgia, hitches a ride to California (312). If she landed in San Francisco, she may have been dismayed by the vibrancy of blackface minstrelsy there, which was not limited to performances in public parks that she witnesses in the South in the novel. In San Francisco, minstrelsy was a cultural industry that developed in the early 1850s and continued to flourish after the Civil War. As seen by the influence of the San Francisco Minstrels, who left a mark in minstrel history in the mid-1860s, minstrelsy outlived the South and slavery in San Francisco. In 1870, San Francisco made minstrel history again. That year, Thomas Maguire, the man who single-handedly made blackface minstrelsy a thriving cultural industry in the West, gifted the city with a minstrel troupe that would become one of the greatest successes in blackface minstrelsy in the United States.

Maguire spearheaded this "most important event in Western history," according to Lawrence Estavan (*Tom Maguire* 84), by forging a partnership with William (Billy) Emerson to form the Emerson Minstrels. The troupe went on to enjoy an unprecedented three-year run at Maguire's eponymous theater and became *the* minstrel troupe associated with San Francisco in the 1870s and beyond. The troupe's first show, performed on November 23, 1870, was described by the *Daily Alta California* thus:

> The theatre was crowded beyond its capacity last night, for some of the later arrivals were almost unable to reach their seats through the densely

blocked aisles and packed vestibule. The Emerson Minstrels have no reason to complain of their reception, nor of their success, which was unequivocal. They are so much superior to the troupe of minstrels who last preceded them that it is a matter of wonder that the others had the impudence to travel as stars in the same country. ("Amusements" 1)

This opening night was so unforgettable for many in San Francisco that an anonymous patron wrote a letter to the *San Francisco Examiner* upon reading the obituary of Emerson more than thirty years later, in February 1902. Using an old diary to recall the opening night of the Emerson Minstrels, the letter writer shared memorable songs from that night and recollected that, in response to Emerson's performance in particular, "the audience went wild, the people arose and yelled, the ladies waved their handkerchiefs and cheered" ("Typescript"). The writer stated that the next day, everyone on the street was singing or whistling the tunes sung by Emerson the night before. The adoring letter was not an outlier. Emerson is said to have been "'the greatest minstrel who ever lived' and certainly the best of his time" (History of Music Project, *Music* 111), and his name was especially legendary in San Francisco. Referring to the height of Emerson's career, during which time he was based in San Francisco, his *New York Times* obituary stated correctly that "he is said to have received the highest salary ever paid to an individual performer in minstrelsy" ("Death of 'Billy' Emerson" 3). In addition to his singing, Emerson was known for his versatility, as he moved the audience to uproarious laughter and doleful tears. While the San Francisco Minstrels were known almost exclusively for their jocularity, the Emerson Minstrels were known not only for humor but also for their return to the sentimentalism of the antebellum minstrel shows, which meant, also, a return to depictions of slavery. If the lawmakers made political decisions during Reconstruction with a look "backward to slavery," as W. E. B. Du Bois argues (*Black Reconstruction* 143), the revival of the minstrel craze in San Francisco through the Emerson Minstrels in the 1870s indicates that the same was happening in popular culture.

Known for his biting journalistic writing and true to his reputation as an iconoclast, Ambrose Bierce was decidedly not one of Emerson's many fans in San Francisco. As a former Union soldier who fought in the Civil War and moved to San Francisco in 1866, Bierce lived and worked as a journalist in San Francisco when Emerson and his troupe were enjoying their heyday there. In 1881, Bierce wrote in his "Prattle" column in the San Francisco *Wasp* that "a Washington journal affronts decency and outrages heaven by [printing] an 'interview' with Billy Emerson, the end-man of a nigger minstrel troupe" (*Unabridged* 297). Bierce described Emerson in the interview as "split[ting] his face and agitat[ing] his tongue like the tail of a spring lamb, but to what purport and purpose I am unable to say," concluding that life is "too short to peruse the record of a nigger minstrel's mind" (297). Using a racist epithet to disparage Emerson, Bierce set himself apart from the unquestioned popularity of the performer in San Francisco.

Bierce's article on Emerson was of a piece with his general opinion on minstrelsy. Unlike Bret Harte, who was ambivalent about minstrel shows, and Mark Twain, who was unabashedly captivated by them, Bierce was categorically against them. In his *Devil's Dictionary* (1906), Bierce included several definitions referring to minstrelsy that he had penned for his various newspaper columns. Originally published in the *Wasp* in 1882, the word "depression" is defined as "the state of mind produced by a newspaper joke, a nigger minstrel performance, or the contemplation of another's success" (*Unabridged* 53).[1] "Gloom" was defined in a similar fashion in the *Wasp* in 1885 as "the mental condition produced by a nigger minstrel, the funny column of a newspaper, a hope in heaven and a devil's dictionary" (97). Finally, he defined "minstrel" in the *New York American* in 1904 as "formerly a poet, singer or musician; now a nigger with a color less than skin deep and a humor more than flesh and blood can bear" (164). In all three definitions, there is a connection between humor—or what Bierce perceived as the lack thereof—and minstrelsy. Unlike Twain, who saw minstrel shows as "a most competent laughter-compeller" (*Autobiography* 2:296), Bierce saw them as cheap, contemptible attempts at humor that failed miserably.

If Bierce's opinion on minstrelsy made him a minor dissenting voice, his writings on the Chinese in San Francisco made him even more so. The anti-Chinese sentiment in San Francisco was at its height in the late 1860s and 1870s. Anti-Chinese violence was a regular occurrence in the city, and in 1877, under the leadership of Denis Kearney, the Workingmen's Party of California was formed, with its recognizable slogan "The Chinese Must Go!" (Lew-Williams 42). As Beth Lew-Williams states, by 1879, 99 percent of California voters declared on a ballot that they were "against Chinese immigration" (40). In this context, Bierce's "lifelong defense of Chinese immigration," according to Bierce scholars David Schultz and S. T. Joshi, "made him very unpopular in California" (*Unabridged* 283). As an avowed agnostic, he was especially critical of white people who professed to be Christian and regularly persecuted the Chinese. In the "Town Crier" column that he wrote for the *San Francisco News Letter* from 1868 to 1872, he regularly criticized both, as seen in an article written in October 1870 that attributed the murder of a Chinese woman to the "galloping Christianity of the malignant California type" (Morris 120). Such unflinching and sustained criticism of the hypocrisies of white Californians is perhaps the reason why Bierce, though respected as a journalist and often included with Harte and Twain in reference to literature of the West, did not enjoy the literary celebrity to the degree that Harte and Twain did in his time.

This chapter reads Bierce's first published short story, "The Haunted Valley" (1871), about a murdered Chinese worker who is described as having "come to 'is death by a healthy Christian sent'ment workin' in the Caucasian breast" (93), as a critique of anti-Chinese racism *and* blackface minstrelsy, which were both part of the dominant ideology in San Francisco in the 1870s. Rather than incorporate the Chinese figure using the minstrel form, as Harte and Twain did, Bierce's story uses the short story form and its reliance on plot as a critique of minstrelsy. Concerning three white men as they attempt to narrate the story of Ah Wee, a Chinese worker who has been dead for five years, "The Haunted Valley" actively refuses a plot while invoking the traditional minstrel format of a performative dialogue between three white performers—the interlocutor and two end men—as they attempt to narrate a racialized other into being. In this fashion, "The Haunted Valley," with its narrator acting as the interlocutor and two other characters acting as end men, can be read as staging a minstrel show. In the process, the story refutes blackface theatrical performances' claim to impart complete and authentic knowledge about their subjects, as it posits that a complete knowledge about the racialized other is impossible through the minstrel form. In addition, the story reveals that minstrelsy is more of a performance of white masculinity than of Blackness or nonwhiteness. As such, the story is counter to the dominant practice of minstrelsy as well as the dominant discourse on the Chinese that produced knowledge about them based on caricatures such as Harte's "heathen Chinee."

Because of Bierce's story's focus on the Chinese worker, a number of Asian Americanists who study the nineteenth century have commented on it, mostly in the context of anti-Chinese sentiments in California that led to the passage of the Page Act in 1875 and ultimately the Chinese Exclusion Act in 1882.[2] Hellen Lee-Keller writes that "The Haunted Valley" "interweaves a critique of the growing anti-Chinese discourse that was gaining legitimacy through the relentless attacks of journalists such as Henry George and through the reincarnation of the Workingman's Party in the mid-1870s under the stewardship of Irish immigrant and labor rabble-rouser Dennis Kearney." She therefore reads the story in the context of the post-1860s economic recession, as white workers in California directed their rising anger against growing monopolies at the Chinese workers. Christine Cynn argues that unlike other anti-Chinese tracts of the day, "The Haunted Valley" posits that racism, and not racial difference or Chineseness, is what perverts proper gender and sexual identities of the men. In saying so, the story "affirms and reinforces a shared heteronormative masculinity as an alternative to shared political action" (Cynn 238). Building on such scholarships, I situate "The Haunted Valley" more broadly to open up a way of reading the anti-Chinese historical context with the history of minstrel shows, particularly in the West, which allows us to examine how the writings about the Chinese and the rising theater culture in San Francisco were directly engaging with and producing popular concepts about race as well as gender in the period.

Bierce's story prompts us to study the contemporaneous discourse of anti-Chineseness in San Francisco along with the city's history of minstrelsy, which constructed and normalized race along with gender, sexuality, and citizenship while disavowing the violence tied to that racialization. "The Haunted Valley" refuses to be complicit in the minstrel form's claim over the knowledge of the racialized other by not only absenting its Chinese character but also refraining from disclosing the character's gender. Through this refusal, the story undoes any knowledge of the Chinese even as that knowledge is being uttered. Moreover, as a story about the murder and absence of a Chinese worker, it exposes the grotesque face of minstrelsy and the horror that its "humor" attempts to obfuscate. Nonetheless, similar to Bierce's use of the antiblack racial epithet to criticize minstrelsy and minstrel actors, by using minstrelsy as a vehicle with which to critique anti-Chinese racism, the story forecloses a critique of antiblackness. Specifically, it fails to account for the antiblack racism and the history of slavery at the heart of blackface minstrelsy. Through an understanding that the minstrel form is a contemptible attempt at humor by white men, the story remains only at the level of exposing the hypocrisy of those men without recognizing the historical connections between minstrelsy, slavery, and antiblackness, particularly in California. Ultimately, Bierce's objection to minstrelsy did not extend to the form's dehumanization and derivation of pleasure founded on Black suffering in slavery.

Subversion of a Plot in "The Haunted Valley"

Most famous for his Civil War short stories such as "An Occurrence at Owl Creek Bridge" (1890), Bierce is not widely known for beginning his fiction-writing career featuring the figure of the Chinese worker. Bierce wrote his first such short story, "The Haunted Valley," for the *Overland Monthly* in July 1871, ten months after the publication of Harte's poem "Plain Language from Truthful James" in the same journal, which had catapulted Harte's career forward.[3] Despite the shared publication venue and subject matter, however, "The Haunted Valley" did not make Bierce a household name or garner him much notice as a budding fiction writer. This discrepancy might be explained by the fact that the Chinese worker figure in Bierce's story confounds an easy consumption and understanding, unlike the "heathen Chinee" reminiscent of Topsy in Harte's poem. The confounding happens precisely through the subversion of the minstrel form that Harte and Twain used to construct their Chinese characters.

To summarize, "The Haunted Valley" is told in first person by a nameless narrator who functions as an intermediary between two men: "Jo." Dunfer and Gopher. The first part of the story introduces the reader to Jo. Dunfer, a white man who lives in a town north of San Francisco and whose most distinct personal trait, other than his love of whiskey, is his "deep-seated antipathy to the Chinese" (Bierce, "Haunted" 88). Dunfer tells the narrator—a visiting Easterner—the story of a Chinese worker named Ah Wee who used to work for him. Dunfer implies that he killed Ah Wee because Ah Wee was not a good worker and was "takin' on airs" (89). After hearing this story, the narrator comes across Ah Wee's grave in a ravine within a valley, inscribed with an enigmatic epitaph that identifies Ah Wee as both a "Chinaman" and a "she" (91). Instead of trying to solve this mystery of gender, the narrator flees the valley and goes back to the East. In the second part of the story, which takes place four years later, we are told that Dunfer has since died also. This time, we get the story about Ah Wee from Gopher, who is described as Dunfer's "White man-servant" (88, 90). Gopher tells the narrator that Ah Wee was a woman who loved Dunfer when Gopher loved her more, and that Dunfer killed Ah Wee in a fit of jealousy when he suspected Ah Wee and Gopher of physical intimacy. Rather than accepting Gopher's story as an answer to the mystery of the epitaph, the narrator dismisses Gopher as mad. By the end of the story, the narrator has no more knowledge about the Chinese worker than he began with, and he is left standing alone in the valley as Gopher rides off into the sunset.

The formal structure of this opaque story, consisting of three white men discussing a missing racialized body, replicates the formal qualities of a minstrel show, especially the ones popularized by the San Francisco Minstrels in the 1860s that highlighted the roles of the interlocutor and two end men. These formal qualities were widely disseminated through the printed minstrel primers, which saw an increase in the period during and after the Civil War. Making the format of a minstrel show familiar to an audience beyond just theatergoers, the primers emphasized the importance of the interlocutor figure, also known as the middle man, to the overall show. Even as late as in 1902, a guidebook on minstrelsy stated, "Your middle man must be possessed with a great deal of dignity and also speak in a clear distinct voice so that the entire audience will hear his repeating or reply of every line spoken by end men. The success of the show generally depends on the middle man" (Haverly 5–6). The middle man, it can be said, performed the role of a conduit between the end men—Bones and Tambo—to make sure that knowledge was properly transferred between what the end men said and the audience. He not only functioned as an interpreter of what was imagined as Black dialect but also made it possible for the audiences to understand the humor, the most important point of the show. Bierce himself recognized the central role of the interlocutor and sardonically defined it as "the barometrical center of depression at a minstrel show" in his *Devil's Dictionary* (*Unabridged* 135).

In "The Haunted Valley," the nameless narrator from the East could be read as the indispensable interlocutor figure. He certainly possesses the qualifications of a traditional interlocutor figure: he is straitlaced, speaks without dialect in an educated manner—unlike Dunfer and Gopher, who act as end men and speak in a dialect—and is prim and proper and patronizing to the end men even though he is usually the butt of their jokes.

The story is also propelled only by his questions and interpretations, as the dialogue between the narrator and the two men—who each only speak to the narrator—moves the narrative forward. The narrator also translates the other men's dialogue, as when Dunfer refers to "Chinagration" and the narrator explains condescendingly, "by which poor Jo. meant Chinese immigration" (Bierce, "Haunted" 88). Despite this condescension, the narrator is seen by the other two characters as "green" (89) and needing edification when it comes to race relations in California. In a later version of "The Haunted Valley," published in Bierce's collected writings in 1909, one of the men describes the narrator as a "spectacular extravaganza" (Bierce, *Collected Works* 3:153), underscoring the narrator's East Coast superciliousness. The term referred to a range of theatrical events that featured the latest technological innovations, from Broadway productions to Buffalo Bill's Wild West shows.[4] And while these extravaganzas were originally associated with the urban lower or working classes, even the upper-class theaters in New York City were offering technologically spectacular shows by the 1870s.[5] The narrator's identification as a "spectacular extravaganza" paints him as harboring East Coast elitism and being ignorant of the reality of things on the ground where the story takes place, all befitting the characteristics of the minstrel show's interlocutor. Although the designation is not used in the original version of "The Haunted Valley," the narrator's and the other characters' associations with theatrical personae are still extensive throughout, as seen in the description of one of the characters as a "consummate actor" (Bierce, "Haunted" 94). Moreover, Dunfer states to the narrator, "Ye don't understand *our play*" (88; emphasis added), casting the Chinese question as a California drama, or a "play," about which an Easterner needs to be educated. With the double meaning of the word "play," the story insists on being read as a theatrical performance, specifically regarding its characters.

As one of the most crucial tasks of the interlocutor is to set up punch lines for the end men's jokes, the narrator in "The Haunted Valley" both performs and subverts the task. The story begins as the narrator walks into a scene in which Jo. Dunfer is chastising his white manservant Gopher for letting a passing "travel-heated Asian" drink water at the horse trough (88). Observing Dunfer's racism, the narrator states, "I ventured to faintly remonstrate with Jo. for his unchristian spirit," which sets up Dunfer to reply, "Ther wusn't no mention of Chinamen in the Noo Test'ment" (88). Dunfer's sassy response could easily have come from one of the joke books and primers with instructions on how to develop the characters of the end men. However, the scene does not end with Dunfer's punch line. Instead, the narrator notes that Dunfer "strode away to wreak his anger upon his little, White man-servant, whom, I suppose, the inspired scribes had likewise neglected to mention by name" (88). Mirroring the physical slapstick comedy of the minstrel show with Tambo and Bones getting into an altercation, the scene ends with the "joke" of Dunfer's violence and the narrator's cheeky supposition that Dunfer's manservant, like the "travel-heated Asian," is also missing from the Bible. But recognizing this joke as funny requires complicity with Dunfer's racism and violence, which the interlocutor tacitly condemns. Though the narrator sets up Dunfer's joke and extends it with his wry commentary, he also thwarts it by revealing that for Dunfer, the joke and his violence are one and the same.

The opening scene sets up the notion that comedy on the minstrel stage depends on violence and also foreshadows the importance of the stereotype of the missing racialized other to the humor. In the scene, the narrator's identification of a gender-neutral "Asian" is converted to a generalized and gendered "China*men*" by Dunfer. The singular Asian becomes pluralized and is made to represent "modernity's economic masses" and, as such, demonstrates the belief that the figure "lacks individuality," as Colleen Lye claims about the figure of the Chinese "coolie" (*America's Asia* 54). This understanding of Asian labor is what prompts Dunfer to respond with violence, and it is also what sets in motion the interactions between the three white men—first between Dunfer and Gopher, second between Dunfer and the narrator, and finally back to Dunfer and Gopher. But despite this crucial role of the figure of the Asian, we are not given any information about the figure. Regardless of the Asian's gender, in the process of being subsumed under the plural, the Asian is automatically assumed to be male, reflecting the dominant understanding that the Chinese were mostly male workers and foreshadowing the ambiguous gender identity of the absent Chinese worker in the story. The dependence on the common understanding of "Chinamen" propels the rest of the story, resembling how the stereotype of what it means to be Black drove an antebellum minstrel show in which actual Black people were missing. Furthermore, the inclusion of an actual Asian figure could be read as demonstrating that when Black performers were finally included in minstrel shows after emancipation, such inclusion did not change the caricatured representations of Blackness.

By absenting the racialized Chinese worker, whether through physical expulsion or discursive stereotyping, "The Haunted Valley" highlights the point that minstrel shows relied on the absence of Black people as noncaricatured human beings in order to fill that absence with the white-produced knowledge of Blackness. That is, the very ethos of blackface minstrelsy negates any "real" Black body. The Blackness being performed on stage always had to be white-mediated. Advertisements for minstrel shows, for instance, often displayed the white actors' faces without the burnt-cork makeup because some white audiences mistakenly believed that the actors were in fact Black—a point that the actors staunchly wanted to correct (Toll 38, 40; see Figure 3.1). The performances needed to remain at the level of acting and imitation for them to be both entertaining and validating of white-imagined notions of Blackness that shore up inequality. What blackface minstrels ultimately promoted was that there was a hierarchized distinction between whiteness and Blackness; and the burlesqued performance of that difference was where the purported humor was.

In "The Haunted Valley," the white characters attempt to construct an understanding of the Chineseness of the missing Ah Wee through their performance. But unlike a minstrel show that firmly maintains a demarcation between whiteness and Blackness, the story ends up blurring the distinction. Following the initial scene of violence that happens outside, the next scene takes place in an exclusively white space of the saloon, where amateur minstrel shows often took place in the West. There, the narrator asks Dunfer to elaborate on his views on the Chinese, prompting Dunfer to launch into something like a stump speech, a satire of political discourse delivered during the second act of minstrel shows. Dunfer claims that the Chinese question is a labor question and a threat to free white labor. But his stump speech is a performance of his hypocrisy, as he proclaims to be prolabor but is described as "a long consumer, who had probably never done an honest day's work in his life," and takes tobacco from a "Chinese tobacco-box" as he tries to convince the narrator of the evils of Chinese labor in California (88). In this way, Dunfer's speech against the Chinese matches the political addresses of the time, which produced knowledge about Chinese workers that was often paradoxical. For instance, Leland Stanford, who was despised by Bierce, claimed in 1862 that China was sending "the dregs of her population" to California (Stanford 4). However, as a capitalist, Stanford also admitted to the "importance of steam communication between California

FIGURE 3.1   Poster for Al. G. Field Greater Minstrels: Fun's Famous Fellows, ca. 1907. Courtesy of Library of Congress.

and Eastern Asia," as well as the "vastly important trade [with] the Eastern world" (4). Dunfer's character embodies this contradictory stance toward the Chinese and China in California. In this contradiction, which is seen in Dunfer's words and actions, we can see cracks in the certitude of Dunfer's own purportedly natural and unchanging racial, gender, and sexual identity.

Even before Dunfer's hypocrisy is revealed through his Chinese tobacco-box, the very core of Dunfer's character is called into question through a destabilization of his gender and sexual identity as a result of his relationship with Ah Wee. In his stump speech, Dunfer states that five years ago, he "hadn't no nice discrimnatin' sense of my duty as a free W'ite citizen; so I got this pagan as a kind of cook, and turned off a Mexican woman—as nice a Greaser as ye ever seen" (Bierce, "Haunted" 89). Racism against Mexican Americans is redirected at the Chinese here, as one racist epithet is replaced with another. Calling to mind the racialization of Chinese workers using the label of the "heathen," Dunfer's use of "pagan" deems Ah Wee to be antithetical to his position as a "free W'ite citizen." But packed into Dunfer's statement is more than just simple racism. His description of Ah Wee as "a kind of cook" without a gender specification raises questions, especially if that role was once fulfilled by a Mexican woman who is described as physically appealing.[6] Dunfer does not say that he *hired* Ah Wee *as* a cook; he says that he "*got* [Ah Wee] as a *kind* of cook," a role that used to be occupied by a woman. It was commonly known that Chinese men performed what was considered women's work in the mining camps and later in places like laundry shops, which fueled the rhetoric that the men were deviant and effeminate, and as such diametrically opposed to white normative masculinity and citizenship.[7] The very work that Ah Wee performs places him out of bounds of masculine gender normativity, making him interchangeable with a Mexican woman. But if that is the case, what does that reveal about Dunfer, who "turned off" a woman "as nice . . . as ye ever seen" in exchange for a male cook? Without addressing the point, Dunfer explains that he only hired Ah Wee before he got into politics and learned about the dangers posed by the Chinese, but once he "got religi'n, over at the Hill" (89), it was too late for him to fire Ah Wee. Dunfer's excuse implies that Christianity and anti-Chinese politics were one and the same for him, as the ambiguity about the nature of his relationships with the Mexican woman and Ah Wee is explained away by his professed allegiance to both the religion and the politics.

If Dunfer's hypocrisy and unstable logic are exposed through his ambiguous characterization of his relationship with Ah Wee—as he implies that "getting" Ah Wee as a "kind of cook" went against Christianity and U.S. political values—they are stabilized by Dunfer's whiteness and Ah Wee's nonwhite position. In the same way that any transgressive performance of racial crossing on the minstrel stage was glossed over by asserting a racial line between whiteness and Blackness that could not be crossed over through the exclusion of actual Black people on the stage, whatever is nonnormative in the story is normalized through race. That is, the structural enforcement of white supremacy stabilizes Dunfer's unstable logic. We see such assertion of white supremacy in Dunfer's stated reason for the murder of Ah Wee. Dunfer tells the narrator that he killed Ah Wee because Ah Wee refused to chop wood as instructed. Dunfer had made this same confession in court, and the jury acquitted him, ruling that Ah Wee "[came] to 'is death by a healthy Christian sent'ment workin' in the Caucasian breast" (93). But while the legal system buttresses Dunfer's whiteness, "The Haunted Valley" exposes it as a discursive performance that relies on the presumed knowledge about its racialized other, which turns out to be unfounded.

In performing his whiteness, Dunfer does not shore up white supremacy by affirming a clear distinction between whiteness and nonwhiteness as blackface minstrels did. Instead, Dunfer's performance blurs that distinction, mostly because the knowledge he ostensibly has about the Chinese is shaky at best. Beyond his use of familiar anti-Chinese epithets such as "pagan" (89), "yeller devils" (89), and "Chinaman" (89), the information he provides is not specifically about them and is always in relation to whiteness. When explaining how Ah Wee died, Dunfer begins by pairing Ah Wee and his white manservant together, as he states, "I set Ah Wee and a little W'ite, named Gopher, to cuttin' the timber" (89). In addition to the fact that they were both under his employ, he strengthens the association between the two by using the word "little" to describe Ah Wee, just as he calls Gopher a "little W'ite." He states, "I didn't expect Ah Wee to be of much account, 'cause he wus so little" (89). If such characterization destabilizes Gopher's whiteness, it also associates Ah Wee with whiteness. Dunfer extends this association even further by making a connection between Ah Wee and the narrator, as he tells the narrator that Ah Wee had a "face 'most as fair as yourn, and big, black eyes that somehow I seem to see 'em yet" (89). Dunfer's description of a male Chinese worker using the words "fair"—which could mean either beautiful or light in complexion—and "big, black eyes" would not have been the common descriptors of a male Chinese worker at the time, and does not quite correspond with his characterization of the Chinese as a stereotypical pagan. But the description does highlight a connection to Dunfer's use of the word "yeller" to describe Ah Wee. As I discuss in Chapter 4, the term "yellow" was not widely used to describe Asians as a race in the United States until the end of the nineteenth century. Instead, in 1871, when Bierce published "The Haunted Valley," the term would have been more closely associated with mixed-race Black people, particularly Black women. During slavery, "yellow girl" was used to describe mixed-race Black women, and the figure of the "yaller gal" was defined and popularized through blackface minstrelsy. As Robert Toll writes, "To give their love songs greater emotional appeal for white audiences, minstrels . . . created the alluring 'yaller gal,' who had the light skin and facial features of white women combined with the exoticism and 'availability' of Negroes" (76). As the "yellow girl" was an object of desire on the minstrel stage, and the descriptions of black eyes in particular were quite common in minstrel songs about "yaller gals," Dunfer's labeling of the Chinese as "yeller devils" reveals his dialectical revulsion and desire for the Chinese other, similar to those seen in blackface minstrelsy.

Charged with comprehending and narrating Dunfer's confounding story, the narrator seeks recourse in grammar and proper speech. He quickly dismisses Dunfer's comparison of Ah Wee and himself as "trenchant thrust at syntax and sense" (Bierce, "Haunted" 89). The charge against Dunfer's "syntax" as well as "sense" is curious, as if a different ordering of Dunfer's words would have made more sense. With no such grammatical aid forthcoming, the narrator fully embodies the interlocutor role, as he provides crucial commentary and details about Dunfer's actions to supplement Dunfer's storytelling. Just as Dunfer mentions Ah Wee's eyes—which Gopher later claims were also "like mine" (94)—the narrator notes that Dunfer "fixedly regarded a knot-hole in the thin board partition, as if that were one of the eyes whose size and color had incapacitated his servant for active usefulness" (89). If we were listening rather than reading the words in the story, the "knot-hole" would be heard as "not-hole," aided by Dunfer's pantomiming of looking at it "as if [it] were" Ah Wee's eyes. That is, Dunfer glares at the knot-hole as if it is not a hole but Ah Wee's eyes. While doing so, Dunfer flares in anger (which the narrator describes as "an appearance of rage" that was not convincing), and says, "I tell ye that Chinaman was the perversest scoundrel you ever dreamed of!" (89). In the revised version, the word "Chinaman" in the sentence is replaced with "Chink," further driving home the notion that the knot-hole is no longer a hole but is Ah Wee, or a "Chink in the wall." But even though it is the narrator who provides this description, he does not share in its understanding. He does not know that Dunfer will soon die out of terror that the knot-hole had really transformed into Ah Wee's eye. The plot of the story, if there was any to begin with, falls apart with the appearance of Ah Wee's eyes—both in Dunfer's description and possibly in the knot-hole.

The narrator, moreover, does not realize the exact nature of the story that Dunfer is telling him. In his flippant approach to Dunfer, the narrator expects to hear a comical story, one he can dismiss lightheartedly. What the narrator does not realize is that Dunfer is narrating Ah Wee's death. Dunfer tells the narrator that Ah Wee was a horrible woodcutter, saying that he tried to instruct Ah Wee the correct way but that Ah Wee disobeyed him again and again. Dunfer reenacts looking at Ah Wee, who pretends to follow instructions but goes back to his "Mongolian" way when Dunfer looks away. Dunfer also explains that he became enraged by Ah Wee's insistence on chopping wood "girdleways" (89). This perplexing gendered descriptor is later echoed by the narrator when he comes across the trees in what he calls the "haunted valley" and states that some have indeed been cut in "the most unwoodman-like manner" (91). As with the descriptor of "[k]not-hole," descriptors of Ah Wee such as "unwoodman-like" are notable for their negation. This void is filled by not just words but also through substitution. For instance, in acting out how he looked at Ah Wee, who would not cut wood like a man, Dunfer turns and looks at the narrator, using the narrator as a stand-in for Ah Wee. In Dunfer's performance, we see an incessant attempt to reconstruct the missing racialized other—through words, gestures, and even affect such as "appearance of rage."

Superficially, this scene could be read as a comical one in which a disobedient or incompetent worker who pretends to do a chore one way does something contrary when the boss turns away—a scene that could very well have been performed at a postbellum minstrel show. In Bierce's story, however, the scene takes on a horrifying tone when we realize that Dunfer is not just narrating but actually reenacting the scene of Ah Wee's murder, in which the narrator is cast as Ah Wee. Though the narrator does not realize the nature of Dunfer's performance (because he does not know yet that Dunfer killed Ah Wee), he states that the look that Dunfer gave him "was singularly well calculated to arouse the gravest apprehension in the breast of any unarmed person so reproached" (89–90). The narrator is able to dismiss Dunfer's narrative by simply not believing his words, but he cannot do the same for Dunfer's physical performance in which he is cast—that is, seen by Dunfer—as the racialized, murdered victim. Outwardly citing frustration and boredom more than fear, belying his confession of feeling "the gravest apprehension," the narrator decides to retreat from the situation in which he is no longer in control. This scene, which is far from comical by this point, concludes not with a finale of hilarity and punch lines but with confusion and chaos, much like the conclusion of a stump speech in a minstrel show that resulted in physical comedy. "If the stump speaker did not fall off the podium onto the floor to punctuate his oration," during such a speech, "the audience felt cheated" (Toll 56). In a similar fashion, as the narrator gets up to leave, Dunfer lets out a loud yell and falls back, "as a cannon recoils from its own thunder" (Bierce, "Haunted" 90). Echoing the earlier language of combat, in which the narrator compares himself to an "unarmed person," the simile of a cannon to describe Dunfer's fall implies that this is a scene of power play not far removed from war. Here, power belongs to whoever is the subject of seeing, rather than to an object to be seen. Dunfer is dehumanized, as though "he had been stricken down like a beef" (90), because he becomes that object. As the narrator follows Dunfer's stare, he *also* sees "that the knot-hole in the wall had indeed become a human eye—a full, black eye, that glared into my own with an entire lack of expression more awful than the most devilish glitter" (90). Both the narrator and Dunfer, instead of being active agents who heretofore carelessly regarded the knot-hole "*as if* that were one of the eyes" belonging to Ah Wee, are now on the flip side of that gaze. The knot-hole, which is human yet has an entire lack of expression, might be understood as a metaphorical representation of the racialized other in minstrel shows, fabricated in the white imagination. Being stared down by the humanity of the other is a moment of utter terror for the white men in this scene. As they become objects of Ah Wee's gaze, they see the other's willful refusal to be understood, through the eye's "entire lack of expression," which for the narrator is "more awful than the most devilish glitter." They can no longer sustain their belief in the facile knowability of the other.

As what breaks the terrifying spell ends up being the "little, White man-servant, coming into the room" (90), this scene plays on the common motif of mistaken identities popular in minstrel shows, which Harte and Twain also exploited in their yellowface play, *Ah Sin*. Seen through this motif, the eye in the hole could be explained away as Gopher's and not the ghost of Ah Wee's. Gopher himself later explains to the narrator that Dunfer died "when I looked in at 'im through the knot-hole" (94). But rather than achieving a comic effect, the motif here is nightmarish enough to cause the narrator to flee, and to cause Dunfer's death. Furthermore, unlike conventional minstrel shows in which mistaken identities are always set right in the finale, "The Haunted Valley" does not provide a satisfying resolution. Dunfer knew Gopher well. How could he have seen Gopher's eye as so abjectly other? Was it Gopher's eye itself that frightened Dunfer—as well as the narrator—or did the knot-hole somehow transform it to look like Ah Wee's? And what exactly causes Dunfer to die, and when does he die? Was he dead when the narrator left him? Was the death caused by fright, or was he poisoned by the narrator, as Gopher suspects? Why would the narrator poison Dunfer, and what would make Gopher think that? The first half of the story raises these questions, only to confound them even more in the second half. Without Ah Wee to validate what really happened, the story has no plot. And a story without a plot, "The Haunted Valley" seems to suggest, is exactly what a minstrel show is.

The Civil War as the Climax

The lack of a resolution in the first half of the story is in part caused by the narrator, as he flees Dunfer's saloon and abandons his role as the master of ceremonies in the previous scene. Without explicitly stating why, he decides to leave the West at this point and does not return. Before leaving, he goes to the haunted valley, his favorite spot in a ravine, to contemplate his "pet superstition" about the place (90). He does not explain what this super-stition is but describes his reflection on the place using war metaphors—"convenient troops and squadrons," along with a "great noise of chariots and general intellectual shouting" (90)—as if they are the only means of representing what is unrepresentable. After describing his mental state us-ing abstract military language, the narrator states that "an indefinable dread came upon me" (90).

If "The Haunted Valley" is a deliberately failed minstrel show, and the scene of Dunfer's fall and the narrator's abandonment of his post as an interlocutor are key moments in that failure, what is the significance that the two are described using the vocabulary of defeat in a war? How does the language of war fit into the minstrel form? The answer is that it does not, and this may be part of the story's critique. As the sentimentalism found in antebellum minstrel shows was almost completely replaced with comedy after the war, the memory and horror of war were not popular subject matters of minstrel shows during Reconstruction. As a former Union soldier, Bierce is the preeminent literary writer who had combat experience in the Civil War and actually wrote about it (see Blight 244–251). By fusing together the language of war with the language of theater in a story about the follies of white men in California, Bierce forges a connection between Southern Reconstruction and the white supremacist anti-Chinese racism in the West as part of a narrative on how the nation was recovering after the war.

In "The Haunted Valley," the language of war anticipates the place of the narrator's reflection as a site of death. As William Conlogue writes, the ravine, or the location of the narrator's haunted valley, is "a major symbol of death," as it is a "topographical feature well known to Bierce from his work as a topographical engineer in the American Civil War" (28). The deaths in Bierce's usual renderings of the war are almost exclusively white. However, in suggesting a place of haunting and mysterious forces, Bierce's story evokes the Southern gothic tradition, whose influence was seen even in minstrel shows, in skits such as "Spirit Rappings" or "The Haunted House" (Rice 46). And this nod to the gothic is the closest that "The Haunted Valley" comes to naming slavery, in the sense that the gothic's subject matters dealing with untimely death and haunting cannot *not* be about race. As Teresa Goddu writes, borrowing from Toni Morrison's view of the American gothic as a way to address slavery, however obliquely, "The gothic's focus on the terror of possession, the iconography of imprisonment, the fear of retribution, and the weight of sin provided a useful vocabulary and register of images by which to represent the scene of America's greatest guilt: slavery" (Goddu 133). If the commonplace understanding is to see the gothic and minstrelsy as two opposite forms of representation of the horrors of slavery, Bierce's story shows that there is horror in the comedy and comedy in the horror. The weight of slavery is something that cannot remain repressed or be laughed off but surfaces in this moment in the story that seems to have nothing to do with slavery.

The narrator does not explicitly make a connection between the secret that he seeks in the valley and Dunfer's narrative. He states, "It is strange that in all this time I had not once thought of connecting Mr. Dunfer's drunken narrative with what I now sought" (Bierce, "Haunted" 91). But they do turn out to be related, for the narrator's war metaphor leads him to the revelation that the haunted valley is also the place where Ah Wee and Gopher were chopping wood, and where Ah Wee died and is buried. The place in which slavery surfaces in the story is the place of a racialized Chinese worker's death. Put differently, it is the place of the deliberate absenting of a racialized worker. To make up for this physical absence, the story gives us fragments of Ah Wee. Acting as a buttress to Dunfer's incomplete narrative of Ah Wee, a grave materializes in front of the narrator. Upon seeing the grave, the narrator states that he "regarded that lonely tombstone with something of the same feeling that Columbus must have had when he saw the hills of San Salvador" (91). The narrator as a minstrel interlocutor now becomes a colonizing figure. The subject position taken on by the narrator as a white man describing the mystery of the valley becomes expansionist and imperialist.

In going from a scene that connects memories of war to the absenting of the Chinese worker to a scene that underscores the performative and colonizing role of the narrator, the story enables us to see that representing the racial other is akin to blackface minstrelsy and that that representation is an imperialist practice. But this practice is limited by the constraints of representation. When he sees the grave, the narrator notes that the inscription on the grave had "the exaggerated eccentricity . . . which I can not hope to reproduce without aid from the engraver" (91). He then gives us the exact words on the grave, which I also reproduce here:

AH WEE—CHINAMAN
Aig Unnone. Wirkt last fur Wisky Jo. This mon-
ment is ewrected bi the saim to keep is memmerry
grean and liquize a wornin to Slestials notter take on
ayres like Wites. Dammum! She was a good eg. (91)

I translate this inscription to be saying:

AH WEE—CHINAMAN
Age Unknown. Worked last for Whiskey Jo. This monu-
ment is erected by the same to keep his memory
green and likewise a warning to Celestials not to take on
airs like Whites. Damn them! She was a good egg.

The grave inscription is, as the narrator says, supposed to speak for itself. But as an epitaph, it represents a genre that is usually written by another/ not-self. That is, even though the epitaph says "Ah Wee" and even defines Ah Wee as "Chinaman," it is obviously not Ah Wee. The engraving of Dunfer's composition requires a translation and a rewriting in order for it to be properly understood—something that would not have been the case had Dunfer spoken the words. The epitaph is also self-contradicting, as it goes from calling Ah Wee "Chinaman" to a "She," a play on gender. In minstrel shows, jokes about epitaphs were common—calling to mind the joke about a dead Black servant in Mark Twain's story "Riley—Newspaper Correspondent," discussed in Chapter 2—as were jokes that relied on homonyms. Illustrating both, the following minstrel joke, called "Epitaphs for All," exemplifies such use of catachresis for comic effect.

> Int. (Interlocutor)—I have noticed that there are epitaphs for nearly all walks in life.
> Bones and Tambo.—Yes, that's true.
> Int.—Now, Bones, give me an epitaph for a brewer.
> Bones.—"A well-known brewer lieth here, His ails are over, he's on his bier." (Wheeler 21)

As the staged utterance of the above joke would not have distinguished between "ails" and "ales," "bier" and "beer," the slippage in "Chinaman" becoming a "she" could be read as mimicking the minstrel practice of not only crossdressing but also engaging in bad wordplay that makes two unrelated words equivalent because the speaker does not have knowledge about one of them.[8]

In all these ways, Ah Wee's epitaph embodies the minstrel form that speaks for and defines the other. Moreover, the story implies that minstrelsy is an imperialist practice. Minstrel shows try to represent "the exaggerated eccentricity" enacted by the white actors. The subject matter of minstrel shows—race, gender, sexuality, citizenship, and so forth—constitutes itself through performance. But when minstrel shows are written out, as in the joke books that were also immensely popular after the war along with the minstrel primers, they are revealed to be just bad jokes that require the "grotesque essence" of the imagined and absent racialized other.[9] In purporting to accurately represent the missing Ah Wee even as it reveals itself to be doing so in a contradictory and inadequate way, the epitaph encapsulates the spirit of minstrelsy.

The discovery of the epitaph lays bare the way in which the horrifying face of white supremacy is bolstered by racial violence and death. The narrator's inability to understand the epitaph or laugh off what he calls its "ludicrous transition of gender and sentiment" (Bierce, "Haunted" 91) also reveals the limits of white knowledge. The narrator is no longer the imperialist, all-knowing subject who is able to narrate anything into being or explain away any mystery. Instead of trying to figure out the truth behind Ah Wee's epitaph, he simply states, "I felt that any further discovery would be a pitiful anti-climax, and, with an unconscious regard for dramatic effect, I turned squarely about and walked away" (91). The narrator does not take on the task of interpreting for the audience here. Rather, by not pursuing the truth about Ah Wee's death, he becomes complicit with Dunfer's white supremacist racial violence as he sees Ah Wee's grave as only "dramatic effect" and a climax in a story without a plot.

"A Queer Little Man" and Madness in the Haunted Valley

In place of a plot, "The Haunted Valley" provides the reader with two acts, as in a play. The discovery of Ah Wee's grave marks the climax of the first act. In the second act, the role of completing the story shifts to Gopher, who is repeatedly described as a "queer little man" (Bierce, "Haunted" 91, 92) in addition to being described as a "consummate actor" (94).[10] Whereas he is passive and silent in the first act, Gopher becomes a crucial actor in the second half. One means through which he occupies this active position is by being the author of Dunfer's epitaph. When the narrator returns to the haunted valley after being away for four years, he comes across Gopher there. Gopher tells the narrator that Dunfer is dead, and offers to take him to Dunfer's grave. After Dunfer's death, Gopher not only replaces Dunfer's authorial role but also subjugates Dunfer to a passive position, as he writes on Dunfer's gravestone, "Jo. Dunfer.—Done for!" (93). The narrator deems the newer epitaph "inferior" and "even repulsive in its terse and savage jocularity" (93), but he still defers authority to Gopher by asking him to narrate the story of Ah Wee and Dunfer. Gopher confirms that Dunfer had indeed killed Ah Wee and confessed to it. When the narrator presses further and asks whether it is true that Dunfer killed Ah Wee because of the latter's refusal to cut down trees the correct way, Gopher affirms it as "the legle trooth" (93) that cleared Dunfer in court. However, Gopher distinguishes between "the legle trooth" and his "knowin' better" (93) and exclaims, "But the real fact is . . . that Jo. wus jealous o' me!" (93). Here the narrator steers the reader to read Gopher's words as a theatrical performance, as he states, "And the little wretch actually swelled out, and made a comical show of adjusting a merely hypothetical cravat, noting the effect in the palm of his hand, which he held up before him to represent a mirror" (93). Gopher's story becomes increasingly theatrical and performative, reminiscent of Dunfer's pantomiming of his interactions with Ah Wee to the narrator, obscuring once again that the topics at hand are murder and death, far from comical.

Gopher's physical performance of his narration also glosses over any homoerotic tension in his narrative or in the larger story of "The Haunted Valley." In addition to the comment that Dunfer was jealous of Gopher, Gopher states that "Jo. thought dead loads o' that Chinaman. Nobody but me ever knowed how'e doted onto 'im" (93). He then recounts that just as Dunfer had told the narrator, he and Ah Wee were set out to cut wood together. But in contrast to Dunfer's story, Gopher states that Dunfer came across Ah Wee and Gopher taking a break and mistakenly thought that they were in an embrace when Ah Wee was merely sleeping and Gopher was trying to pick out a tarantula from Ah Wee's sleeve. In his jealous anger, Dunfer grabbed an ax and tried to strike them both. Gopher was able to dodge the blow but Ah Wee was not. Dunfer saw just then that Gopher had indeed been bitten by the spider that was in Ah Wee's sleeve, and as he held the dying Ah Wee, Ah Wee gave Dunfer a long stare, which explains why Dunfer was so fixated on Ah Wee's eyes. As Gopher tells the story, the narrator states that Gopher, whom the narrator now temporarily identifies as "the narrator," had become "transfigured." The original narrator observes, "Gradually the comic—or, rather, sardonic—element had been eliminated, and, as with bowed head and streaming eyes he painted that strange death-scene, it was with difficulty that I repressed an audible sob" (94). The death scene performed and narrated by Gopher is a familiar one from heteronormative sentimental dramas, but it is made unfamiliar by the fact that the two characters cast in the roles of lovers are not only two men but also two men of different races.[11] The narrator downplays this difference as simply "strange," and states that the main point he got from Gopher's narration is not an identification with the dead victim Ah Wee—or even a reaction to the tale of a love triangle between three men that resulted in an ax murder in a fit of jealousy—but rather sympathy for Gopher. He admits that the audible sob was not for Ah Wee, the victim in the "death-scene," or the regretful and bereaved Dunfer, but Gopher, as "this consummate actor had somehow so managed me that the sympathy due to his *dramatis personae* was really bestowed upon himself" (94). The narrator is seduced by Gopher's performance to the point of identifying and sympathizing with Gopher completely, but he insists that it is Gopher's performance, and not the actual story that Gopher is telling, that so affects him. Trying to firm up this slippery distinction, the narrator employs the notion of performance as a foil to disavow any sort of homoeroticism. He states, "I don't know how it was done, but when he had concluded, I was just upon the point of taking him in my arms, when suddenly a broad grin danced across [Gopher's] countenance, and with a light laugh he continued" (94). The narrator's impulse to take Gopher in his arms is buried in the shifting descriptions of Gopher's performance, as if the narrator were merely responding involuntarily to Gopher's masterful acting as Gopher swings from melodrama back to "sardonic" comedy.

Through Gopher's character, "The Haunted Valley" suggests that the capacity to manipulate emotions, which might be thought of as admirable talent for a "consummate actor," is akin to lunacy. When the narrator asks Gopher about Dunfer's death, Gopher accuses the narrator of having killed Dunfer by poisoning his drink. The narrator represses a violent desire to strangle Gopher when he realizes that Gopher is mad. He coolly asks Gopher, "And when did you become insane?" (94). Gopher, uncharacteristic of those who are deemed mad, dramatically responds that he became insane "nine years ago!" (94). With that response, Gopher delivers a long speech that acts as the second act's climax. He shrieks as he falls on Ah Wee's grave:

> [Ni]ne years ago, w'en that great broote killed the woman who loved *him* better than she did *me*!—me who had disguised myself an' follered 'er from 'Frisco, w'er' he won 'er from me at poker!—me who had watched over 'er fur years, w'en the scoundrel she b'longed to wus ashamed to acknowledge 'er an' treat 'er well! (94; emphasis in original)

Here, we see that the same sentence in which Gopher admits that he is mad is the one in which he first identifies the murdered victim as "the woman."

Crucial to note is that Gopher never says, "Ah Wee was a woman." Given that Dunfer told the narrator that he killed Ah Wee five years ago when the narrator last saw him, and given that there is no other murder mentioned in the story, we can surmise that "the woman" "killed" by "that great broote" and Ah Wee are one and the same. But what is the significance of the fact that Ah Wee's name is missing in Gopher's dramatic revelation? And why did Gopher have to follow Ah Wee and Dunfer in a disguise? Is the description that Gopher was "little" like Ah Wee hinting at the possibility that Gopher was also a woman?[12]

To state that Ah Wee was a woman in Gopher's narrative would have meant admitting that Ah Wee was a *Chinese woman* and that two white men, or one white man and one white woman, loved her. By having Gopher not utter these words, the story implicitly articulates what was unspoken in the white representation of the racialized other, which is a transgressive desire for the other that reveals whiteness to be a sham. In their desire for the "perversest scoundrel," Dunfer and Gopher are exposed to be the perversest scoundrels of them all. "The Haunted Valley" hinges on the allure and anxiety over interracial mixing explored in blackface minstrelsy, which is evident in the preponderance of cross-dressing in the shows. Unspoken in these representations is the sexual logic of slavery, or the contradictory dual practice of slavery, which Du Bois characterized as "the deliberate commercial breeding and sale of human labor for profit and . . . the intermingling of black and white blood" (*Black Reconstruction* 80). Evidencing the "monstrous intimacy" of slavery (Sharpe, *Monstrous* 2), the performances of white men in blackface and drag crossed racial and sexual lines and perpetuated the violence of the "peculiar institution."

To circumvent replicating such violence, "The Haunted Valley" ultimately refuses to proclaim knowledge about Ah Wee or corroborate the white characters' knowledge about Ah Wee through Ah Wee's gender ambiguity. There are at least three contrasting stories about Ah Wee's gender. First, Ah Wee is a male Chinese worker, or a "Chinaman," as narrated by Dunfer. Second, Ah Wee was a "Chinaman" who was a "She," as seen in Ah Wee's epitaph. Third is Gopher's story that Ah Wee was a "Chinaman" but also a "woman who loved *him* [Dunfer] better than she did *me* [Gopher]!" (Bierce, "Haunted" 94). As seen in these versions, what makes Ah Wee's gender ambiguous is the racial category of the "Chinaman," highlighting that the category had not yet fully crystallized in meaning, though was well on its way. In 1870, just one year prior to the publication of the story, California passed an act that prohibited the importation of "Mongolian, Chinese, and Japanese females for criminal or demoralizing purposes," and the same act also prohibited the trade in "coolie slavery" (Chan, "Exclusion" 98). The wording of this law had a great impact on the 1875 Page Act, which outlawed "immigration of any subject of China, Japan, or any Oriental country, to the United States" under contract for "lewd and immoral purposes," and more generally promulgated "that the importation . . . of women for the purposes of prostitution is hereby forbidden" (qtd. in Peffer 115). The Page Act also spoke out against the violation of the "cooly [sic] trade." This practice of the simultaneous interdiction against the figures of the Chinese female prostitute and male coolie is mirrored in the ways in which "Chinaman" was understood as what Robert Lee calls the "third sex"—the "ambiguous, inscrutable, and hermaphrodite" (85). The Chinaman category was meant to be understood as a generalizable sign of gender nonnormativity.

In this moment of inchoate definitions and stereotypes, Bierce's story refuses to participate in the process of producing knowledge about the Chinese through Dunfer, who did not "acknowledge 'er" (Bierce, "Haunted" 94), and Gopher, who does not name her in his story. The story's unnaming of Ah Wee's gender is a refusal to give authority to these men. It also forecloses knowledge about Ah Wee's sexuality, keeping the knowledge about Ah Wee's desire a secret. And through this refusal, the story—instead of upholding the racial logic of slavery that relied on the constructed knowledge of the racialized "slave" as naturally unfree—reveals the fissures in that logic and the constructed knowledge. But most of all, "The Haunted Valley" reveals that the inconclusive narrative about Ah Wee is like a minstrel show—a performance of the precariousness and anxiety of white masculinity, which amounts to a show of madness. Moreover, quite different from a comic performance or exposé of racialized difference or a narrative about interracial romance that would not become popularized for decades, "The Haunted Valley" is a horror story, leaving its main characters either dead, mad, or stuck in the place of haunting.[13] If to be haunted is "to be frequented by and possessed by a force that not always bears a proper name," as Ann Stoler writes (1), "The Haunted Valley" seems perfectly content with keeping this haunting alive through its refusal to disclose knowledge about Ah Wee or use that knowledge to establish a plot.[14]

The Absence of Blackness in a Critique of Blackface Minstrelsy

Even while "The Haunted Valley" provides a critique of minstrelsy and anti-Chinese racism, it stops short of undertaking a critique of antiblackness. In this way, the story is also haunted by slavery, which it fails to name and locate as the originating point of blackface minstrelsy. When Dunfer tells the narrator that he needs to explain "this whole [Chinese] question" because "none of ye . . . understand our play" (Bierce, "Haunted" 88), he does not realize the connections between the race "questions" during Reconstruction: the "Negro problem," the "Chinese question," and the "Indian problem." Specifically, the anti-Chinese racism that Dunfer embodies, as Alexander Saxton argues about white working-class racism in California during Reconstruction, can be read as "replaying the script of an older drama," which was "largely shaped by previous responses to Indians, to immigrants, and especially to Negroes and Negro slaves" (*Indispensable* 19). This connection is something that Bierce misses as well, even though the histories of the Chinese racialization and minstrelsy in San Francisco attest to it. Bierce seems to have harbored animosity for minstrelsy as something of a fad in the 1870s, but its history in San Francisco stretches back to the founding of California. Understanding this history, particularly in conjunction with the history of the Chinese in California, is crucial to seeing the stakes in the shortcomings of Bierce's critique in "The Haunted Valley."

The history of the Chinese in California runs parallel to the history of minstrelsy there, as both were the result of the imperialist westward expansion of the United States and the signing of the Treaty of Guadalupe Hidalgo with Mexico in 1848 that ended the Mexican-American War (1846–1848). Shortly thereafter, gold was discovered in what became California, resulting in mining camps and the need for workers. The unequal Treaty of Wanghia in 1844, which China was forced to sign with the United States after losing the first Opium War, facilitated the migration of Chinese labor to the mining camps. Coupled with the Taiping Rebellion of 1850, which drove the impoverished laboring class in China to go overseas for work, the Chinese population in California increased steadily throughout the 1850s, even in spite of legal impositions such as the Foreign Miners Tax as early as in 1850. By the end of the 1850s, the Chinese were the largest nonwhite population in the city.[15]

To understand how Chinese workers were racialized in San Francisco in the 1840s, we can look to the premier San Francisco newspaper, *Alta California*. After having operated as a weekly for a year, the newspaper began printing triweekly issues because of high demand. In its very first issue as a triweekly, on December 10, 1849, *Alta California* printed a piece about the Chinese on its front page. Titled "Meeting of the Chinese Residents of San Francisco," it reported a gathering during which the Chinese voted to pass a resolution that appointed a white lawyer as their counselor and adviser. There is much in the evidence of mutual goodwill on the part of the Chinese and the white authorities who were present at the meeting in this first *Alta California* item about the Chinese. This sentiment was repeated in another friendly article, called "The China Boys," in May 1851, after the newspaper became *Daily Alta California* in 1850.

Praising the Chinese as being "among the most industrious, quiet, patient people among us . . . except the Germans," the 1851 article affirms that they were, just like the German immigrants, "quiet and valuable" ("China Boys" 2). Contradicting the future argument that unlike European immigrants, the Chinese were unassimilable because their laws and customs were so foreign, the article states that "they seem to live under our laws as if born and bred under them, and already have commenced an expression of their preference by applying for citizenship, by filing their intention, in our courts" ("China Boys" 2). This legal participation on the part of the Chinese is not condemned with hostility but approved as a natural course in "amalgamation," as "the China Boys will yet vote at the same polls, study at the same schools and bow at the same Altar as our own countrymen" (2). As with the previous article on the meeting of the Chinese in San Francisco, the article still contains condescending and offensive descriptions, including the characterization of the Chinese language as "peculiar gibberish" (2).[16] These peculiarities aside, the article fully embraces the inevitability and desirability of assimilation—what it calls "amalgamation" (2)—as it draws a connection between the Chinese and European immigrants.

In two years, that friendly tone of *Daily Alta California* changed drastically in an article published in June 1853 in a weekly column called "Saturday Morning." Couched as an editorial among other reflections, the section in question begins in a neutral tone describing the passage of a law in Illinois that prohibited free Black people from entering or residing in the state. The editorial deems that Illinois's exclusion of Black people was justified because "fugitive and liberated blacks [are] a class whose presence is unprofitable and undesirable" in that state ("Saturday Morning" 2). It then postulates that California also has a class of people whose labor is undesirable, but, unlike in Illinois, they are not Black. Black people in California constitute too small of a number, and, besides, the article states, they have "a useful purpose [in California] as domestics and servants" (2). If the Black population were to increase in California, then the state may need to decide "what additional disabilities they shall be put under in order to check their too free immigration" (2). But for the time being, the class of people who should be excluded were the Chinese, as the article asks, "If the presence of an inferior class is not for the advantage of the free white population in Illinois, can the Chinese, who are in most respects more objectionable and are totally unfit to be domestics or servants, be in California?" (2). In response to this question, the editorial states, "Every reason that exists against the toleration of free blacks in Illinois may be argued against that of the Chinese here" (2).

This early call for the exclusion of the Chinese in California—the first one of its kind to be published in a previously friendly *Daily Alta California*—was therefore modeled after the exclusion of free Black people in Illinois before the Civil War. But while ostensibly endorsing Black inclusion in California, the article also reveals the state's ambiguous relationship with slavery. California entered the Union as a free state after the Compromise of 1850, but it passed the Fugitive Slave Act in 1852, which deemed that all those who escaped slavery or were brought as enslaved people to California prior to 1850 were now fugitive "slaves." According to historian W. Sherman Savage, "This action did not mean that the state legislature had sanctioned slavery but that California would not free the slaves who had been brought in before 1850" (31). As most of the enslaved people who were brought to California were "body servants and domestic servants" (Savage 30), *Daily Alta California*'s approval of Black people as serving a "useful purpose as domestics and servants" could be read as an implicit endorsement of conditions of forced Black servitude ("Saturday Morning" 2). What we can draw from the *Daily Alta* article, then, is an attitude toward slavery and a belief about who can be free workers and who can freely choose what work they want to engage in. The racism against Chinese workers in the article was crucially tied to a preconception about Blackness and Black people's putative fitness for freedom under slavery. Demonstrating this connection, the article includes the following description:

[The Chinese] are more clannish than the blacks, and therefore more dangerous. They are more cunning and deceitful and are less fitted to be menials or servants. They are not so improvident as the negro, but they are more vicious and offensive in their habits, and are mentally far inferior to our own people. ("Saturday Morning" 2)

At the same time that the article makes a case for Chinese exclusion, it fixes Black people in the roles of "menials and servants." All the reasons that are cited as evidence for why the Chinese should be excluded already apply to Black people, as the article separates both nonwhite groups from "our own people."

Crucial to the construction of white San Franciscans as "our own people" were the minstrel shows there. As scholars such as David Roediger and Eric Lott have shown, blackface minstrelsy was pivotal to the formation of a white, particularly working-class, identity in the nineteenth-century United States. In San Francisco, it was equally crucial in the formation of a dominant culture in addition to a working-class identity. The racial attitude of white San Franciscans in the late 1840s and early 1850s can be extracted from the popularity of minstrel shows in the city and the mining towns around it. In the same issue of *Alta California* that first reported on the Chinese in 1849, it was reported that "Jim Crow Rice"—also known as "Daddy Rice" in minstrel history and recognized as the man who populated the dance called Jim Crow—"appeared for the last time in the drama of life" ("Mortality" 2). Though in error, since Rice did not actually die until 1860, the report demonstrates that as early as 1849, minstrelsy was a part of the popular cultural discourse in San Francisco. As discussed in Chapter 2, minstrelsy quickly became integral to San Francisco's cultural scene. The May 12, 1852, issue of *Daily Alta California* reported that the "celebrated troupe of negro melodists" called the New Orleans Serenaders "are performing at Columbia to crowded houses" ("Theatrical" 2). The routine announcements in the *Daily Alta California* for minstrel shows likewise speak to their unwavering popularity. In August 1853, it was said that Tracy's Serenaders—a "band of minstrels"—"drew a good house, and gave, if possible, more satisfaction than on their previous evening's performance" ("Musical" 2). A year later, in August 1854, the Backus Minstrels, formed by Charles Backus who would go on to form the famed San Francisco Minstrels, performed in San Francisco to "a crowded house," providing what was said to be "a delightful entertainment"

("Musical" 2). If San Francisco was relatively a new part of the United States, the preferred form of entertainment by its residents was not.

In addition to the shows performed in theaters as mentioned in *Daily Alta California*, some troupes in San Francisco, such as the New Orleans Minstrels, "gave concerts in the principal towns and visited the mines where they were compelled to perform in tents, which were overcrowded, notwithstanding the price of admission was three dollars a ticket" (Slout 92).[17] When they returned to San Francisco after traveling to other cities and states, "they performed for fifty consecutive nights to crowded houses" (93). Consistent in the descriptions of both the shows performed in theaters as well as those performed in makeshift tents is that the shows were crowded, if not overcrowded, resulting in some individuals putting on informal shows in gambling saloons to try to meet the public demand (Estavan, *Minstrelsy* 38). White San Francisco denizens could not get enough of minstrelsy in the 1850s, and it was a feature of their main socializing space, the saloons, which functioned as "semiofficial working-class institutions" (Lott, *Love* 74). This fact has resonance in Bierce's "The Haunted Valley," as much of the first part of the story takes place in a saloon.

Although some scholars of minstrelsy claim that the songs from the minstrel shows attempted to elicit sympathy for the enslaved Black people in the North, such feelings were not prevalent in the West.[18] After the publication of Harriet Beecher Stowe's *Uncle Tom's Cabin* in 1852, a stage version was written by George L. Aiken and performed for the first time in New York City in 1853. The play was "so popular that it ran an unprecedented 325 consecutive performances" (Toll 90). During this long run, Henry J. Conway wrote a pro-Southern version, which opened in San Francisco in 1854 and played on the West Coast for two years (Toll 92). If the Aikens and Conway versions of *Uncle Tom's Cabin* represented two competing views on slavery, the view that was embraced by the audience in San Francisco was explicitly proslavery.

Exemplifying the attitude of one white transplant in the West whose enjoyment of minstrel shows informed his attitudes toward nonwhite people—especially the Chinese—was Charles De Long, a New Yorker of French descent, who moved to San Francisco in 1850. In his diary from 1854 to 1863, we see that his views on nonwhite people extended to his everyday practices of work and pleasure, such as going to the theater. In particular, De Long's diary entries show a direct connection between his job as a tax collector and his enjoyment of minstrel shows. In early 1855, De Long switched from his mining career and other temporary means of livelihood to become a deputy sheriff and was responsible for collecting the fees for the Foreign Miners Tax, mostly from Chinese miners. In the October 20, 1855, entry, he wrote, "A negro minstrel performance at home went to it and took some girls" (Wheat 346). In the entry for the very next day, he wrote, "Loafing around doing nothing but picking up a few Chinamen whom their bad luck and my good threw in my way" (346). These disparaging views about the Chinese and other nonwhite people can be seen in his diary entries even before he took the job. In the September 17, 1854, entry, he complained that the store he was keeping at the time was "full of Kanakas, Spanish, Indians & Negroes & Chinese. Buying their Dust and trying to jabber their language" (206). De Long's reference to Native Hawaiians as "Kanakas" disavows settler colonialism by folding in Kanakas into other groups representing a generalized nonwhite other, including "Indians" in California. After taking on the job that relied on the presence of noncitizens—he writes about also collecting from "Frenchmen, Niggers, Chinamen &c" (343)—De Long seems to have taken particular pleasure in what he called "hunting" the Chinese miners. He speaks of having "shot a China man [*sic*]" in March 1855, and having a "hell of a time" as a result (338), and in October 1855, of once again having a "great time" collecting, and terrorizing the Chinese—as he writes, "Chinamen tails cut off" (346). These descriptions of De Long's violence against the Chinese are interspersed with his going to "Negro concerts" (340).

That De Long's diary includes entries about attending minstrel shows alongside references to the Chinese is not merely a coincidence. The popularity of minstrelsy in San Francisco flourished alongside white songwriters setting the melodies from minstrel shows to lyrics about the Chinese. The lyrics to "John Chinaman's Appeal" (1856), one of the earliest U.S. popular songs to be written exclusively about the Chinese, were influenced by "A Negro's Appeal" (1848),[19] which was sung on minstrel stages in blackface, just as "John Chinaman's Appeal" was meant to be sung in the voice of Gee Sing, a Chinese worker who laments over his harsh treatment in California, by a white performer in yellowface (Moon 34). Many of the songs popular in California included a verse about the Chinese, including and not limited to, "Joaquin, the Horse-Thief," "Prospecting Dream," "The Happy Miner," "California as It Is and Was," "The California Stage Company,"

"The Great Pacific Railway," "The Heathen Chinee," "A Chinatown Bal-
lad," "Twelve Hundred More," "Kearney, the Workingman's Friend," and
"John Chinaman" (see History of Music Project, *San Francisco* 43, 54, 66,
75, 86, 121A, 131, 143, 144, 145). Most of these songs, specifically "Joaquin,
the Horse-Thief" and "John Chinaman," were sung to the tune of songs
from the minstrel stage. Moreover, Charles Backus performed as a Chinese
laundryman as early as 1854 in California and later in New York (Moon 43).
Just as it did not take long for blackface minstrelsy to establish its foothold
in San Francisco, there was not much stalling in the incorporation of the
Chinese worker figure into the popular form. Anti-Chinese racism found its
expression in partaking of the minstrel form, as the songs depicted violence
against Chinese characters. This history, as well as the history of Thomas
Maguire, the San Francisco Minstrels, and the Emerson Minstrels in the
1860s and 1870s, provide the necessary backdrop for Bierce's "The Haunted
Valley" to highlight what Bierce misses in his critique.

In critiquing the minstrel form and aligning it with the genre of horror,
Bierce does not account for the preexisting condition of antiblackness that
makes such form and the horror possible. In this way, he deracializes the
form. This deracialization can be also seen in Bierce's "The Affair at Coulter's Notch" (1889), a short story about the horrors of war. In the story, Coulter, a Union soldier, is ordered to launch an attack on a Southern plantation
home suspected of housing the Confederate army. After the attack, which
leaves many dead, the men on Coulter's side are described as dehumanized: "The men?—they looked like demons of the pit! All were hatless, all
stripped to the waist, their reeking skins black with blotches of powder and
spattered with gouts of blood" (116). If the question mark after "the men"
indicates that the characterization of the soldiers as such was debatable, the
description of their "reeking skins black with blotches of powder" buttresses
that notion. The war's dehumanization of the men is portrayed as a process
of blackening. Similarly, at the conclusion of the story, when it is revealed
that the house under attack was actually Coulter's, Coulter is discovered by
his superiors, who see him embracing his dead wife and child and observe
that "his complexion was coal black; the cheeks were apparently tattooed in
irregular sinuous lines from the eyes downward. The lips, too, were white,
like those of a stage negro" (120–21). Reading the story as Bierce's trenchant
critique of sentimentalized narratives of the Civil War rampant in the late
nineteenth century, Wade Newhouse states, "When a man will knowingly

destroy his own home rather than protect it, when battlefield success reveals not the destruction of the enemy but that enemy's identity as part *of* the ideological self, and when northern conquerors assume the likeness of slaves as part of the military campaign that freed those slaves, then much of the vocabulary that underlies the larger war effort war becomes open to further revision" (Newhouse; emphasis in original). While it is true that Bierce's overall aim is to challenge the vocabulary with which to write about the war, what is telling is the ready availability of Blackness and blackface minstrelsy—the ability to "assume the likeness of slaves"—as a metaphor of utter *white* abjection. "An Affair at Coulter's Notch" thus exemplifies Bierce's stories that employ "the symbolic register of blackness while displacing actual black identities," as Jordan Weber writes (46). Weber's proposed reading practice for Bierce's stories is to build on Toni Morrison's notion of reading for the "Africanist presence," a "dark and abiding presence, there for the literary imagination as both a visible and an invisible mediating force" (Morrison 46). This Africanist presence, a product of the white imagination as its other, pervades U.S. literature and culture in discussions of race, even when Blackness is not explicitly mentioned. In the pervasive presence of the minstrel form in Bierce's and other white writers' works, we see evidence in support of Morrison's argument. In particular, in "The Haunted Valley" we see the Africanist presence in the "yeller devils" and the haunted ravine of death described using war metaphors. That Bierce does not actually name the Africanist presence in "The Haunted Valley" or elsewhere in his writings reveals a limitation of his critique of blackface minstrelsy and anti-Chinese racism. He was able to use the minstrel form to expose the horrors of white supremacy, but that use did not extend to his seeing Black suffering in slavery that made blackface minstrelsy possible.

Keeping in mind Morrison's notion of the Africanist presence, we might read Bierce's one other short story featuring the Chinese worker, titled "The Strange Night-Doings at Deadman's" (1874), as positing an unspoken Blackness as a precursor to a Chinese characterization.[20] In the story, a man is haunted by the ghost of a Chinese worker who was not only murdered but also had his queue cut off after his death and comes back every night to claim it. Before the ghost appears on this particular night, however, the story prestages him with a "swarthy little man, very prepossessing of exterior, dressed with faultless taste, and nodding to the old man with familiar and most engaging smile" (Bierce, "Strange" 70). Both the "swarthy little

FIGURE 3.2   Louise Glackens, "A Skeleton in His Closet." From *Puck*, January 3, 1912, p. 2. Courtesy of the Library of Congress.

gentleman" (70) and the Chinese worker are ghostly, but only the latter is "ghastly," as he attempts to get his queue hanging on the wall with his "horrible yellow teeth" in a silence described as "hideous" (70). The movements of the former are described as pleasantly light and nimble, while the latter moves in a "frenzy," "like a corpse, artificially convulsed by means of a galvanic battery" (70). However, the two seem to work together, as the swarthy little man keeps time for the ghost and disappears when the ghost successfully gets his queue back and crawls back into the dark hole from where he came. As the Chinese ghost is described as "another actor appear[ing] upon the scene" (70) after the appearance of the swarthy little man, I read this scene in the story as another staging of a minstrel show, with "swarthy" coming closest to Bierce's naming of Blackness. A ghost story about a wronged Chinese worker, also with a confounding plot line—if it can even be called as such—"The Strange Night-Doings at Deadman's" reveals that what is haunting the white imagination is not just the horrors of anti-Chinese racism, as in a 1912 Louise Glackens political cartoon (Figure 3.2), but also the ongoing horrors behind the "familiar and most engaging smile" of the imagined Africanist presence.

PART TWO

"Pioneers" of Asian American and African American Literatures at the Turn of the Twentieth Century

CHAPTER FOUR

Representations of Gender and Slavery in Sui Sin Far's Early Fictions

In Ambrose Bierce's "The Haunted Valley," a character narrates the tale of another character's sexually ambiguous relationship with a Chinese worker in a voice described as "of a low pitch of singular sweetness" (125). Edith Eaton, who is better known by her pen name, Sui Sin Far,[1] wrote in "The Smuggling of Tie Co," published in 1900, about a Chinese worker with an ambiguous gender identity as having a "boyish voice sounding clear and sweet" (103). The similarity in the two descriptions may not have been accidental. Sui Sin Far's brother-in-law, Walter Blackburn Harte (no relation to Bret Harte),[2] who edited some of her first stories published in the United States, idolized Bierce and considered him "at once wit, philosopher and genius" (W. Harte, "Tribute" 680), and the two men had an amicable correspondence by letter until Blackburn Harte's death in 1899. Although no known record of Sui Sin Far's direct acquaintance with Bierce exists, taking into account the numerous exchanges between Blackburn Harte and Bierce, as well as the former's writings about the latter in various articles, it is quite likely that Blackburn Harte would have discussed Bierce's stories with Sui Sin Far, a mixed-race writer with a Chinese mother and a white father, particularly those stories featuring the Chinese.

This chapter reads Sui Sin Far's early literary writings in the United States as being influenced by the high-profile white writers such as Bierce, Mark Twain, and especially Bret Harte and their representations of the Chinese.[3] Sui Sin Far herself compared her writings directly to those of Harte, who was most readily associated with the Chinese in U.S. literature during this time. In October 1896, she published a story called "A Love Story of the Orient" under the name "Sui Seen Far" in the *Lotus*, a magazine edited by Blackburn Harte. In an editorial note, which, according to Mary Chapman, was most likely written by the author herself, since she was helping out Blackburn Harte, who was gravely ill at the time, Sui Seen Far is formally introduced as the author of "A Love Story."[4] The editorial describes Sui Seen Far as having "a real and intimate knowledge of the inner and social life of the Chinese at home and in their exile in this country which has never been shown before in American fiction" (W. Harte, "Bubble and Squeak" 217). It does not explicitly identify Sui Seen Far as a mixed-race Chinese woman—it does not even disclose "whether [Sui Seen Far is] a man or a woman" (217)—but its description that she had "knowledge of the inner and social life of the Chinese" sufficiently establishes Sui Seen Far as both an insider and a pioneer, as the first North American writer of Chinese ancestry to write fictional stories about the Chinese in English. This unique insider position of one who has authentic embodied knowledge of the Chinese sets apart Sui Seen Far from the white dominant literary establishment, one represented specifically by Bret Harte. The editorial devotes an entire paragraph to the point, which is worth reproducing in its entirety:

> It is true that Bret Harte, in his early days, wrote of John Chinaman in California, but Harte's sketches were written in the Dickensian mood, and they were too colored by caricature to hold the touch of psychological reality that gives permanence. It is in this particular matter of insight that Sui Seen Far excels, and on this particular ground excels Bret Harte, for the writer of "A Love-Story of the Orient" writes with keen sympathy and knowledge to touch a pity that lies close to the surface in response to all human feeling. Harte, on the other hand, did not bring to the Chinaman the broad humanity he had for the gambler and the outcasts of Poker Flat. He wrote of John as if he did not exactly belong to humankind, but was an isolated puzzle that appealed to one's sense of ludicrous and mysterious. Of course Bret Harte is a sure master of his art, and Sui Seen Far or the writer of these lines would not dream of instituting any whisper of rivalry. (217)

With its repeated and various uses of the word "human," the editorial implies that Harte's "master[y] of his art" was inadequate and that his representations of the Chinese was dehumanizing because he did not have true "insight" and "knowledge" about them. It therefore wrests the task of representing the Chinese other away from the non-Chinese Harte and places it in the able and knowledgeable hands of Sui Seen Far.[5]

Over the course of her writing career, Sui Sin Far seems to have been particularly preoccupied with what she perceived as Harte's dehumanized characterization of the "heathen Chinee" in his most famous poem, and how the poem's racialization of the Chinese effected an exclusion that was both literary and political. In "Tian Shan's Kindred Spirit," a story written for the *Mrs. Spring Fragrance* collection in 1912, Sui Sin Far wrote, "Had Tian Shan been an American and China to him a forbidden country, his daring exploits and thrilling adventures would have furnished inspiration for many a newspaper and magazine article, novel, and short story" (152). As a Chinese man, however, "he was simply recorded by the American press as 'a wily Oriental, who "by ways that are dark and tricks that are vain," is eluding the vigilance of our brave customs officers'" (153). Although Sui Sin Far cites Harte's poem, worth clarifying here is that the citation is from the "American press." That is, she is not quoting Harte's poem but a newspaper article that uses a line from the poem to describe a "wily Oriental." The article does not even do so accurately, as the actual line is *"for* ways that are dark and tricks that are vain" (Harte, "Plain" 287; emphasis added). Sui Sin Far's newspaper quotation seems to have been based on depictions of Chinese border crossers in cities contiguous with Canada and the United States, such as Buffalo. The *Buffalo Evening News*, for example, also cites Harte's poem in its characterization of Chinese illegal border crossing and unmistakably resembles Sui Sin Far's rendition of the "American press" (E. Lee 169; see Figure 4.1). With the heading "Wily Tricks Played by John Chinaman and His Smugglers," the depiction includes a putatively direct quotation from "Plain Language from Truthful James": "Which is Why I Repeat (and I'm Free to Maintain) That for Ways That Are Dark and for Tricks That Are Vain, the Heathen Chinee is Peculiar." The piece mixes up the lines of the poem by inserting the final line "I'm Free to Maintain" in the beginning, emphasizing the "free" status of the speaker and the "ways that are dark" that make the Chinese worker "peculiar." By alluding to such use of Harte's poem in U.S. newspapers, Sui Sin Far's "Tian Shan's Kindred Spirit" highlights the influence of the poem on the racialization of the "Oriental" as the exclusion-worthy other that was central to the political discourse policing the border in the United States.

Sui Sin Far's familiarity with Harte even at the start of her literary career in the United States indicates the hegemonic role of U.S. literature—particularly in Canada—as well as the transnational reach of Harte's poem. Sui Sin Far, like Walter Blackburn Harte, began her writing career in Canada

FIGURE 4.1   Illustration from *Buffalo Sunday Morning News*, February 1, 1903, p. 16.

when there was an exodus of Canadians who migrated to and took literary jobs in the United States. As Nick Mount states, Canadian writers were attracted by the increased opportunities in the United States at the turn of the twentieth century resulting from the printing boom and the abundance of newspapers, magazines, and books that were being published in cities such as New York and Boston (10). These writers would have grown up already familiar with U.S. literature and authors who were popular in the United States. Less than one year after Harte's "Plain Language from Truthful James" was published in the *Overland Monthly* in 1870, for example, the poem was reprinted in Canada and advertised along with other writings by Harte and Twain, demonstrating the wide reach of the two writers that would extend throughout and beyond the 1870s. As the April 1879 cover of the *Canadian Illustrated News* shows, the image of the "heathen Chinee" was invoked in Canada when the calls for Chinese exclusion were at their height in both Canada and the United States (Figure 4.2). The Chinese worker on the cover is shown to protest his treatment by speaking in a dialect often used by Harte, which had originated in blackface minstrelsy but by 1879 became more familiarly associated with the Chinese: "Why you

FIGURE 4.2 "The Heathen Chinee in British Columbia." From *Canadian Illustrated News*, April 26, 1879. Courtesy of University of British Columbia Library Open Collections.

send me offee?" In the caption below the image, Amor De Cosmos, a Canadian journalist and politician, replies that it is because the Chinese will not assimilate, meaning, "You won't drink whiskey, and talk politics and vote like us." The hypocrisy hinted at in De Cosmos's words notwithstanding, the size difference between the two men establishes De Cosmos as a figure of authority that the Chinese man cannot stand up to, let alone face.

This chapter studies Sui Sin Far's foray into publishing short stories about the Chinese in the United States as an attempt to subvert the representational practices popularized by white U.S. writers such as Harte, particularly in the figure of the "heathen Chinee." Building on the argument that the "heathen Chinee" is a minstrel figure that both calls upon and obfuscates the history of antiblackness rooted in U.S. slavery, as seen in the Chinese worker's dialogue in the *Canadian Illustrated News* above, I examine the narrative strategies that Sui Sin Far used to humanize and rewrite the figure through the lens of blackface minstrelsy in the United States.

To begin, I read "The Gamblers" (1896), her first story published in the United States—which replicates Harte's delineation of the Chinese worker as always male—as a straightforward rewriting of the gambling and cheating comic "heathen Chinee" character into a tragic one. After "The Gamblers," however, Sui Sin Far moved on from simply revising the male "heathen Chinee" character to replacing the figure altogether with a Chinese woman. Crucial to note about this process of rewriting is that Sui Sin Far used the label "slave" metaphorically to describe the Chinese female characters. In doing so, she implied that the label insufficiently described the characters, as they were not *really* slaves, though treated as such. A common practice by white suffragists in the United States, the naming of slavery as a metaphor for patriarchy, which equated "woman" with "slave," not only obfuscates the understanding of what chattel slavery was in the United States but also effects the erasure of the racialized Black female captive. Hortense Spillers calls this practice the "ungendering" and "misnaming" of the Black female captive and identifies it as a core antiblack technique of the transatlantic slavery (72, 78, 66). In "Ku Yum" (1896), Sui Sin Far's first major publication in the United States, we see the implicit erasure and misnaming of the Black woman first through the label of "slave" to refer to Chinese women and second through the story's oblique use of a vaudevillian dialogue influenced by blackface minstrelsy. The latter underscores the point that while the lampooned performance of Black womanhood on the minstrel stage by cross-dressing white men began the process of erasure and dehumanization of Black women in U.S. popular culture, it was not only white men who kept the process alive.

As a means of reading "Ku Yum" not for Sui Sin Far's purported insider authentic knowledge that humanizes Chinese women but for understanding how representational practices of racial slavery continued to influence literary and cultural imaginations in the (mis)construction of the figure of the Black woman in the United States and beyond, I pair my reading of "Ku Yum" with a reading of "Away Down in Jamaica" (1898), Sui Sin Far's only short story with prominent Black characters, who are also women. In the latter story, the use of minstrel figures and dialogues in the delineation of Black female characters is undeniable. Published soon after Sui Sin Far worked as a reporter in Kingston, Jamaica, from December 1896 to May 1897, "Away Down in Jamaica" provides a heuristic for how we might read the enduring presence of slavery and empire in literature through the figure of the misnamed Black woman. The racialization and gendering of such women are shown to be incomparably different from the Chinese female "slaves" featured in Sui Sin Far's stories written around the same time. If Sui Sin Far used the metaphor of slavery to humanize and rewrite the caricatured "heathen Chinee" worker, that humanization came at the expense of the erasure of the Black female captive figure.

My reading of Sui Sin Far's "Ku Yum" and "Away Down in Jamaica" together, while also putting them in conversation with canonical texts by white writers, is inspired by Lisa Lowe's call to "read *across*" archives that are purposely organized to obscure "connection[s] and convergence[s]" in empire—what she calls the "intimacies of four continents" (5, 4; emphasis in original). Sui Sin Far seems to have meant for the two stories to be read in different registers, publishing "Ku Yum" in a Los Angeles magazine in the United States under her pen name at the time, Sui Seen Far, and "Away Down in Jamaica" in a women's newspaper in Canada—the *Metropolitan*—under her given name Edith Eaton. If we were to focus only on how she is articulating an Asian North American identity, the stories would seem unrelated, since "Away Down in Jamaica" does not feature any characters who are explicitly Asian. However, a focus on her formal strategies shows both stories to be important archives that reveal the process of defining slavery and misnaming the Black woman figure in North America after the abolition of slavery, especially through the enduring antebellum U.S. cultural form of blackface minstrelsy.

By reading Sui Sin Far's early fictional writings this way, I contravene the effort to align Sui Sin Far exclusively with the Asian North American literary tradition and contribute to the growing scholarship on Sui Sin Far that calls for wide-ranging ways of reading her work.[6] Such reading practice is made possible by the recent archival work of scholars such as Chapman, who published a treasure trove of Sui Sin Far's previously overlooked writings in *Becoming Sui Sin Far*, including "Ku Yum," and Martha Cutter, who rediscovered "Away Down in Jamaica."[7] Rather than pointing to these stories to forge a narrative of a (re)discoverable Asian North American past, my intertextual and against-the-grain reading practice juxtaposes them alongside the dominant U.S. literary and cultural modes of representation that sustained the minstrel form after slavery. In other words, I place the stories in the larger tradition of antiblackness in the U.S. empire. Employing such a reading practice, I am not interested in adjudicating whether or not Sui Sin Far was antiblack or antiracist. My interest lies in broadening our understanding of the history of comparative and ultimately incommensurable racializations of Black and Asian women in the United States, specifically in the context of how slavery and freedom were defined in the nineteenth century and beyond. Finally, by tracing the afterlife of slavery in Sui Sin Far's early fictional writings, I posit literature not as a site of "triumph" against "systemic racist repression" (Ammons 105) but as a critical site of struggle over the meaning of slavery in empire.

Sui Sin Far's Narrative Strategies in "The Gamblers" and "Ku Yum"

In 1903, in a letter to the *Century Magazine* editor Robert Underwood Johnson, Sui Sin Far wrote, "I have read many clever and interesting Chinese stories written by American writers, but they all seem to me to stand afar off from the Chinaman—in most cases treating him as a 'joke'" (White-Parks 44–45). Sui Sin Far's first fictional story published in the United States demonstrates an effort to move away from such figurations of the Chinese character as a "joke." Mirroring the subject matter of gambling in Harte's poem "Plain Language from Truthful James," "The Gamblers" features a protagonist named Ah Lin, resembling the name Ah Sin from the poem. Far from being imitative, however, the story revises the Chinese worker character from a lampooned figure to a tragic one, as Ah Lin and another

Chinese worker die from fighting each other out of their shared desperation for money. In her depiction of Ah Lin, Sui Sin Far provides a suggestion on how he should be read. For example, Ah Lin is described as wrapping his queue around a "Yankee hat" as a "peculiar means by which he prevented the last-mentioned part of his costume from being blown off by the wind and rain" (Sui Seen Far, "Gamblers" 141). Even though this "peculiar" fashion prompted "jocose remarks and amused smiles" from the white passersby, reminiscent of Harte's comical description of Ah Sin as "peculiar" and the white people's ridicule of Chinese clothing in Twain's "John Chinaman in New York," discussed in Chapter 2, we are told that Ah Lin "paid no heed" to them (141). By presenting the reader with a character who actively dismisses the humorous reactions of those around him, the story discounts the white perspective of the passersby and privileges Ah Lin's. Furthermore, in addition to "peculiar," the words repeated from Harte's poem such as "remark" and "smile" undermine Harte's disparagement of the figure of the Chinese worker rather than reinforce it.

In the next story that Sui Sin Far wrote as Sui Seen Far, she broke away from Harte's mold of the "heathen Chinee" altogether by rewriting the Chinese worker figure as a woman. "Ku Yum" appeared in the June 1896 issue of the *Land of Sunshine*. Published out of Los Angeles, the *Land of Sunshine* was a much bigger venue than the magazines edited by Blackburn Harte, and Sui Sin Far's publication there may have been because of Blackburn Harte's connection to Bierce.[8] Though it was a regional magazine, it had a circulation of 9,000 and 12,000 at the end of 1895 and 1896, respectively. And even though those numbers were not quite "startling," as Edwin Bingham writes, the distribution of *Land of Sunshine* was "national, even international, in scope" (64).

Featured in the magazine with such grand aspirations, "Ku Yum" was not only Sui Sin Far's major literary debut in the United States but also possibly the first time that Chinese women appeared as full-fledged fictional characters in U.S. literature. "Ku Yum" is about the eponymous daughter of a wealthy merchant in China who is betrothed to a man in San Francisco. On the way to the United States, Ku Yum switches identities with her maid in order not to bring shame on her father, who led his future son-in-law to believe that Ku Yum's beautiful maid, and not the plain-looking Ku Yum, was the bride-to-be. After the identity switch, Ku Yum is abused by the maid acting as the wealthy merchant's wife in San Francisco and kills herself out of misery. Her body is sent back to China, and even after realizing that the body is his daughter's, Ku Yum's father buries her "among the slaves" so as to preserve the honor of his family name (31).

In the story, Sui Sin Far composes her Chinese female characters using the designation "slave" to denote the literal status of Ku Yum's maid and "chattel" to describe the figurative status of Ku Yum (Sui Seen Far, "Ku Yum" 29). The former description denotes the literal presence of slavery in China. According to James Watson, "Until the foundation of the People's Republic in 1949 China had one of the largest and most comprehensive markets for the exchange of human beings in the world" (223). Chapman has found that Sui Sin Far's own mother was enslaved as a girl ("Sui Sin Far in Solidarity"), a point to which Sui Sin Far refers in her autobiographical essay when she states, "I am never tired of listening to the story of how she was stolen from her home" ("Leaves" 128). But in addition to the literal use of "slave," the story also employs it as a metaphor. Even before Ku Yum becomes a maid in San Francisco, she thinks of herself as "chattel," bemoaning the fact that "she would no longer be reckoned as belonging to her father's family, but then and for evermore would be the chattel of a stranger" (Sui Seen Far, "Ku Yum" 29). Hence, Chinese "slavery" is a factual descriptor as well as a metaphor in "Ku Yum."

In 1894, two years before she published stories in the United States using a Chinese pseudonym, Sui Sin Far employed the figure of the Chinese female slave in one of her earliest writings on the Chinese in North America. She wrote an unsigned article for the Montreal *Daily Witness* called "Girl Slave in Montreal" with the dramatic opening line, "There is a slave in Montreal—a ten-year-old Chinese girl—the property of Mrs. Sam Kee" (Chapman, *Becoming* 44). Writing more than fifty years after slavery was abolished across the British Empire in 1838,[9] Sui Sin Far explained later in the article that the girl "is treated more like a sister than a slave, [and] indeed it is the custom in China to look upon slaves as family" (Chapman, *Becoming* 45), implying that the designation of a Chinese slave meant something different than what a Canadian reader would assume from the word. For North American readers, such an understanding would have been impossible without the historical fact of the transatlantic slave trade—a fact that Sui Sin Far relies on when she makes the sensational claim that "there is a slave in Montreal" who is someone's "property." The assertion that the "slave" in question "is treated more like a sister than a slave" therefore requires an a priori understanding of the word *slave*, inseparable from the transatlantic slavery that Sui Sin Far calls forth only to suppress a connection to it in order to report on the "new" knowledge of Chinese slavery.

In "Ku Yum" and other early short stories written around this time, Sui Sin Far expanded on the figure of the Chinese female slave who is not *really* a slave as a literary device, using the figure in her fictional writings and not in journalistic ones.[10] Just as the word "slave" performed the work of a sensational headline and lent authority to its writer in the Montreal *Daily Witness* article, words associated with slavery in Sui Sin Far's early fictional writings signaled not just authority but also newness.[11] Sui Sin Far herself promoted this idea, stating of her short story "Ku Yum," "I do not think anything of the sort has ever been put before the public" (Cutter, "Sui Sin Far's Letters" 265). If this promotion of newness was an attempt to distinguish her writing from Harte's and other white writers' representations of the "heathen Chinee," her metaphorical use of slavery as the means through which that distinction happened requires a critical examination.

The Rhetorical Use of Slavery in the U.S. White Suffragist Movement and "Chinese Slavery"

Because it likens the positions of a wife and daughter under patriarchy to chattel, Sui Sin Far's "Ku Yum" provides a textual link to the discourse of the U.S. white suffragist movement that used the language of slavery to refer to women. From the very founding of the suffragist movement in the United States, there were appeals to parallels between (white) women's conditions of rightlessness and slavery. As Emily Collins, one of the early suffragists and participants of the Seneca Falls Convention in 1848, wrote, "All through the Anti-Slavery struggle, every word of denunciation of the wrongs of the Southern slave, was, I felt, equally applicable to the wrongs of my own sex" (Stanton, *History* 89). At the Seneca Falls Convention, Elizabeth Cady Stanton read the "Declaration of Sentiments," which invoked the language of slavery to describe marriage by stating that through marriage, the man becomes "to all intents and purposes, her master" (Stanton, *History* 70).[12] At the 1850 Ohio Women's Convention in Salem, Ohio, the third of its kind after Seneca Falls, J. Elizabeth Jones explicitly equated "woman" with "chattel," stating, "Woman, over half the globe, is now and always has been but a chattel. Wives are bargained for, bought and sold, as other merchandise, and as a consequence of the annihilation of natural rights, they have no political existence" (Stanton, *History* 109). Though Jones extended the condition of "woman" as chattel to "half the globe," assumed in her and the other suffragists' rhetorical invocation of slavery is that such women are white and that therein lies the injustice.

The universalized and deracialized metaphor of chattel dehistoricizes the specificity of the history of African chattel slavery in the United States, a point underscored by the presence of formerly enslaved Black people in attendance at the suffragist conventions, particularly Frederick Douglass and Sojourner Truth. In 1845 and 1850, respectively, Douglass and Truth had published their autobiographical narratives in which they described their former conditions under chattel slavery. *Narrative of the Life of Frederick Douglass* describes the marketplace of enslaved people, in which Black humanity was equated with the nonhuman, stating, "Men and women, old and young, married and single, were ranked with horses, sheep, and swine. There were horses and men, cattle and women, pigs and children, all holding the same rank in the scale of being, and were all subjected to the same narrow examination" (48). J. Elizabeth Jones's claim that women were bought and sold, along with Collins's and Stanton's statements, divulges either a complete ignorance of the condition of racial slavery or a willful misunderstanding of it as a process of literal dehumanization that Douglass describes.

In *Narrative of Sojourner Truth*, we see the specificity of this process of dehumanization for the female captive. As told to Olive Gilbert, Truth's narrative includes a wrenching account of Truth's relationship with Robert, a man whom she "truly loved," and her forced "marriage" to another man (Truth 35). Robert belonged to a different enslaver who forbade him to see Truth because the enslaver did not want anyone else's "property but his own should be enhanced by the increase of his slaves" (34). As a result, Robert and Truth were both forced to "marry" captives under their respective enslavers, and it is stated that "in process of time, [Truth] found herself the mother of five children, and she rejoiced in being permitted to be the instrument of increasing the property of her oppressors!" (37). The appearance of the word "increase" in the narrative signals the fact that children of enslaved women were actually called "increases" and that, as historian Jennifer Morgan states, the women "embodied both productive and reproductive potential" as instruments of bringing about that increase (90, 92). Driving home the idea that words like "children" and "mother" are thrown into dis-array in this system, Truth's narrative goes on to opine on enslaved women who "willingly" bring children into slavery: "*beings* capable of such sacrifices are *not mothers*; they are only 'things,' 'chattels,' 'property'" (37; emphasis added). Truth's account stresses the role of the female captives in reproduc-ing the system of slavery, specifically through the process of ungendering that casts them as "beings" and "not mothers."

If Truth's narrative shows that the blurring of productive and reproduc-tive labor of the Black female captive and the process of ungendering hap-pened together in slavery, the forcefulness and enormity of that fact are undermined by a text that is commonly attributed to Truth as the "Ar'n't I a Woman" speech. With the well-known refrain, the speech ascribes a desire for inclusion into a universal womanhood, a desire that Truth may have never expressed at all. At the Akron, Ohio, women's convention in May 1851, Truth delivered a speech, of which no written transcript exists because she could not read or write. A few weeks after the convention, Marius Rob-inson published a version of the speech in the Salem *Anti-slavery Bugle* after going over it with Truth.[13] Almost twelve years later, suffragist Frances D. Gage published a different version of the speech in the New York *Indepen-dent*, which is the version that became the most well known. In addition to peppering Truth's speech with the *n*-word, Gage added the refrain, "Ar'n't I a woman?"—neither of which appears in the Robinson version. Gage also published the speech in a Southern dialect, even though Truth had been en-slaved in New York and had a Dutch accent. As Naomi Greyser writes, the "ventriloquized" question in Gage's rendition of the speech "circulates as a plea for categorical recognition of an African American woman in the con-text of white women's culture" (283, 282). In contrast, in the Robinson ver-sion, Truth does not make claims for womanhood, in the same way that her autobiographical narrative uses "beings" to describe female captives instead of "women." Instead, Truth compares herself to a man, stating, "I have as much muscle as any man, and can do as much work as any man. I have plowed and reaped and husked and chopped and mowed, and can any man do more than that?" (Podell). Truth's characterization is in line with other Black women who were formerly enslaved. Louise Terrell testified in an in-terview conducted after emancipation that "the women had to split rails all day long, just like the men." Nancy Boudry likewise stated that she used to "split wood jus' like a man" (qtd. in Jacqueline Jones 17). Repeated again and again is the statement that the women had to work "just like a man." Emphasized in these testimonies, as well as the Robinson version of Truth's speech, is that it is the condition of slavery that produced the "I" that is "just like a man" or "as any man." The question of whether or not that "I" is a woman is secondary to the import of how gendering—or, more precisely, ungendering—functioned under slavery to exclude the enslaved women from the categories of woman and human.[14]

The discrepancy between the Robinson version of Truth's speech and the more famous Gage version encapsulates what is at stake in Hortense Spillers's theorization of ungendering in her essay, "Mama's Baby, Papa's Maybe: An American Grammar Book." In the essay, Spillers argues that the subject positions of "male" and "female" do not have meaning in slavery (66). She describes the Middle Passages of the transatlantic slavery as a process of ungendering through which the captive persons were "culturally 'unmade,'" so that "one is neither female, nor male, as both subjects are taken into 'account' as *quantities*" (72; emphasis in original). Spillers tracks this ungendering in the afterlife of slavery, in which the dominant white culture continues to "misname" the Black woman (80).[15] The task at hand for this misnaming of the Black female, then, Spillers argues, is not necessarily to have the subject "join the ranks of gendered femaleness," but to "make a place for this different social subject" (80)—meaning, Spillers's call to action is both a critique of how the Black female captive has been represented in the U.S. dominant white culture and a recommendation for how to read that subject.

By casting Sojourner Truth as a Black woman who is seeking membership in universal womanhood, Gage's version of the speech precludes a "place for [the] different social subject" of the Black female by denying the process of ungendering in racial slavery—what Spillers calls a "peculiar American denial" (80). This denial can be seen in Gage's characterization of *Narrative of Sojourner Truth*, which she tellingly misidentifies as *Life of Sojourner Truth* (Stanton, *History* 115). Gage describes Truth's autobiography as "a narrative of her own strange and adventurous life," deeming Truth's racialized and gendered oppression as an "adventure" instead of naming it as slavery (115). Moreover, Truth's ungendering is antithetical to the process of gendering through legal rights that white women such as Gage and Elizabeth Cady Stanton were fighting for, using the metaphor of slavery. In other words, it is not just the process of ungendering and the subsequent misnaming of Black female captives that is denied when slavery is used as an ahistorical metaphor to describe universal womanhood. The process of racialization and gendering of white women as legitimately and authentically "free" also gets denied and naturalized, as seen in Stanton's antebellum definition of "women" as "the mothers, wives, sisters and daughters of freemen" (*History* 680). In maintaining what Sarah Haley terms the "racial-gendered order" (3) of the nineteenth-century United States, the white suffragists' appeals to womanhood not only excluded Black women from the protected "woman" category but also negated their capability for freedom.

Alongside the ungendering of the female captive, the rhetoric of white suffragists who used slavery as a metaphor gendered the category of the "slave" as male. In her 1860 speech titled "A Slave's Appeal," Stanton detailed the white woman's plight as a "slave" in a lengthy comparison to the Black male captive, stating that the "negro has no name. He is Cuffy Douglas or Cuffy Brooks, just whose Cuffy he may chance to be," just as the "woman has no name. She is Mrs. Richard Roe or Mrs. John Doe, just whose Mrs. she may chance to be" (Stanton, *History* 680). Given this comparison, after emancipation, particularly after the passage of the Fourteenth and Fifteenth Amendments, which granted citizenship and voting rights to Black men, the gendered former Black male captive easily became an antagonistic figure.

During Reconstruction, moreover, the threatening and unbefitting Black male vote could be generalized to apply to immigrant and nonwhite men, including Chinese men. In 1869, prior to the passage of the Fifteenth Amendment the following year, Stanton warned, "Think of Patrick and Sambo and Hans and Yung Tung, who do not know the difference between a monarchy and a republic, who can not read the Declaration of Independence or Webster's spelling-book, making laws for Lucretia Mott, Ernestine L. Rose and Anna E. Dickinson" (qtd. in Newman 5). Stanton's rhetorical inclusion of "Yung Tung" to refer to Chinese men is disingenuous, because unlike European immigrant men, Chinese men could not become citizens or vote, precisely through their alignment with the formerly enslaved anti-black figure "Sambo" during the debates on the passage of the Fourteenth Amendment in 1868.[16] Unlike the metaphor of slavery that was used as a call for political inclusion by white feminists, the notion that Chinese male workers were slavelike was used for their exclusion during and after

Reconstruction. As Moon-Ho Jung writes, the lawmakers understood that "a vote for Chinese exclusion would mean a vote against slavery" (11). However, as Jung explains, the antislavery rhetoric of Reconstruction and post-Reconstruction did not translate into pro-blackness. The racialization of male Chinese workers as servile, unfree, unassimilable, and worthy of exclusion perpetuated antiblackness by keeping alive the figure of the inherently unfree slave, racialized as Black and gendered as male. The warning tenor of Stanton's speech relies on both of these racializations.

The comparative racializations of the male Chinese worker and the male Black former captive took on a different gender twist when it came to the racialization of Chinese women as unfree.[17] Given the history of the U.S. empire's interest in and scouting of Chinese labor after China lost the first Opium War and was forced to sign the unequal Treaty of Wanghia in 1844, the population of the Chinese in the United States in the nineteenth century was disproportionately male and mostly workers. From the earliest days of the significant presence of Chinese labor in the United States in California after the discovery of gold, the few Chinese women who were in the state were associated with prostitution—forced or otherwise. When Horace Greeley wrote about the Chinese in his influential *New-York Tribune* in 1854, he stated, "*every* female is a prostitute, and of the basest order" ("Chinese Immigration" 4; emphasis in original). This logic led to the passage of the 1875 Page Act, which stated "that the importation into the United States of women for the purposes of prostitution is hereby forbidden" and also prohibited the "cooly trade" (qtd. in Peffer 115, 116). The law emphasized that immigration had to be "free and voluntary," with the implication that the women who were "imported" for the "purposes of prostitution" were unfree, just like the Chinese male workers racialized as "coolies" (115). The presumed unfree status of Chinese women was central to the discourse of Chinese slavery, gendered and racialized to mean sex trafficking of Chinese women, which proliferated in the latter half of the nineteenth century in the United States.[18] As Yu-Fang Cho has shown, Chinese slavery—also referred to as yellow slavery—became a "national obsession," and "slavery" "automatically serve[d] as a shorthand of the circumstances of all Chinese women: rich or poor, married or single, 'enslaved' or free" ("Yellow" 44).[19]

The discourse of Chinese slavery thus sexualized all Chinese women as "prostitutes," yet also cast the women as victims in need of rescue.[20] In this narrative of rescue and liberation, U.S. slavery in the South was invoked as a point of comparison to argue that Chinese slavery was qualitatively more objectionable, just as Stanton had argued that the conditions of white women "are not surpassed by any slaveholding code in the Southern States; in fact they are worse" (*History* 680). As Cho states in a discussion of how Sui Sin Far's story "Lin John" challenges the narratives of rescue, Chinese prostitution was cast as a "new" problem, not only "dissociated from the 'past' of African slavery" but also exceptionally reprehensible (Cho, "Yellow" 41). In one of the most sensational and influential articles about Chinese slavery, M. G. C. Edholm made the following comparison: "The negro of ante-bellum days was a prince in fortune to the luckless Chinese slave: the former was sold to work, while the latter is selected, bought and handed over for a use compared to which death would be a happy release" (159). Edholm's statement genders the "negro" as a male "prince," while glossing over the dehumanization of African chattel slavery by casting it only as a condition of work. With the claim that Chinese slavery was "a stain upon the American flag" (159), Edholm's essay inspired others using a similar rhetoric, such as a *San Francisco Chronicle* article published later in the year. The *Chronicle* article describes Chinese slavery as a "blot upon the escutcheon of our civilization" and claims that "slavery is not altogether a thing of the past, but that human beings are today bought and sold into a worse kind of slavery than ever Uncle Tom knew of" (qtd. in Kang 128). This statement echoes Edholm's argument, that "all the horrors of negro American slavery do not begin to compare with [those of Chinese slavery]" (159). In the gendering of "the negro of ante-bellum days" as "prince" and "Uncle Tom," and the Chinese "slave" as a woman, the rhetoric of Chinese slavery comparing the two figures elided the history and the figure of the Black female captive. Through comparison, the Afro-Asian analogy, like the marriage-slavery analogy, discounted the historical violence against Black women in the United States.

The figure of the Chinese "slave" in Sui Sin Far's "Ku Yum" is therefore overdetermined by multiple histories of slavery as metaphor in the United States, all of which depend on the exclusion of the figure of the Black female captive. The story attempts to unload these histories, however, by not only casting the figure of the slave and Chinese slavery as strictly Chinese but also disconnecting slavery of any kind from the United States. Contrary to Ku Yum's initial worry that she will become her husband's chattel, the position of a wealthy merchant's wife ends up being one of privilege and freedom, which Ku Yum's maid, A-Toy, occupies in the United States. Since A-Toy assumes the position of her "former mistress" (Sui Seen Far, "Ku Yum" 30) and Ku Yum is actually who A-Toy pretends to be, the category of the Chinese "slave" is destabilized in the United States and dissolves completely when Ku Yum commits suicide. The same does not apply in China, as seen in Ku Yum's father's declaration: "The body that arrives must be buried as the body of A-Toy, the slave" (31). The conclusion of the story underscores the point that the words associated with slavery, such as "chattel" and "slave," are strictly Chinese and incongruous with what is possible in the United States, as the figurative "body of A-Toy, the slave" gets buried in China while A-Toy lives on as the wife of a wealthy merchant in San Francisco. This point can be seen in other stories by Sui Sin Far featuring the word "slave." In those stories, we are told that "in this country it is against the law to buy a woman for a slave" (Sui Seen Far, "Daughter" 222), and "the purchase of slave-girls, which is just and right in our own country, is not lawful in America" (Sui Sin Fah, "Chinese" 48). Recalling the description of the "girl slave" in the Montreal *Daily Witness* article, a character in another story who is described as "a sweet little adopted daughter" is called a "slave" by "some Chinese," but the narrator states, "that was not my name for one who was loved as was she by those around her" (Sui Sin Far, "Son" 127). As seen in these characterizations, Sui Sin Far never used "slave" to mean "prostitute" but used the term to denote class or connote a metaphorical status of a wife or daughter.[21] Even as she underscored the specificity of Chinese patriarchy, Sui Sin Far's use of the term *slave*, therefore, was closely aligned with the white U.S. suffragists' metaphorical use of the term, which was invoked to humanize white women's suffering at the expense of the Black women's erasure as well as the disavowal of chattel slavery in the United States.

In spite of this disavowal, however, the story contains an unintended trace of that slavery's afterlife as it betrays an important historical connection between late-nineteenth-century representations of race and antebellum slavery, particularly in the form of blackface minstrelsy and its cultural legacy. As Trav S.D. writes, "Minstrelsy's songs, sketches, monologues, and overall format laid the foundation for the character of American show business for all time. American popular music of every conceivable type (ragtime, jazz, blues, bluegrass, country) owes something to it, as do all American solo, improv, and sketch comedy" (S.D. 37). In particular, the format of a minstrel show featuring a serious "middle man"—or "interlocutor"—and silly "end men" engaged in a "rapid-fire interplay" called "crosstalk" (38) influenced the dialogues in vaudeville shows that became popular in the late nineteenth century. Early vaudeville shows always included blackface performances, and the two forms are so closely linked that one can be said to be a "relative" of the other (6).

Sui Sin Far wrote about her love of vaudeville shows when she was living and working in Jamaica. In the January 28, 1897, "The Girl of the Period" column in *Gall's Daily News Letter* that Sui Sin Far wrote as "Fire Fly"—a "pleasantly chatty persona" (Ferens 69) presumed to be a white Canadian woman—she stated, "I confess to a partiality for light opera, and a Vaudeville Theatre is my delight" (Chapman, *Becoming* 119). In vaudeville shows, the mark of blackface minstrelsy could be seen in the use of dialogues that delivered punch lines in the form of question and answer. Jokes such as "Why did the chicken cross the road?" originated on the minstrel stage and would have been common in vaudeville shows. And this type of crosstalk is what we see in the final climactic dialogue between Ku Yum's parents in China after they receive a letter from their supposed son-in-law. With minimal interruption from the omniscient narrator, the dialogue begins with Ha You, Ku Yum's father, speaking the first line to his wife, A-Chu:

> "I have received a letter from Tie Sung," said Ha You to his wife. "He seems to be very pleased with Ku Yum's appearance, and compliments us highly on her beauty."
>
> "I always thought Ku Yum lovely," replied A-Chu, complacently.
>
> "He says, however," continued Ha You, "that her temper is not as good as he would like it to be."
>
> "He's out of his mind," retorted A-Chu with asperity. "Ku Yum's temper is of the sweetest."
>
> "What do you thinks he means when he says he is surprised to find that her feet are large, not at all like a lady's?"
>
> "I think he must be joking! Ku Yum's feet could not possibly be smaller." (Sui Seen Far, "Ku Yum" 31)

The exchange here, particularly with the insertion of the word "joking," exemplifies the dramatic irony that was employed in minstrel or vaudeville shows for a laugh, as the characters on the stage said things that sounded ludicrous given what the audience already knew. Ku Yum's parents' obliviousness to the fact that Ku Yum switched places with A-Toy makes possible the humor behind the query, "What do you think he means when he says he is surprised to find that her feet are large?" and at the same time suggests a certain complicity in the horror that the humor effects.

Even though the morbid humor of the dialogue depends on Ku Yum's parents' obliviousness, however, what is really being made fun of is that a "slave," with "large" feet, "not at all like a lady's," is pretending to be a lady. The humor derived from the figure of a woman who is not an authentic woman—with a particular focus on exaggerated body parts—is integral to the history of blackface minstrelsy and its male practice of cross-dressing to represent the misnamed figure of the Black female captive. Despite the lack of direct engagement with the history of chattel slavery in the United States in "Ku Yum," that history makes an appearance through the employment of the minstrel form—represented by the vaudevillian dialogue—in the delineation of a Chinese worker character as a slave. What we find in tracking that history is the specificity and incomparability of the Black female captive figure. These factors are in full view in "Away Down in Jamaica," the only one of Sui Sin Far's short stories known thus far to include Black female characters who occupy more than a fleeting role, particularly in the story's use of the minstrel dialogue and figures.[22]

The Histories of the "Yellow Girl"

In "Black-Asian Counterintimacies: Reading Sui Sin Far in Jamaica," Christine "Xine" Yao argues that "Away Down in Jamaica" illustrates Sui Sin Far's affinity for "affective connections that center peoples of color," particularly through the figure of the "yellow girl" as a "figure of the mixed-race woman" in the story (199, 200). In support of the argument, Yao points to the aforementioned article in *Gall's Daily News Letter* about theater and vaudeville shows that Sui Sin Far wrote while living in Jamaica, but she does not mention Sui Sin Far's professed love of vaudeville. Rather, Yao cites Sui Sin Far discussing the yellow girl in a poem that begins, "Are you, my dear, the yellow girl, / Of all our author folks / At whom we decent people hurl / Anathemas, and jokes?" (200). Based on the fact that Sui Sin Far then moves on to the topic of a women's prison in Jamaica, Yao surmises that given how "state violence overwhelmingly impacts black and mixed-race women," "Sui Sin Far shares the song [about the yellow girl] in a self-aware sense of kinship with these other 'yellow girls' who are both exoticized and criminalized" (201). In short, even though she admits that Sui Sin Far shows an understanding of "how 'yellow girls' of black and Asian descent" (201) are differently racialized and criminalized, Yao posits the yellow girl figure as a symbol of Afro-Asian unity in Sui Sin Far's story.

In what follows, I provide a reading of "Away Down in Jamaica" that problematizes that Afro-Asian unity, also through the figure of the yellow girl. In the *Gall's Daily News Letter* that Yao cites, Sui Sin Far introduces the yellow girl as a vaudeville figure in the context of professing her love of theater and vaudeville shows. Before she launches into the poem cited above, she states of theater that "next to literature it is the most potent influence that is working in the modern world," and adds, "Why not, here's to the Vaudeville girl" (Chapman, *Becoming* 119). For Sui Sin Far, the yellow girl *is* "the Vaudeville girl," which is tied to her love of vaudeville. There is no mention of race in the article—not in the section on theater and not in the subsequent discussion of a women's prison. Instead, by placing the poem in a discussion about literature and theater, Sui Sin Far offers up the "yellow girl of all our author folks" as a literary and theatrical *representation*, through which knowledge was produced about those who are identified as "yellow girls." And this representation has a messy and contradictory genealogy that proves that the yellow girl figure, far from being one of Afro-Asian unity, signals precisely the opposite.

Meant to denote mixed-race women during slavery, the term *yellow girl* euphemizes the history of chattel slavery in the United States. The figure of the yellow girl was performed on the minstrel stage to connote sexual desire for and by the figure as well as to provide "emotional appeal for white audiences" (Toll 76). As mentioned in Chapter 3, the figure, called "yaller gal," was meant to represent those "who had the light skin and facial features of white women combined with the exoticism and 'availability' of Negroes" (76), according to Robert Toll. Toll's description that the "yaller gal" was created as a symbol of romance is revealing of one of the most grotesque representations in blackface minstrelsy that masks the history of rape and sexual violence against Black female captives and the exploitation of those captives' productive and reproductive labor in slavery. Not only was the "yaller gal" an object of desire; she was also cast as a desiring subject through her "coquettish flirtations" (76). This representational practice is seen in the popular song "De Yaller Gal wid a Josey On" (1854), describing a "darling yaller gal" who casts a "tender glance" on the speaker, only to run away with the "Jo, the cattle drover [*sic*]," after the narrator marries her (Christy and White 52). Moreover, the "yaller gal" figure shored up white supremacy, as the figure was differentiated from the "black" or "colored" woman figure, who was depicted to be monstrous and subhuman. For example, in the song "Gal from the South" (1854), the "colored gal" is described in a physically perverse way, with "Her hair it curled so very tight / She could not shut her mouth. / Her eyes they were so bery small, / They both ran into one, . . . [and] Her nose it was so berry long, / It turned up like a squash" (Christy and White 85). Typifying the process of ungendering of the "black woman" figure, the "colored gal's" bodily features are overemphasized and masculin- ized, reminiscent of the description of A-Toy's feet in "Ku Yum" as "large" and "not at all like a lady's." The song shows how such aberrant features are also perversely sexualized, through its chorus about the "colored gal's" gaping mouth, as well as its finale in which the figure swallows everyone in sight. Unlike such characters derogatorily referred to as "wench," the "yaller gal" was highly mannered and never coarse, and always "sweet [and] grace- ful" (Toll 76)—again calling to mind the description of Ku Yum's temper as "the sweetest."[23] The "yaller gal," then, was distinguished from the "black women [who] furnished the laughs," as the former role was initially not meant to be comedic (76). Though both Ku Yum and A-Toy are Chinese, we can see a trace of this history of blackface minstrelsy in the final dialogue of "Ku Yum," as the misnaming of Black women as both the "yellow girl" and the "wench"/"colored gal"/"black woman" affirmed the ideal woman as not-slave and not-black.

The distinction of the yellow girl as not-quite-black is perhaps how, at the turn of the twentieth century, the figure was whitened as European or Bohemian. In fact, the poem that Sui Sin Far recites about the figure in the *Gall's Daily News Letter* article was called "To M'lle Bohemia" (1896), by Waitman Barbe, though she does not mention that citation.[24] It was pub- lished right before Sui Sin Far's "The Gamblers," in the February 1896 issue of the *Fly Leaf*, edited by Blackburn Harte. "To M'lle Bohemia" equated the "yellow girl" with the "Bohemian girl," a figure that was decidedly white and European, as seen in Willa Cather's 1912 short story of the same name.[25] In the inaugural issue of the *Fly Leaf* in December 1895, Blackburn Harte had also included an essay discussing the "yellow girl" as a European phe- nomenon and a "figure for fin de siècle literature" in his magazine (Chapman, *Becoming* 119). The writer of the essay, identified as Ben Franklin Jr., defended the figure—which he explained was an "import" from Paris— from its critics in England, who denounced the figure as "bare armed, bare throated, great hatted, with parasol a-kimbo, with flapping gown of gold, and snakey boa bristling in the breeze, with tripping toes a la Chinoise, with waspy waist, with painted cheeks and sparking, wine-fed eyes, and a monkey grin of daftest daftness—there flaunts the Yellow Girl, the she Baal, the new born goddess of Today, laughing the amazed to scorn" (Franklin 14). Unlike the "yaller gal" from minstrel shows, the European "yellow girl"— adorned with Orientalist trappings—was a figure marked by lightness, disparaged as a "hair-brained [*sic*] comedienne," though Franklin credited her for putting "a splash of color into the dulness [*sic*] of city life" (14, 15).

Significantly, the yellow girl was never racialized as Asian, despite the fact that in the latter nineteenth century, "yellow" was increasingly used to designate such.[26] In addition to the "yellow slavery" discourse about the sex trafficking of Chinese women, the threat posed by the rising Japanese empire was called "yellow peril" circa 1895 (Keevak 7). But on the minstrel stage and in literature, the dominant representations of the Chinese in latter nineteenth century depicted them as male workers and rarely included women, and never depicted those women as the yellow girl. In fact, as mentioned in the introduction, the minstrel song called "Nigger Versus Chinese" (1870) explicitly stated that the reason why the Chinese were less desirable than Black people was that "dey've got no pret-ty yellow gals wid de nice lit-tle su-gar lips" (Lorraine 4). From her specific subject position as a mixed-race woman—a "Eurasian," as she would later call herself ("Leaves" 125)—Sui Sin Far could have been especially interested in the fact that the yellow girl could be Black or white but not Chinese, though in her short story "Its Wavering Image," a mixed-race protagonist is described as "a Bohemian" (62). Reflective of this fact that the yellow girl could be either Black or white but not Asian, the restaging of the vaudeville dialogue in "Away Down in Jamaica" features both the white and Black iterations of the yellow girl, and the story as a whole does not include any characters who are explicitly Chinese or Asian. Despite Julia Lee's cogent claim that Sui Sin Far's experience in Jamaica, particularly recollected in her autobiographical essay in which she claims to be "of the 'brown people' of the earth" ("Leaves" 130),[27] "cannot be understood outside the discursive racial politics and representations of the day that consistently intertwined 'Asiatics' with 'Negroes'" (J. Lee 98),

Sui Sin Far did not radically align the "yellow" race with the "brown girl" figure, the Jamaican version of the yellow girl. Similarly, she did not use her Chinese pseudonym in the fictional meditation on the figure in "Away Down in Jamaica." The story thus circumvents Afro-Asian analogy as well as Afro-Asian unity. Such impossibility is all the more reason why "Away Down in Jamaica" is an important archive in Asian North American studies and why we need to read it alongside Sui Sin Far's stories about Chinese women who are called "slaves," particularly as she was attempting to write against stereotypical depictions of the "heathen Chinee." By animating the flexibility and malleability of racial discourse in the U.S. empire-state's "hierarchical differentiation of people" (Moon-Kie Jung, *Beneath* 67) that are evident in such shifts and vicissitudes in the word "yellow," Sui Sin Far's story highlights the specificity of the nonanalogical Black racialization as well as the enduring cultural legacy of slavery that informs it.

Narrating the Black Female Figures in "Away Down in Jamaica"

Like "Ku Yum," "Away Down in Jamaica" does not explicitly refer to the transatlantic chattel slavery. Despite this absence, we see glimpses of its afterlife through cultural forms to which the story alludes. Just as "Ku Yum" reveals the afterlife of slavery through vaudeville dialogue, "Away Down in Jamaica" betrays the ongoing effects of slavery through its engagement with cultural forms such as minstrel songs, vaudeville theater, and British and U.S. novels written during slavery. The connection to the novelistic form is especially strong in "Away Down in Jamaica," as despite the brevity of the short story, it is broken into four "chapters." In thinking about the novel as a "cultural artifact of bourgeois society," Edward Said posits that the form of the British novel and British imperialism are "unthinkable without each other" (71). As many of the formal qualities of "Away Down in Jamaica" resemble Emily Brontë's 1847 novel, *Wuthering Heights*—and, to a lesser degree, Charlotte Brontë's *Jane Eyre* (1847)—I argue that Sui Sin Far's story also shows insidious and ever-lurking antiblackness to be just as intricately connected to culture and empire, particularly through its present-day imperializing presence of Canada and the United States in Jamaica. Moreover, we can see how Sui Sin Far attempts to represent the specificity and incommensurability of the misnamed Black woman through the story's resemblance to *Wuthering Heights* and its evocation of other cultural forms such as blackface minstrelsy. The story ultimately provides a glimpse of the mis-recognition—including the story's own—that structures the representation of Black women as part of the ongoing afterlife of slavery.

The skeletal plot of "Away Down in Jamaica" is this: Kathleen Harold, an American woman, is engaged to be married to Wickliff Walker, who is not identified by nationality or race, in Kingston, Jamaica.[28] Wickliff has an ex-lover, Clarissa, a Jamaican woman described as a "brown girl" (Eaton 4), whom he seduced, and then abandoned. Kathleen also has an ex-lover, Phil Everett from Canada,[29] whom she "wooed" (13) then scorned when he reciprocated her affection. Kathleen actually *does* love Phil (13) and does not love Wickliff but cannot resist an attraction to Wickliff. Phil dies from an illness, and Kathleen dies immediately after, poisoned by the flowers that Clarissa had brought for her. Clarissa is deemed mad by doctors and is "locked up" (13), but she escapes and goes into hiding.

If we were to read "Away Down in Jamaica" "univocally" (Said 47), according to Said's theorization of a dominant form of reading practice, focusing only on what the story presents as the main characters and plot points, we might say that this is a tale of a fickle, "frail" (Eaton 13) woman named Kathleen and a domineering man named Wickliff who have both wronged their ex-lovers, Phil and Clarissa. Phil suffers a greater consequence than Clarissa, as the rejection of Kathleen may have contributed to the decline of his health. Both Kathleen and Wickliff are punished by Clarissa's revenge, though Kathleen pays the heftier price with her death. In this reading, Kathleen and Phil, the only characters who are described using the adjective "fair" (13), are cast as victims, with Phil being totally innocent. With her poisoning of Kathleen, Clarissa could be seen as the antithesis of Phil and read as a villain, not unlike the "black buzzards" outside Phil's window that torment him as he accuses them of "draw[ing] life from death" (13) as he lies dying.[30] Phil attributes his poor health to "this beastly Jamaica" (13), and so Clarissa and Jamaica could both be read as the cause of the downfall of all the non-Jamaican characters. "Away Down in Jamaica" might then be read as a cautionary tale about colonialism.

However, the story itself provides a counterpoint to this univocal reading through its figuration of the characters' race and gender and their differing relationships to different modes of narrating culture and empire. In what Said calls a "contrapuntal" reading practice, which I employ here, one must pay attention to "those other histories against which (and together with which) the dominating discourse acts" (51). Specifically, I read the story by focusing on the Jamaican characters of Clarissa and Rachel—the only characters who are not given last names. Rachel, in particular, is left out in my recounting of the story's main plot, yet plays a crucial role. In what follows, I read "Away Down in Jamaica" as illustrating a tapestry of uneven and unequal relationships wrought by slavery, British colonialism, and U.S. and Canadian imperialisms. Through this illustration, the story teaches us that an essential component in the study of the afterlife of slavery must be an examination of empire's literature and its effects in culture, particularly in representations of the "misnamed" Black women.

To see how Sui Sin Far's story represents its Black female characters, we must read the story's characters comparatively. To begin, I read Clarissa in comparison to Wickliff. Although scholars have read Wickliff as a "white man" (Cutter, "Sex" 85) in a "conventional bourgeois white love triangle" (Yao 201), the story itself does not identify him as white. In contrast to descriptions of Kathleen as "fair" (Eaton 13) and Phil as "yellow haired" (4) and having "fair hair" (13), Wickliff is never described as "fair." Quite the opposite: Wickliff is described as having a "dark, handsome face" (13). When he discovers the dead bodies of Kathleen and Phil, the latter described as "white as marble" (13), Wickliff is said to "look very black" (13). Later in the story, as Rachel provides the epilogue, she calls Phil using the appellation of "master"—"Master Phil"—but not Wickliff, referring to him as "Mr. Walker" (13).

The sound of Wickliff's name, as well as his overpowering masculinity and description as "dark," calls to mind the Heathcliff character in Brontë's *Wuthering Heights*. Adopted by the white Earnshaw family as a boy, Heathcliff is repeatedly described as having a "dark face" (E. Brontë 73), called "a dark-skinned gipsy [*sic*]" (218) and referred to as "it" (5), as in, "it's as dark almost as if it came from the devil" (29). Heathcliff states of himself, "I wish I had light hair and a fair skin" (45). Nelly, a housekeeper who narrates most of the novel, calls him a "black villain" (88), and Catherine Earnshaw, Heathcliff's love interest, describes him at one point as looking "very black" (42), mirroring exactly the previously mentioned description of Wickliff in "Away Down in Jamaica." Given that *Wuthering Heights* takes place in and prior to 1801, before the British Parliament outlawed the slave trade—but not slavery—in 1807, the racialization of Heathcliff as nonwhite positions the racial transatlantic slavery in the novel as an absent presence. Heathcliff's place of "discovery" in Liverpool by Earnshaw buttresses this point further, as "the English city with the most spirited commerce in slaves was Liverpool" (von Sneidern 171) and "by 1804 Liverpool merchants were responsible for more than eighty-four percent of the British transatlantic slave trade" (172), according to Maja-Lisa von Sneidern. But in spite of such connections, *Wuthering Heights* is not typically read in the context of slavery, and the novel's contemporary reviews made no connection between Heathcliff's character and slavery, whitewashing both the character and the history of slavery. The twentieth-century film adaptations beginning in 1939 cast only white actors to play the part, and it was not until 2011 when Heathcliff was played by a Black actor.

The trace of Heathcliff and Brontë's novel that we see in "Away Down in Jamaica" illustrates that if British imperialism and novel were inseparable, so were slavery and the English novel and its conceptualization of the human. In *Wuthering Heights*, this obvious connection to slavery is downplayed by the fact that Heathcliff's race functions as a metaphor for his ruthlessness and inhumanity. As Wickliff's character is delineated in a similar fashion, what "Away Down in Jamaica" emphasizes is not the antiblackness in the equation of Blackness and villainy but rather the social mobility of the character *even* in spite of his association with Blackness. Neither Heathcliff nor Wickliff is constrained by his nonwhiteness or a possible historical connection to slavery. The two characters are both able to be read as white and move as white. This mobility is cast as strictly masculine.[31] In literature, this means that they are cast as protagonists in romance involving white women. Thus, Heathcliff's and Wickliff's association with Blackness is trumped by patriarchy and heteronormativity.

"Away Down in Jamaica" contrasts Wickliff's racial ambiguity and social mobility—it is implied that Kathleen comes from wealth and that marrying her will afford him "respectab[ility]" (Eaton 13)—with Clarissa's unambiguous identity as a Jamaican "brown girl." Like Wickliff, Clarissa also bears similarities to Heathcliff's character. On top of being explicitly nonwhite, Clarissa, like Heathcliff, was an orphan who was adopted by "some rich white people" (4). But though "they brought her up like a lady," Clarissa is said to have "[run] away from them some years ago" (4). Given that Clarissa from Samuel Richardson's eponymous novel *Clarissa* (1748) is a recognizable literary figure symbolizing female virtue against male corruption, and that the seduction of a manipulative man prompts Richardson's Clarissa to run away from her family, it is not too much of a leap to surmise that the reason that Sui Sin Far's Clarissa ran away from her family "some years ago" is Wickliff, who seduced her. But unlike Heathcliff whose running away from his adoptive family results in newfound wealth and independence, Clarissa's running away results in her destitution as well as abandonment by Wickliff. When Clarissa confronts Wickliff and asks "whether I am really nothing to you now," he responds, "Oh well, Clarissa, that's a queer question to put to a reformed man. You must know that I have given up all my wild ways, drinking, gambling and so forth, and am settling down to a respectable old age—am going to be married in fact" (13). Clarissa's question that casts her as "nothing" and Wickliff's answer are revealing of her exclusion from the genre of romance through his male privilege, as Wickliff deems Clarissa to be part of his "wild ways," associated with *his* actions, and respectability and marriage to be counter to who she is.

The rejection of Clarissa by Wickliff and the exclusion of Clarissa from the genre of romance can both be read as imperializing gestures, and the driving force of this imperialism and romance is not Wickliff but the white American woman, Kathleen. Harkening to the notion of marriage as bondage, Kathleen is said to feel "frightened" (4) when Wickliff proposes to her, and Wickliff's presence is described as an "influence" that Kathleen "rebelled against" in private, but when near him, she finds that she cannot speak the words that could set her "free" (4). Wickliff is said to be "her master, though not through her heart" (13)—the implication being that her attraction for him is more physical than emotional. The focus of the first chapter on Wickliff's romantic courtship of Kathleen, then, acts as the superficial layer of the story that serves to mask the violent history of conquest, genocide, and slavery. That is, the main plot of the story is told in the language of terror and bondage describing the oppression that *Kathleen* feels from Wickliff and their future marriage, explicitly rendering the violent history of the island a non-plot. In their oppressive courtship, Kathleen's outlet is through her relationship with the landscape of Jamaica. Kathleen romanticizes the island, as seen when she is on an outing with Wickliff. As the two are on a mountainside overlooking "orange groves, banana plantations and acres of cane fields stretched far away" (4) and "an old fort standing on a high, rocky promontory running out into the sea" (4), she derives pleasure from the landscape in "fair solitude" (4), negating the history of slavery,

British and U.S. imperialisms, and revolts and wars declared by the Jamaican Maroons. The "plantations," "cane fields," and "old fort" are unpeopled in her imagination. The sea, in particular, allows her to indulge in "vague and melancholy musing," and when she see a ship, she wishes to be on that ship, as "strange imaginings, undefinable and inexplicable floated through her mind as she gazed on that great circle of water" (4). For Kathleen, the sea represents freedom that she does not feel, as she characterizes it as "great, so free, so mysterious" (4). That she sees the sea as a possible source of salvation is underscored by her comparison to it as "a chapter from Revelations" (4), which, Chapman explains, refers to a biblical verse describing "a sea of glass glowing with fire" (*Becoming* 173).

What Kathleen does not consciously see in the sea is what Christina Sharpe calls the "wake of slavery" (*In the Wake* 8) and, as an American, her embeddedness in that wake. Moreover, Kathleen represents the increased U.S. presence in Jamaica at the turn of the twentieth century. According to Matthew Smith, "The United States had replaced Great Britain as Jamaica's major trading partner by the end of the century and was investing heavily in Jamaican economic development" (242). The intimacy in the histories of slavery and U.S. imperialism is not seen by Kathleen in her preoccupation with her romance. In fact, Kathleen's gaze and her characterization of herself as unfree in relation to Wickliff are one and the same as that which glosses over the history of slavery, as "plantations and acres of cane fields" are only seen as part of what she calls an "enchanted country" (Eaton 4). Nonetheless, the wake of slavery cannot be completely expunged, as what gets trivialized as part of Kathleen's daydream asserts itself as "vague and melancholy" and "strange . . . undefinable and inexplicable," in which we might find traces of the history of the slave trade and the Middle Passage. This interruption to the story posed by the haunting of slavery happens through the insertion of an element of the gothic, as Wickliff's name is called out by an unknown voice from the cliffs surrounding Kathleen and Wickliff near the sea. The unidentified voice is later revealed to be Clarissa's, but in the actual scene, Clarissa's calling out of Wickliff's name, whether in an attempt to interrupt Wickliff's romance with Kathleen or to insert herself back in his life, is quickly dismissed by both Kathleen and Wickliff. Despite the fact that they both clearly hear the voice, Wickliff dismisses it as "nobody" (4), reminiscent of Clarissa's earlier characterization as "nothing." Kathleen not only acquiesces to that dismissal but also demands leaving the place at once, not wanting to hear or see anything that might contradict her romantic vision of the "enchanted country."

If the romanticized landscape around Kingston is haunted by slavery, and Clarissa's ghostly voice calling Wickliff's name is a manifestation of that haunting, the fact that Clarissa has a bodily presence in only one scene in the story is significant. In place of her bodily presence, the story obliquely alludes to the figure of the "yellow girl"—an allusion that acts as a distinction among its female characters—through a strange detour in the second chapter with the insertion of a vaudevillian dialogue.

In the second chapter of "Away Down in Jamaica," we see both the U.S. and European iterations of the yellow girl in a scene that restages the vaudeville theater. The scene introduces Rachel and Clarissa through a dialogue between Rachel and Kathleen. Though neither Rachel nor Kathleen is explicitly identified by race in the scene, their differing class works as a code for their race, as Rachel is described as "one of the serving maids belonging to the hotel," who looks on admiringly as Kathleen brushes her hair (Eaton 4).[32] Emphasizing their difference even further, Kathleen asks, "Well, Rachel, my hair is rather straight, is it not?" and adds, "if my hair was only like that which grows on your head, I would be quite happy. How do you manage to make yours so nice and crinkly?" (4). Kathleen's focus on Rachel's hair calls to mind minstrel songs about the "black woman" figure, whose hair was described as "so black and curly" and, as cited earlier, "curled so very tight" (Christy and White 77, 85). In response, Rachel "laugh[s] heartily, showing her white teeth" (Eaton 4), a description that matches minstrelsy's frequent description of the "black woman's" "teeth [as being] so berry white" (Christy and White 77). As seen in such descriptions, it is not just Kathleen but also the story that fixes Rachel in a minstrel role, as she is made to repeat the line, "Missus is so funny," accompanying her "hearty laugh" (Eaton 4). Rachel's jovial laughter provides the support necessary to amp up the ridiculousness of what Kathleen is saying, as Kathleen states that she puts her hair in curlers every night "to make it curly, like yours," then wonders, "But perhaps you think my hair is cold, and I wrap it up to keep it warm" (4), and Rachel responds again by saying, "Missus is so funny" (4). Reminiscent of the insertion of the word "joking" in the final scene of "Ku Yum," Kathleen states that she is not "joking" (4) in this dialogue, as she plays the role of the European "yellow girl" as the (literally) "hair-brained [sic] comedienne," while Rachel plays the servile and lampooned figure of a loyal servant and sidekick. Here Rachel is represented as another misnaming of the Black woman—the "mammy" figure with an origin in the myth of the loyal enslaved person[33]—who does not begrudge Kathleen for the outlandish notions that Kathleen ascribes to her but only views her with "admiring eyes" (4). This figuration of Rachel returns at the conclusion of the story. For now, the hair scene does not have to say that Rachel is Black or that Kathleen is white; Rachel's representation is overdetermined by racist caricatures of the Black woman from slavery and the minstrel stage, and that serves to racialize them both.

Reading Kathleen as the European fin de siècle iteration of the whitened "yellow girl" in this scene is helpful because it spotlights the incommensurability between Kathleen and Rachel and Clarissa. Even as the idea of the "yellow girl" as the white Bohemian girl proliferated, the "yellow girl" of blackface minstrelsy found more enduring expression in minstrel songs at the end of the nineteenth century and well into the twentieth century in literature, no longer just as a figure of romance but more as a figure of lampoonery and hypersexualization. This transformation can be seen in the popular blackface minstrel songs published around the same time when Sui Sin Far wrote about the "yellow girl." The song "De Yaller Gal with Kinky Hair" (1896)—again, with the hair—included the lyrics "Her teef de is so large an' white / Dat when she laughs dey's out ob sight" (Harvey 4–5), reminiscent of the description of Rachel's teeth. Another example of the hypersexualized Black "yellow girl" figure can be seen in Erskine Caldwell's short story called "Yellow Girl" (1933). In the story, a white Southern woman develops doubts about her husband's fidelity after a neighbor warns her about her cook, a "yellow girl," stating, "I reckon I'd heap rather have a black girl and a poor cook, than to have a yellow girl and the finest cook in the whole country" (E. Caldwell 175). If the earlier minstrel representations of the "yaller gal" highlighted her desirability as well as her coquettish desires, the representations at the turn of the twentieth country concentrated mostly on the latter and rendered it aggressive and destructive.

Evidencing different shades of antiblackness, the enduring quality of these representations of the yellow girl highlights the difference between Kathleen and Clarissa. Immediately following the conversation about their hair, Kathleen puts a flower in her hair and asks Rachel who brings in the flowers every day. This prompts Rachel to tell Kathleen about—and introduces the reader to—Clarissa as a "brown girl" (Eaton 4). As stated, Clarissa is the only major character to be explicitly identified by race. In line with her general romanticizing of Jamaica as an "enchanted country" (4), Kathleen characterizes Rachel's story of Clarissa and her race as "Quite a romantic history!" and expresses a wish to "see her" the next time Clarissa comes around (4). Despite this wish, Kathleen does not see Clarissa as anything outside of the "yellow girl" figure, as she objectifies Clarissa as part of her fantastical landscape of Jamaica.

That Kathleen never actually gets to see Clarissa—both literally and figuratively—epitomizes her failure to see the history of slavery in Jamaica. The very identification of Clarissa as "brown" in Jamaica, just like the categorization of "yellow" in the United States, is a legacy of rape of female African captives by white male enslavers, interracial unions, and hierarchization of color on plantations. Explaining the color specifications produced out of slavery in the British Empire in the West Indies, Charmaine Nelson states, "Mixed-race populations were more commonly referred to as 'brown' and 'mulatto' . . . but also frequently as 'coloured' as well as a host of other terms . . . meant to designate specific racial mixtures" (30). Furthermore, as Orlando Patterson writes, there was a "correlation of colour and status" in Jamaica during slavery, as the "free coloured group [was] in a middle caste position between the white and slave group" (*Sociology* 64). The continued use of such racial terms associated with color post-slavery suggests that, as Christopher Charles argues, "the White-Black social structure/racial hierarchy of slavery, . . . evolved into a White-Black class structure" in Jamaica (157).

Though Clarissa thus represents Jamaican slavery's binding of race and color as well as gender, she herself does not identify as a victim or a caricatured and familiarized figure of romance in the story. She is an active agent in her own story—she runs away from her white adoptive family for love, calls out Wickliff's name when he is with Kathleen, gets inside Kathleen's place of domicile by bringing her flowers every day, confronts Wickliff directly and castigates him for his contemptible actions, and poisons the flowers that kill Kathleen. However, these acts are not properly recognized by others in the story. When she calls out Wickliff's name, her disembodied voice is characterized as "nobody" by Wickliff, who also deems her to be "nothing" (Eaton 4, 13). Kathleen cannot imagine that Clarissa will cause her death when she patronizingly casts Clarissa's life story as a "romantic history." Clarissa's resort to the practice of obeah and even her confession of Kathleen's murder—"she said she was glad Miss Kathleen was dead and that she had sent the flowers on purpose to poison her" (13)—are not only mediated through Rachel's retelling but also inappropriately understood, as "the doctors said Clarissa was mad and ordered her to be locked up" (13). The legal bounds of sociality do not apply to her, as her crime is adjudicated by *doctors*, though she ends up being "locked up" nonetheless. The pronouncement that she is "mad" likens her to the Jamaican Creole character Bertha Mason, the "mad" woman in the attic in Charlotte Brontë's *Jane Eyre* (C. Brontë 319).[34] Though Clarissa escapes instead of being confined like Mason, her escape is not exactly emancipation, as she is relegated to go into hiding "where no one can find her" (13). A peripatetic figure, who states of herself that, "like the Devil, I wander to and fro upon the earth" (13), her relationship to the space "upon the earth" is particularly in contrast to Kathleen's. Unlike Kathleen, who sees divine salvation in Jamaica's sea and landscape, Clarissa compares herself to Satan. In the book of Job in the King James Version of the Bible, in response to God's questioning of *his* whereabouts, Satan states, "From going to and fro in the earth, and from walking up and down in it" (Job 1:7). Thus ungendered, Clarissa is out of bounds with Christian middle-class domesticity and normativity. Outside of the familiar frame of "yellow girl," Clarissa and her actions are illegible, as she occupies a position of nonbeing in the story.[35]

If the characterization of Clarissa thus poses a transformative potential in what it shows about representations of Black women that do not conform to familiar stereotypes, perhaps embodying what Sylvia Wynter calls "'demonic ground' outside of our present governing system of meaning" ("Afterword" 356), it is counterposed to Rachel's. Much of Clarissa's story is narrated through Rachel, who acts as a mediating interpreter. In the last section of "Away Down in Jamaica," the narrative point of view switches without fanfare.[36] After Kathleen discovers Phil's dead body, the story is broken up with a line space and shifts to Rachel's point of view, as we are told, "Rachel held forth to her friends in the country. The following was her discourse" (13). Rachel explains how Kathleen died and what happened to Clarissa and then abruptly states, "I feel like singing" (13). What follows, and what ends the story, is this:

Oh, there'll be mourning, mourning,
Oh, there'll be mourning, mourning,
Oh, there'll be mourning, mourning,
At the Judgment seat of Christ. (13)

With these lines, the story aligns Rachel's character with not only blackface minstrelsy but also the most well-known novel about slavery in the United States and beyond—Harriet Beecher Stowe's *Uncle Tom's Cabin* (1852), which I argue in Chapter 1 inspired the creation of the "heathen Chinee." As Sui Sin Far does not draw a connection between the figure and the novel, her allusion is all the more provocative.

As Mary Chapman notes, the hymn appears—in a longer version—in *Uncle Tom's Cabin* in a scene involving the villainous enslaver Simon Legree (Chapman, *Becoming* 180). The novel does not explicitly identify the singer of the hymn. Because Cassy, a female captive, is outside taking care of Tom, enslaved by Legree and beaten savagely, the only other possible singer inside the house is Emmaline, another female captive. However, the novel leaves that point ambiguous, only describing the singer as "a wild, pathetic voice," "a mocking echo from the walls," and a "sweet voice," without stating directly that Emmaline was singing (Stowe, *Uncle* 487).[37] The way *Uncle Tom's Cabin* introduces this voice—"Legree stopped at the foot of the stairs, and heard a voice singing. . . . Hark! what is it?" (486)—is strikingly similar to how "Away Down in Jamaica" introduces Clarissa's disembodied voice: "But hark, what was the cry which seemed to echo from the cliffs behind them" (Eaton 4). The detachment of the voice from the body, particularly on the part of Stowe's novel, which does not explicitly identify the singer of "a hymn common among the slaves" (Stowe, *Uncle* 487), provides an opening for imagining the haunting of slavery that materializes in a collective metaphysical voice of condemnation.[38] The hymn terrorizes and torments Legree, who is reminded of his dead, devoutly Christian mother. To get his mind off it, he tries to supplant the hymn with entertainment by his captives: "I'll have Sambo and Quimbo up here, to sing and dance one of their hell dances, and keep off these horrid notions" (488). The description of the forced entertainment that ensues exposes the "terror of the mundane and quotidian" in what Saidiya Hartman calls the "scene of subjection" in slavery (*Scenes* 4). In place of the unidentifiable haunting of slavery communicated by the hymn, Legree opts for something he finds understandable and familiar that carries a trace of the minstrel form, which restores his sense of empowerment.

Sui Sin Far's insertion of the haunting hymn, which is meant to be understood as the complete opposite of the song and dance of Sambo and Quimbo in *Uncle Tom's Cabin*, might be read as signaling what Yao calls the "counterintimacies" in "Away Down in Jamaica," indicating that "instead of a 'friendly' relationship to whiteness, Sui Sin Far seeks alternative intimacies" through "affective kinship with black people" (Yao 198, 202). However, by putting Rachel in the role of singing the hymn—though "others joined in" (Eaton 13)—"Away Down in Jamaica," not unlike Legree, opts for a representational practice mediated by whiteness through its recourse to Stowe's novel instead of providing "a place for [the] different social subject" of the misrecognized Black woman. Rachel in "Away Down in Jamaica" resembles a description of a white character also named Rachel in *Uncle Tom's Cabin*, who is described as "one good, loving woman," having "just the face and form that made 'mother' seem the most natural word in the world" (Stowe, *Uncle* 177).[39] In making Rachel Black, "Away Down in Jamaica" fixes her role not as a "mother" but as the racist and sexist stereotype "mammy," as she cleans up after white people's mess by providing a conclusion to the story.

Ascribing to Rachel an abundance of love for the white characters and whiteness that the mammy figure holds—"Two such beautiful corpses I never did see," she says of Phil and Kathleen (Eaton 13)—the conclusion of "Away Down in Jamaica" calls to mind Frances Gage's description of Sojourner Truth after recounting the ventriloquized version of Truth's speech: "She had taken us up in her strong arms and carried us safely over the slough of difficulty turning the whole tide in our favor" (Stanton, *History* 116–17). The misnamed figure of the Black woman thus performs indispensable work—affective and otherwise—in narratives about "us" in slavery and its afterlife. In "Away Down in Jamaica," a story that is decidedly not *about* Rachel—or even Clarissa—a trace of the yellow girl and black woman figures from the minstrel stage that we see in "Ku Yum" gets fully animated, as Sui Sin Far joins in the rank of "all our author folks" trying their hand at (mis)naming the Black woman.

As a means of showing the incommensurability of the figure of the misnamed Black woman to a "Chinese slave," I conclude my discussion of "Away Down in Jamaica" by returning to the Wickliff-Heathcliff connection. In *Wuthering Heights*, in addition to the descriptions of Heathcliff as "dark" and "black," the ethnicity that he is tied to—other than the derogatory epithet of "gipsy"—is Asian. In response to Heathcliff's wish for whiteness, Nelly tells him, "Who knows but your father was Emperor of China, and your mother an Indian queen. . . . And you were kidnapped by

wicked sailors and brought to England" (E. Brontë 45).[40] Combined with
the description that as a foundling he would only speak "some gibberish
that nobody could understand" (29), the novel implies a foreignness on top
of Heathcliff's racial otherness. And this foreignness mitigates his Blackness, acting as a soothing salve for his impossible wish for "light hair and a
fair skin" (45). If we read Wickliff as a reiteration of Heathcliff, we might
read Wickliff's character as not only not-white but specifically Asian. That
is, the character with whom Asianness is most aligned in "Away Down in
Jamaica" is not Clarissa or Rachel but Wickliff. This reading further thwarts
the attempt to read "Away Down in Jamaica" as a story about Afro-Asian
solidarity on the basis of Sui Sin Far's mixed race, and highlights the incommensurability of Blackness and Asianness. But this reading is based on a
conjecture that cannot be proven. The story outwardly remains mum on
the presence of Asian labor in Jamaica.[41] That silence encapsulates the misnaming of Asian workers after slavery, which is a different story and a different misrecognition in the intimate histories of slavery, colonialism, and
labor migration.

. . .

The rhetorical use of slavery in Sui Sin Far's fictional writings in her attempt to rewrite the "heathen Chinee" figure must be read as part of the
afterlife of slavery, in which slavery is dehistoricized and antiblackness is
perpetuated through the use of slavery as a metaphor. Charting the multiple
histories of that metaphor shows that the figure of the Black female captive
persistently gets misrecognized and elided in the effort to claim freedom
counter to the category of the "slave." As a means of productively reading
that misrecognition and denial, I paired Sui Sin Far's "Ku Yum" with "Away
Down in Jamaica," arguing that the latter illuminates how the gendered
racial logic of slavery continues through representations of the figure of the
misnamed Black woman, for whom the Chinese or white woman oppressed
by patriarchy is not a commensurable other. As we read Sui Sin Far's rich
archive of writings, we must pay attention to how the writings participate in
the knowledge production of what it means to be not just a gendered Asian
North American subject but also the (un)gendered Black female subject in
the ongoing afterlife of slavery.[42]

Toward the end of her life, Sui Sin Far seems to have gone through a shift
in how she used the word *slave* in her stories. In early 1897, she published

a story called "The Daughter of a Slave." The only one of Sui Sin Far's fictional stories that contains "slave" in its title, it is also the only one in her collection of short stories, *Mrs. Spring Fragrance*, published two years before her death in 1914, to have gone through a significant title change.[43] In the 1912 title, "The God of Restoration," the focus on the word *slave* as determining the status of a woman was taken out and replaced by a religious reference. Though the content remained the same, and the word *slave* still appears several times in the body of the story, the title change in 1912 is also reflected in the revisions to the dialogue of the female protagonist, Sie. In the original 1897 version, when Sie expresses a misguided gratitude to her childhood lover for marrying her and thus buying her father's freedom when it was her lover's cousin who did so, she states, "My dear, good father—he has worked so hard all these years; he has ever been so kind to me. To think that he will no longer be a slave" (Sui Seen Far, "Daughter" 220). In the 1912 revised version, Sie states, "My dear, good father—he has worked so hard all these years. He has ever been so kind to me. How glad am I to think that through me the God of Restoration has decreed that he shall no longer be a slave" (Sui Sin Far, "God of Restoration" 138). Commenting on the 1912 version, Hsuan Hsu states, "Sui Sin Far may be alluding to the frequent association of God and Christ with restoration throughout the Bible" (Sui Sin Far, "God of Restoration" 138n1). While it is true that many of Sui Sin Far's stories touch on themes associated with Christianity in general, this particular insertion of a Christian reference is an incongruous moment in the text, all the more noteworthy because Sui Sin Far considered the reference significant enough to change the title.

Both the change in the title and the allusion to Christianity in the 1912 version of the story may be read as indicating Sui Sin Far's conversion of a sort to more expressive feelings of racial solidarity, particularly with Black authors and even more specifically with W. E. B. Du Bois.[44] In August 1910, Sui Sin Far published "Her Chinese Husband," about a white woman named Minnie who marries Liu Kanghi, a Chinese man, as a sequel to her March 1910 story, "A White Woman Who Married a Chinaman." In "Her Chinese Husband," we see a possible allusion to Du Bois—specifically, his concept of the "veil"—in the scene in which Minnie gives birth to her mixed-race baby, Little Kanghi. Minnie states that when she saw her son for the first time, she noted that "the boy was born with a veil over his face" (Sui Sin Far, "Her Chinese" 361). This description is similar to a passage from Du Bois's "Of the Passing of the First-Born" in *The Souls of Black Folk* (1903).[45] In observing that even though his infant son had hair "tinted with gold" and eyes with a hint of blue, Du Bois wrote, "In the Land of the Color-line I saw, as it fell across my baby, the shadow of the Veil" (*Souls* 507). Du Bois also employed the metaphor of the veil to theorize the concept of double consciousness in *Souls*: "The Negro is a sort of seventh son, born with a veil, and gifted with second-sight in this American world,—a world which yields him no true self-consciousness, but only lets him see himself through the revelation of the other world" (364). Implied in the two passages is that the concepts of the veil and double consciousness are specifically based in the United States. Minnie's association of the veil with her U.S.-born son and not her Chinese husband reflects this notion.

In the 1912 version of "Her Chinese Husband," however, Sui Sin Far extends the concept of double consciousness to the description of the Chinese husband as well. In that version, Minnie states, "There was also on Liu Kanghi's side an acute consciousness that, though belonging to him as his wife, yet in a sense I was not his, but of the dominant race, which claimed, even while it professed to despise me. . . . [I]t was there between us: that strange, invisible—what? Was it the barrier of race—that consciousness?" (Sui Sin Far, *Mrs. Spring* 108). Sui Sin Far's repeated use of "consciousness," particularly to characterize "the barrier of race," lays bare how Minnie and Liu Kanghi are differently racialized. That is, the revision in the 1912 story is remarkable in its attunement to racial, rather than cultural, difference between Minnie and Kanghi. It thereby insists on seeing Chineseness *and* whiteness as racial categories and suggests that the veil of race as a marker of nonwhiteness is not confined only to Blackness and in the United States.

Sui Sin Far's refined global view of race in 1912 was most likely influenced by Du Bois's "The Souls of White Folk" (1910), which was published in the same *Independent* issue containing "Her Chinese Husband."[46] In the essay, Du Bois expounds on the notion of a global white supremacist racial ideology that works against not just Black people but also all those who are racialized as "un-white," including those from countries such as Japan ("Souls of White Folk" 339, 340). By incorporating the notion of double consciousness as it applies to the Chinese-born Liu Kanghi, the revised "Her Chinese Husband" steps in line with Du Bois's proclamation that the "color line belts the world" ("Color Line" 33), not just as a means of oppression but also as a means of connecting "yellow races" with "brown and black races" (34).

But even with such influence by Du Bois, the two main characters in either version of "Her Chinese Husband" do not express a desire for any sort of solidarity with Blackness; nor do they put anything resembling antiracism into practice. Such work, as well as that of positing a glimmer of hope for the future, is relegated to the midwife who nurses Minnie, described as an "old mulatto Jewess" (Sui Sin Far, "Her Chinese Husband" 361). In contradistinction to Minnie, who weeps upon realizing the baby's nonwhiteness, the midwife announces the baby's birth by exclaiming, "A prophet! A prophet has come into the world" (361).[47] The brief appearance of the "mulatto Jewess," who expresses a desire for racial solidarity by celebrating the mixed-race Chinese baby, pronounces the birth of Minnie and Liu Kanghi's son as a moment of exaltation and promise for a better future. She is in the story only to perform a particular work, which is to nurse Minnie and to validate and define Little Kanghi as a prophet. This label revises the derogatory label of "oily little Chink" that Minnie's white ex-husband uses to describe Liu Kanghi (Sui Sin Far, "White Woman" 522) and the caricatured minstrel figure of the "heathen Chinee." Like Rachel in "Away Down in Jamaica," the nameless midwife is imbued with love for Little Kanghi for no apparent reason, characteristic of two-dimensional representations of Blackness that serve as "narrative gearshifts" in dominant white U.S. literature that Toni Morrison calls the "Africanist presence" (x, 6). While Sui Sin Far may have held ideas about race influenced by Du Bois later in her life, her representations of Blackness, particularly of Black women, still disclose a more deep-rooted influence by the white literary imagination that renders Black women as not much more than "surrogate, serviceable black bodies" (Morrison 28). As Sui Sin Far is most commonly read as humanizing the Chinese at a time of their dehumanized representations, her writings featuring Black female characters urge us to read with an eye toward who performs the work of that humanization and by what means.

Reading the Minstrel Tradition and U.S. Empire Through Charles Chesnutt's *The Marrow of Tradition*

If blackface minstrelsy was the most popular form of entertainment in the nineteenth-century United States, what did it look like at the end of the century? Did its transition into vaudeville shows, as discussed in Chapter 4, signal its demise? One opinion, put forward by Robert Toll, is that blackface minstrelsy reached a symbolic "final culmination" (263) in May 1895, in a production aptly called *Black America*. The production was the brainchild of Nate Salsbury, a white theater manager famous for his Buffalo Bill's Wild West Show, which was in high demand from its creation in the 1870s all the way to the 1920s. In *Black America*, Salsbury turned to the South and staged a show at a park in Brooklyn, New York, consisting of a replica of a Southern plantation that was billed as "A Gigantic Exhibition of Negro Life" (R. Hall, "Black" 49). Its cast included five hundred Black people, whom Salsbury advertised as "'genuinely southern negroes' brought 'direct from the fields' of Virginia and the Carolinas" (Toll 262). Salsbury emphasized that *Black America* was distinctly not a minstrel show and that the audience would see "no imitation, nothing but what is real" (qtd. in Toll 262). Toward this promise of authenticity, Salsbury referred to the Black people in the show only as "participants," never as performers or entertainers (Toll 262). Despite the proclaimed distinction, *Black America* did not mark a clean break from minstrel shows. Roger Hall cites a contemporaneous review in the *New York Times* that reported that "*Black America* was arranged 'somewhat like a minstrel show' with a first part of songs, chorus, and cakewalk, and a second part of specialties" (R. Hall, "Black" 55). As a spectacle of slavery that disavowed the minstrel form and presented itself as something new even as it performed the same song and dance about caricatured Blackness, *Black America*, writes Toll, "embodied the ultimate in white fantasies about Southern Negroes" and "left nowhere else for the plantation-centered blackface minstrel show to go" (263).

As unprecedented as *Black America* was in the sheer size of its all-Black cast, it is one in a series of unprecedented moments at the turn of the twentieth century that signaled an important shift in—but not the complete demise of—blackface minstrelsy. Contrary to Toll's claim that it "left nowhere else" for blackface minstrelsy to go, *Black America* pointed the way to a different turn in its history. Salsbury's show was not a wild success, but it may have inspired John W. Isham, a Black theater manager who sometimes passed as white, to make history by staging the first show on Broadway composed entirely of Black performers the following year in 1896. The show was the first to "entirely break away from the slapstick and burlesque of the minstrel show" (Sampson, *Blacks* 27), even as it loosely followed the minstrel format, opting instead to finish with a grand finale of well-loved operatic arias that lasted for forty minutes. In a review of the show on November 9, 1896, the Washington, D.C., *Morning Times* praised it as "one of the strongest" of its kind (Sampson, *Blacks* 100). The review continued, "Among the many features of the great show were a Japanese dance" and "the maids of the Oriental Hussars" (104). Although these two acts were minor components, they gave "credence to the show's title" (Hill and Hatch 146), which was *Oriental America*. The direction after *Black America* for Black artists who had been in the industry of minstrelsy after the Civil War was a move away from "Black" to "Oriental," not necessarily in a turn to yellowface but a turn to whiteface performing in yellowface. As seen in the show's promotional poster featuring the "Japanese" dancers, *Oriental America* differed from *Black America* and its claim of authentic, unmediated Blackness, as the former included a Black cast who did not necessarily perform Blackness (see Figure 5.1). It follows, then, that perhaps *Black America* was not the terminal point of blackface minstrelsy; rather, with an all-Black cast pictured in promotional posters as white and Asian, *Oriental America* was an inflection point that would take blackface minstrelsy in a new direction in the twentieth century.

The significance of the first Broadway show with an all-Black cast being named *Oriental America*, possibly in an effort to move away from the

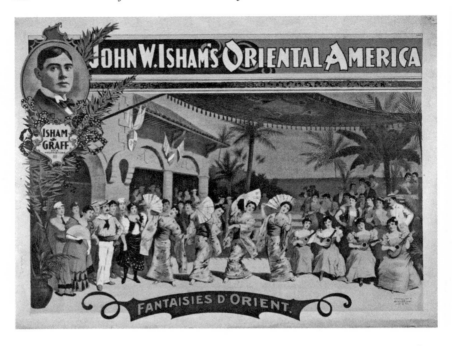

FIGURE 5.1   Poster for John W. Isham's *Oriental America*, ca. 1896. Courtesy of Library of Congress.

staging of slavery as a spectacle in *Black America*, has not been duly noted in the history of minstrelsy. Also understudied is that in what came after *Oriental America*—in the rise and success of Black musicals and musical comedies that ultimately replaced blackface minstrel shows—we see the same recourse to white and yellowface by *Black* performers who also acted in blackface.[1] *Oriental America* was critically lauded but, like *Black America*, did not achieve wide fame in the United States. Nonetheless, James Weldon Johnson, one of the most prominent writers of the New Negro Renaissance, wrote in 1930 that Isham's show "broke all precedents" (J. Johnson, *Black Manhattan* 97). Johnson's description is in line with theater historian Henry Sampson's future assessment that the show was an "important [link] in the development of black theatricals in America" (Sampson, *Blacks* 102). *Oriental America* paved the way for Black minstrel performers to stage all-Black shows that transitioned out of minstrelsy and birthed the genre of Black musicals. Specifically, white managers were inspired by *Oriental America* to recruit Black performers and songwriters to compete against the show. Two such performers, Billy Johnson and Bob Cole, who got their start in black-face minstrelsy, eventually left their white management, and what resulted was *A Trip to Coontown*—the first all-Black produced and "first complete original black musical comedy on the American stage" (Sampson, *Blacks* 287), which debuted in 1898. Unlike *Black America* and *Oriental America*, *A Trip to Coontown* was a major commercial success. Whereas the two previous shows were described as being too ahead of their time for the contemporary audiences to appreciate, *A Trip to Coontown* appealed to what was already in vogue and familiar.

The title, *A Trip to Coontown*, was a riff on *A Trip to Chinatown* (1891), a nonminstrel musical comedy by Charles Hoyt with an all-white cast that was the longest-running show on Broadway until 1919. *A Trip to Chinatown* had no Chinese characters—in yellowface or otherwise—and none of its songs had anything to do with the Chinese. The only connection to Chineseness was the premise that a group of white San Franciscans was going to have a wild night in the city's Chinatown (but never make it there) and, as Michael Saffle states, "in act 2, a widow named Mrs. Guyer appears in orientalized costume and 'does Chinese specialty' (whatever that means)" while claiming to wear "a Chinese dress" that vouches for her knowledge of Chinese customs (101). As Saffle's research shows, this brief reference to Chineseness in *A Trip to Chinatown* was part of a larger fascination with the Chinese and the "Orient"—the latter understood as referring to both Asia and the Middle East—at the end of the nineteenth century in the United States, a fascination in which *Oriental America* also participated and tried to capitalize on. Taking its name from the wildly successful *A Trip to Chinatown*, then, *A Trip to Coontown* took the fascination with Chineseness one step further. It included Chinese characters and featured songs about them, one of which was called "The Wedding of the Chinee and the Coon" (1897), about the marriage of a Chinese woman and a Black man, described as "A mighty jubilee Way down in Chinatown" (Cole and Johnson, *Wedding* 1; see Figure 5.2). Almost thirty years after the publication of Harry Lorraine's song, "Nigger Versus Chinese," in which the narrator complains that the Chinese have "got no pret-ty yellow gals" (Lorraine 4), Cole and Johnson's song answered back with a "pretty Chinese girl" (1). In the process, the song also revised the figure of the "heathen Chinee" by literally marrying the caricature with another caricature, the "coon," as it stated, "All Diplomats

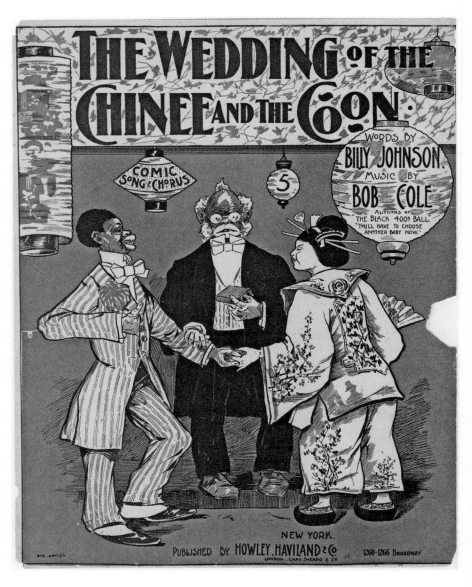

FIGURE 5.2 The cover image for *The Wedding of the Chinee and the Coon* score (New York: Howley, Haviland, 1897), Music Division, New York Public Library, http://digitalcollections.nypl.org/items/510d47de-1878-a3d9-e040-e00a18064a99.

from coon-ville must be ready / To join in with the band of the heathen chinamen," as "The coon Parson joined the Chinee and the coon" (1).

Cole and Johnson's use of "heathen" and "Chinee" to refer to the Chinese and "coon" to refer to Black people reveals that the afterlife of slavery at the end of the nineteenth century, seen through the history of black-face minstrelsy, was indeed peculiar. Even though the "band of the heathen Chinamen" and the "Chinee" bride are unrecognizable from Bret Harte's "heathen Chinee" that was reminiscent of Harriet Beecher Stowe's minstrel figure of Topsy, we see the long life of the association between the word *heathen* and the Chinese in Cole and Johnson's song. And just as Harte's "heathen Chinee" signaled the newness of the U.S. West, the Chinese characters in Cole and Johnson's song also embodied a novelty, which was not just foreignness. Unlike *Oriental America*'s Japanese dancers, the Chinese in "The Wedding of the Chinee and the Coon" are domestic figures, living in "Chinatown" in the United States (1). The caricature of the "heathen Chinee"—a product of Reconstruction when the racialization of the Chinese as a "new" presence proliferated, as seen in Harte's, Twain's, and Bierce's writings and dominant cultural representations such as "Nigger Versus Chinese"—serves to exoticize the song while also making it familiar. "The Wedding of the Chinee and the Coon," therefore, could be understood as a post-Reconstruction Black cultural production that relies on the racialization of the Chinese in order to stake out a new space in U.S. popular culture. As Julia Lee argues, "'The Wedding of the Chinee and the Coon' provides a particularly rich example of how the figure of the Asian was vital in mediating the relationship between blackness and the 'American' national identity, and in turn how blackness was key in imagining Asian racial difference in relation to the nation" (25). The song also reveals that just as the "heathen Chinee" provides a way of examining the construction of U.S. literature during Reconstruction through the minstrel form, the Chinese figure in post-Reconstruction popular culture provides a way of studying self-expressions of Blackness through Black performances as well as Black literature before the New Negro Renaissance.

This chapter examines the figure of the Chinese worker in Black cultural productions at the turn of the twentieth century in the context of the shifts in the blackface minstrel form to see how Black performers and writers influenced and responded to the changes. I begin with a study of the proliferation of songs at the end of the nineteenth century that were collectively

called "coon songs," many of which were written by Black artists. I point to
a connection between these songs and the development of African American literature as a cultural institution at this time. Writers whom we readily
associate with the New Negro Renaissance, such as Paul Laurence Dunbar
and James Weldon Johnson, wrote the lyrics for many of the songs, such
as "The Hottest Coon in Dixie" (1898) and "Sambo and Dinah" (1904),
respectively. That these writers, who are thought of today as having been
"race men" for their activism in calling for Black equality, were employing
the minstrel form in their artistic endeavors illustrates the complexities of
that paradox. As a proposal for how we should understand this paradoxical
moment, this chapter presents Charles Chesnutt as a Black author who explicitly tried to write African American literature that was not only distinct
from but also antithetical to the tradition of blackface minstrelsy by demonstrating the violent antiblackness at minstrelsy's core.

Such effort by Chesnutt can be seen most clearly in his 1901 novel *The
Marrow of Tradition*, which concludes with a fictionalized race massacre that
had actually occurred in Wilmington, North Carolina, in 1898. The white
people in Wilmington sought to drive out and terrorize the city's Black
residents, twenty of whom were killed. Chesnutt sets the stage for the massacre through three prior incidents in the novel: a reference to the role of
the "coon song" (*Marrow* 238) that shapes the dominant understanding of
Blackness in the fictional town of Wellington and the United States, the
practice of blackface performance by a white man that nearly results in the
lynching of a Black man, and a scene on a Jim Crow train in which a Chinese worker rides in the white section from which a Black doctor had just
been expelled. With these three incidents, the novel provides the heuristic
with which we can understand the complex strands of the 1890s discussed
above: the flourishing of Black-written and -produced songs and shows in
U.S. popular culture, the question of Black self-expression through the arts
in a country at whose core—or marrow of tradition—was an understanding
of race structured by antiblackness and slavery, and the role of the Chinese
worker figure in the period's "race question," particularly in relation to the
state-sanctioned Jim Crow laws and extralegal violence against Black people. For *The Marrow of Tradition*, the minstrel form is not an enabling tool
through which Chesnutt could assert his identity as a racially unmarked
writer as it was for Sui Sin Far writing "Away Down in Jamaica" as Edith
Eaton. Instead, the form is revealed to be inextricably tied to the terror

of antiblack violence and what Ruth Gilmore describes as "vulnerability to premature death" (28) in the afterlife of slavery. Moreover, rather than employing the Chinese worker figure to keep alive antiblack literary and cultural forms through blackface minstrelsy, or to highlight the innovative newness of Black representation of Chineseness, Chesnutt marks the figure as ambiguously racialized in the Black-white binary in the United States, focusing instead on the incommensurabilty of Blackness rooted in the racial logic of slavery as well as the formal specificity of *The Marrow of Tradition* as a Black novel in U.S. literature and empire.[2] In what follows, I analyze the novel's deliberations on race, violence, and performance and conclude with its critical reception in the *North American Review*, which reveals the antiblack contours of the U.S. empire and the complicity of U.S. literature in it.

Subverting the Minstrel Form Through "Coon Songs"

The liberal use of the word "coon" in songs written by Black songwriters aptly illustrates the structured domination in U.S. popular culture and the extremely limited freedom those artists had for creative expressions because of the enduring legacy of blackface minstrelsy. Even though traditional minstrel shows were being replaced by vaudeville shows, the most popular form of entertainment in the United States at the turn of the twentieth century was still unquestionably a remnant of minstrelsy. Collectively known as "coon songs," one of the first such songs was printed in 1880, according to James Dormon, and by the mid-1880s, the coon song had become a national craze—in the same way that blackface minstrelsy had been decades earlier. Dormon states that "over six hundred of them were published during the decade of the 1890s, and the more successful efforts sold in the millions of copies" (453). Many of the songs, like Cole and Johnson's and some of the most famous ones such as "All Coons Look Alike to Me" (1895), were written and performed by Black songwriters for what were pejoratively called "coon shows." The craze of such songs therefore coincided with the national ascension of Black performers who sang and performed them in blackface: in addition to Cole and Johnson, these artists included Ernest Hogan, who wrote "All Coons Look Alike to Me," and Bert Williams, the legendary performer from the West Indies who along with his partner George Walker would famously bill themselves as "Two Real Coons" (Chude-Sokei 5).

These performers and songwriters—whom Amma Ghartey-Tagoe Kootin labels as participating in "blackbody minstrelsy" (4)—all became household names during this time.

The blackbody minstrels who performed as "coons" were not simply continuing the tradition of blackface minstrelsy, even though they have been understood that way. In the conclusion to *The Souls of Black Folk* (1903), W. E. B. Du Bois groups together "contemporary 'coon' songs" with "the Negro 'minstrel' songs" in order to cast both as "debasements and imitations" of what he calls the "sorrow songs" of the enslaved, which he sees as a "singular spiritual heritage of the nation and the greatest gift of the Negro people" (251).[3] Characterizing the sorrow songs as a distinctly Black cultural form, Du Bois implies that minstrel and "coon songs" were interchangeable, as he deems Black artists who performed as "coons" and white people who performed as "minstrels" to be. However, as scholars of blackbody performances argue, the Black songwriters and vaudevillian performers of "coon songs" saw themselves as decidedly different from white blackface performers. Karen Sotiropoulos writes that "Black vaudevillians pleased white theater managers and white audiences with their antics, but they were just as concerned with furthering race progress as they were with their own fame and fortune" (4). Sotiropoulos specifically cites Bert Williams, who said minstrelsy was "a thing of the past . . . to cork your face and talk politics is not minstrelsy" to make this point (4). As Williams understood his blackbody act and his lines to be subverting dominant white racism, he saw his performance as inherently political and distinguishable from blackface minstrelsy. In line with such understanding, Louis Chude-Sokei states that Williams "appropriated from whites the very right to perform and symbolically possess 'the Negro'" (5). Williams and his partner Walker wrote songs about and performed as "*real* coons" (5; emphasis added) which ultimately destroyed the fiction of Blackness that had been created by blackface minstrelsy. In donning the persona created by the antiblack form of minstrelsy and claiming the bona fide nature of *their* characterizations, blackbody minstrel performers undermined the legitimacy of white blackface performers.

The notion that blackbody performers destabilized the form of blackface minstrelsy through their performance can be seen most patently in cases where they donned not just blackface but also whiteface and yellowface. In *A Trip to Coontown*, the partners Cole and Johnson developed a character in whiteface named Willie Wayside, played by Cole.[4] Willie Wayside became a popular tramp figure, inspiring many imitations. In fact, Cole's and other actors' performances in *A Trip to Coontown* prompted one reviewer to state, "There are many white comedians who could sit at the feet of these Negro actors and learn a thing or two" (qtd. in Sampson, *Ghost* 149). In thus outperforming whiteness, actors such as Cole not only exhibited the performativity of race but also exposed white racism in and through the minstrel form. In a song called "No Coons Allowed" (1897) written by Cole and Johnson, Cole sang the following words in whiteface: "This place is meant for white folks that's all / We don't want no kinky-head kind, / So move on darky down the line / No coons allow'd in here at all" (Cole and Johnson, *No Coons* 3). Associated with whiteness in the song is the imperious nature of white privilege that restricts Black people from participation in civil society, seen through the treatment of a Black man in the song who tries to dine at the "swellest place in town" (1). Performing white racism on stage had to be done strategically, however, as the song also lampoons the Black man by repeatedly calling him a "coon" and a "darky" (1). The very label of "coon" has its origin in blackface minstrelsy, as Zip Coon was a minstrel character personifying purported free Black people—usually dandies—who put on airs and always got their comeuppance. Songs such as "No Coons Allowed" present the dialectical nature of blackbody performances that called out white racism through a performance in whiteface while also appearing to keep Black people in their place, as the song's Black protagonist repeatedly tries to claim white spaces restricted to him, only to be denied—even at the courthouse in the final scene.

These songs that subtly invoke the rise of Jim Crow laws against Black people suggest that perhaps the only way that Black performers could participate in theatrical representations in dominant popular culture was through the vehicle of minstrelsy and asserting their ability to perform race. In this regard, performances in yellowface were very common in Black-written songs and shows at the turn of the twentieth century. As stated, beginning with *Oriental America*, the Chinese/Oriental presence pervaded nearly every single moment of precedence in Black musical theater history during this time.[5] Like the "coon" caricature, the Chinese character—usually a laundry worker or a cook, and most often male—was a familiar one that afforded the shows a way to showcase impersonation as a special talent of certain performers. Black actors such as George Caitlin, Tom Brown, Sam Cook, and Frank Walker (better known as "Chinee" Walker), built their reputations as performers by honing their Chinese impersonation skills. They performed in yellowface not just in Black musicals but also blackbody performances in vaudeville shows. These performances were enjoyed by both white and Black audiences. They were also reviewed in Black newspapers, which provided an opportunity for Black criticism of Black performances and the articulation of a distinct Black culture.

After viewing the vaudeville performance of Sam Cook and Jim Stevens, for example, a Black theater critic named J. D. Howard wrote in the *Indianapolis Freeman* in October 1909 that Cook's Chinese impersonation was a "unique feature" of their act. He stated, "Ordinarily the announcement of a stage Chinaman is a signal to cringe, and when it is coupled with a sketch that suggests a laundry it means to cringe all the harder. But Cook and his partner, Jim Stevens who presents a Negro character that serves as an excellent foil to the Chinaman, make their sketch, No Check-ee, No Wash-ee, the hit of the bill" (Howard 5). Howard's description of "the announcement of a stage Chinaman [as] a signal to cringe" hints that white performances of the Chinese figure in traditional blackface minstrel shows had perhaps been insufferable. In fact, other than Charles Parsloe, who performed the role of Ah Sin in Mark Twain and Bret Harte's collaboration *Ah Sin*, no other white blackface performer was widely known for his impersonation of the Chinese as were the blackbody performers named above. In particular, what made Cook's performance so appealing in contrast to the "ordinar[y] . . . stage Chinaman," according to the reviewer, was that "Cook apparently has discarded the traditional stage Chinaman in to-to" (5). As the reference to the "traditional stage Chinaman" connotes white performances in yellowface, the reviewer suggests that Cook was not merely imitative of such performances but has instead "discarded" that tradition "in to-to," specifically by having "gone out into Chinatown and studied the Chinaman from life, and then created and embellished a character true to life and, more importantly, to stage art" (5). The reviewer states that Cook's performance is based on real "life," implying that white performers' impersonations were not. Yet the performance was especially successful because of the embellishments that Cook himself added that were true to "stage art," evidencing his unique artistic touches on real life that the reviewer found "irresistible" (5). In other words, the reviewer highlights Cook's artistry in performing the Chinese role and suggests that it is precisely that artistry that signals a total break from the traditional blackface minstrelsy of white performers.

Insinuated in both Black performances of Chineseness and reviews of them was the notion that blackbody performances as "stage art" were superior to unartistic white blackface performances.

The blackbody performances of Chineseness, therefore, were not as much about making fun of the Chinese or participating in white racism as they were about performing a part that had been off-limits to Black performers when minstrelsy was a strictly white cultural form. The blackbody performances were a part of the process in which Black artists integrated theater by participating in one of the few venues in U.S. popular culture that allowed for such participation. The aim of such process was not to replicate white racism but to articulate what it meant to be Black through yellowface performance as an artistic self-expression. We see this articulation in a song by Alex Rogers and Bert Williams called "Chink, Chink, Chinaman," which was performed in *Mr. Lode of Koal* (1909). The song is performed in yellowface, as the narrator laments that he used to run a "chop suey house on street where heap white boys, / All time sing 'bout chink chink chinee all time make heap noise" (B. Williams 1). To escape this noise, the narrator moves to a different street, which to his chagrin has "got heap black boys, / Him all same sing chink, chink, chinee him all same make noise" (1). The narrator curses the "clazy song," and concludes, "White boy, black boy loud as can sing / chink, chink, chink, chink, chineeman" (3). Whereas Krystyn Moon, in her study of yellowface performances in popular music in the United States, argues that the song "brings African Americans and whites together because they enjoy singing the same racist ditties" (136), I read "Chink, Chink, Chinaman" as speaking not to anti-Chinese racism but the inseparability of antiblackness and blackface minstrelsy, specifically in San Francisco.

Bert Williams and his partner George Walker had met in theater circuits in San Francisco in 1893 before moving to New York and finding their fame there. *Mr. Lode of Koal* was the first play in which Bert Williams appeared without his partner George Walker, who had fallen ill. The song "Chink, Chink, Chinaman" could be read as not just an homage to the history of their partnership but also a statement about the availability of performing opportunities for Black artists in San Francisco in contrast to New York. The Chinese character's move to a different street in the song could be reflecting Williams and Walker's move to New York and the practice of performing songs about—and as—the Chinese there. Similarly, the

Chinese character's initial place of dwelling could refer to San Francisco and the white-dominant theater scene in the city. Even though the main point seems to be the Chinese character's detestation of the anti-Chinese song that both the "white boys" and "black boys" sing, the song has a subtler message. Operating implicitly in the song is strict segregation and the insinuation that the black boys could not sing in the same place where the white boys sang. With the understanding that the initial place where the white boys live is San Francisco, we can draw the connection that the existence of a segregated space of "singing" probably extended to the condition of antiblackness that Williams and Walker lived in, which made them leave the city to seek a better opportunity in New York. As Lynn Hudson writes, "Eager to capitalize on the popularity of the minstrel stage, the *San Francisco Examiner*, in the 1890s, began running a special Sunday supplement with 'coon songs'" (181). The popularity of minstrel shows in San Francisco, which had been constant since the early 1850s, found a new expression in the "coon songs" as the songs were incorporated into everyday practices like reading the newspaper as well as special occasions, such as a banquet for the new president of the University of California at Berkeley at the city's Palace Hotel in 1899 (181). When read between the lines, "Chink, Chink, Chinaman," combined with Williams and Walker's self-appellation as "real coons," points out the hypocrisy that the pair who would become widely recognized for their writing and performance of "coon songs" found San Francisco an inhospitable place to perform them. This reading emphasizes the crucial difference between the white "coon songs" and the Black ones: the former were integral to and buttressed the structure of white supremacy that relied on the racial logic of antiblackness, while the latter challenged that structure and its racial logic through mimicry and an articulation of Black culture.

The figure of the Chinese worker was vital to that attempt to transform the antiblack minstrel form to Black "stage art," as a vehicle through which to demonstrate Black self-expression and artistry. In this way, Black performances of Chineseness can be understood as what Daphne Brooks calls "Afro-alienation acts," the practice of Black artists "defamiliarizing their own bodies" to "rewrite the ubiquitous master narrative of minstrelsy, with its colonizing and constrictive figurations of grotesque and immobile 'blackness'" (4, 5–6). As the success of Williams and Walker's career indicates, New York City, described by many as "black Bohemia" (J. Johnson, *Black Manhattan* 74) at the turn of the twentieth century, was central to this self-expression.[6] Just as the figure of the Chinese worker was enlisted in the writings of the white authors who called themselves "Bohemians" in San Francisco during Reconstruction, the figure was embedded in what was considered to be the "center of colored bohemians" (J. Johnson, *Autobiography* 102) in post-Reconstruction New York City, enabling a rearticulation of what it meant to be Black and white in the United States in spaces that were formerly exclusively white.

Subversion of the Minstrel Form in The Marrow of Tradition

If the "coon songs" written by Black artists attempted to undermine antiblack racism through a subversive reworking of the minstrel form and incorporations of the Chinese character, Charles Chesnutt's *The Marrow of Tradition* (1901) argues that a successful challenge against antiblackness could not be through the minstrel form or the figure of the Chinese worker. Chesnutt believed that literature was the form through which to challenge white racism and expose the specificity of antiblackness as the "marrow of tradition" in the United States. As he wrote in a letter to Booker T. Washington, he thought that "the medium of fiction offers a golden opportunity to create sympathy throughout the country for our cause" (Chesnutt, *"To Be"* 167). Speaking as a Black man who grew up in the South, Chesnutt understood "our cause" as the race question as it pertained to not just Black people in general but more specifically Black people in the South.

Chesnutt was born in Ohio in 1858 but grew up in Fayetteville, North Carolina, having moved there as an eight-year-old with his parents who were free Black people originally from the city. After teaching at the Fayetteville State Normal School for Negroes for three years, Chesnutt was working as a principal at the school when he began considering a career in writing in 1880. That year, in a journal entry on March 16, the twenty-two-year-old Chesnutt wrote, "Judge Tourgee has sold the 'Fool's Errand,' I understand, for $20,000. . . . The work has gained an astonishing degree of popularity, and is to be translated into the French" (Chesnutt, *Journals* 124). In 1879, Albion W. Tourgée, a white Ohioan who was a supreme court judge in North Carolina during the Radical Reconstruction (1867–1872) and would go on to be Homer Plessy's lawyer in *Plessy v. Ferguson* (1896), had published his novel *A Fool's Errand*, based on his experience with the failures of Reconstruction in North Carolina. Tourgée's novel was a best seller, and Chesnutt found inspiration in the fact that a novel about race could be received so favorably by the U.S. reading public. Giving himself a pep talk to achieve similar success, he declared in the same journal entry, "If Judge Tourgee, with his necessarily limited intercourse with colored people, and with his limited stay in the South, can write such an interesting descriptions, such vivid pictures of Southern life and character as to make himself rich and famous, why could not a colored man, who has lived among colored people all his life . . . if he possessed the ability, write a far better book about the South than Judge Tourgee or Mrs. Stowe has written?" (*Journals* 125). Aligning Tourgée with Harriet Beecher Stowe for motivation, Chesnutt's pep talk to himself perspicaciously named the fact that the two best-selling novels about race written in the nineteenth-century United States were by white authors.

Even with this recognition, the young Chesnutt was optimistic about his future as a literary writer. In particular, he deemed that his life experiences as a Black man who grew up in the South gave him a certain advantage, "especially with all the phases of the slavery question" (125). Acknowledging the representations that he was writing against, Chesnutt explicitly vowed not to "record stale negro minstrel jokes" in his literary endeavor (126). Unlike Bret Harte, Mark Twain, Ambrose Bierce, and Sui Sin Far, Charles Chesnutt specifically set out to base his literary writing on the "slavery question," and he saw the minstrel form as antithetical to this effort. *The Marrow of Tradition* is a remarkable showcase of Chesnutt's attempt to represent the "hard facts" (126) of slavery and its afterlife.

Chesnutt's novel contends that to understand its present moment at the turn of the twentieth century, we need to know its past. The novel centers on two families in the fictional Wellington, North Carolina,[7] whose histories are deeply intertwined: the Carterets and the Millers. Philip and Olivia Carteret are white. William and Janet Miller are Black. Olivia and Janet are half sisters. Olivia's mother died when Olivia was a young girl, and Olivia's mother's sister, Aunt Polly, assumed the responsibility of the house. But when Olivia's father, Sam Merkell—"Mars Sam"—insisted that Julia Brown, a Black house servant, should manage the household, Aunt Polly left and took Olivia with her. When Merkell died unexpectedly, Aunt Polly came back, took charge of the house, and banished Julia and her daughter Janet. Not too long afterward, Julia died, and Janet—whose father is Merkell—was educated by a philanthropic Northern woman. She came back to Wellington and married Adam Miller's son, William Miller, who is a doctor. Adam Miller, who was formerly enslaved by the Carterets, bought the Carteret mansion when it had to be sold after the war, so that when Adam died, Janet and Dr. Miller became the new property owners. Philip Carteret harbors antiblack racism and sees the Millers as actively having taken what is rightfully his estate and inheritance. Olivia also blames her estrangement from her father when she was growing up on Janet and is ashamed and vexed whenever she sees Janet around town.

While the intertwined histories of the Carterets and the Millers may seem to suggest that the antiblackness harbored by both Philip and Olivia Carteret is personal and localized, it is actually structural and deeply rooted in slavery. A former Confederate soldier, Philip Carteret—consistently called Major Carteret in the novel—stands in for the Southern planter class who profited from the institution of slavery and whose lives were upended by the war. The novel describes that Carteret's "elder brother had sacrificed his life on the bloody altar of the lost cause," which made their father die "broken and chagrined" soon thereafter (Chesnutt, *Marrow* 2). The notion of the "lost cause," first introduced in Edward Pollard's 1867 book of the same name, glorified the valor, bravery, and manhood of Southern soldiers who fought against an overwhelming Union force, which the South believed was greater only in number and resources but not in spirit. By beginning the novel with a reference to the lost cause, Chesnutt sets up and historicizes Carteret's antiblackness during and after Reconstruction as part of the effort of the white South to justify fighting for slavery as valorous and to validate the notion of white redemption from the so-called "Negro domination" during Reconstruction. Carteret's status is restored after his marriage to Olivia, but as evidenced by the precarious health of their baby, the marrow of their family is diseased by slavery. The novel is thus in direct conversation with the "counterrevolution" of the white South, which sought to make sure, as David Blight argues, that "the war may have been lost but Reconstruction was won—by the South and by a reconciled nation" (111). By refusing to forget and keep silent on the antiblack violence unleashed after emancipation, Chesnutt's novel takes on the challenge of transforming a racial discourse injurious to those specifically racialized as Black, which is revealed to be deeply entrenched as "tradition."[8]

Published when "coon songs" were widely popular, *The Marrow of Tradition* critically engages with the popularity of the songs, as well as the minstrel form of white people performing in blackface, in order to spotlight the role those cultural forms played in the American tradition of antiblackness. The novel specifically mentions the songs in the context of the "constant lynchings" (Chesnutt, *Marrow* 238) in the South, stating that the white Northerners who "derived their opinions of [Black people] from the 'coon song' and the police reports" (238) were blind to what was going on. As Sandra Gunning states, the period from the 1890s to the 1910s saw the highest number of lynchings and white mob violence, and anti-lynching activists such as James Elbert Cutler and Ida B. Wells estimated the number of Black victims ranging from 3,337 to 10,000 (5). Most of the victims were lynched as a means of upholding the system of Jim Crow apartheid but were purported to have been deserving of the deaths because of some made-up threat they posed. By citing the depictions of Blackness in "coon songs" and police reports of Black violence in the North, Chesnutt indicts them for indirectly supporting the lynchings.

As part of Chesnutt's consideration of "all the phases of the slavery question," specifically regarding violence in slavery's afterlife, *The Marrow of Tradition* provides a heuristic for how the violence depicted in "coon songs," particularly those written by Black artists, might be understood. As strategic as the blackbody performances and songs may have been in trying to challenge the white supremacist form of blackface minstrelsy, they often replicated caricatures and stereotypes of Blackness. Many songs depicted Black people as violent, specifically by featuring razors symbolizing that violence. In their song "The Coon's Trade Mark," for instance, Williams and Walker sang, "Four things you'll always find together, Regardless of condition of sun and moon— / A watermelon, a razor, a chicken and a coon!" (qtd. in Dormon 456). The razor appears in "The Wedding of the Chinee and the Coon" as well, when the families of the Chinese bride and the Black groom get into a debate about who should officiate the wedding, and all of a sudden, there are "razors in the air," which results in the "Chinese preacher los[ing] his cue" (Cole and Johnson, *Wedding* 4) and the job of officiating going to the "coon Parson" (4–5). As Dormon writes, the violence in these songs was "uniformly perpetrated by blacks on blacks" (460)—or in this case, by Black people on nonwhite people. Dormon states that the violence was never perpetrated on white people, and that to "involve whites would eliminate the comic veneer altogether, and one simply did not write or perform comic songs about race riots" (460). The threat of Black violence, therefore, was subtle. But why was there such a hint of violence to begin with?

Rather than deny the existence of Black violence altogether, *The Marrow of Tradition*, a novel precisely about a race riot, recasts the razors found in "coon songs" as a violent legacy in the United States of not just slavery but also Reconstruction. The word *razor* is used just twice in the novel, in connection with two characters who epitomize the postemancipation violence against Black people—one as a perpetrator and the other as a victim and avenger. The perpetrator is a white character named George McBane, who is described to have "sprung from the poor white class, to which, even more than to the slaves, the abolition of slavery had opened the door of opportunity" (Chesnutt, *Marrow* 34). The most vocal antiblack racist in the novel, McBane is introduced as being slovenly dressed, and though clean shaven, having "here and there a speck of dried blood due to a carelessly or unskillfully handled *razor*" (32; emphasis added). McBane's outward appearance of being clean shaven cannot hide the violent antiblackness simmering beneath, revealed in the razor and specks of dried blood that stand as an ineffaceable reminder of his murder of Black men as a member of the Ku Klux Klan during Reconstruction. The blood on his face also foreshadows the blood that would be shed during the race massacre at the end of the novel that he instigates and organizes with Carteret and another prominent white man in town. McBane's character is reminiscent of Jo. Dunfer's in "The Haunted Valley" discussed in Chapter 3. The gaudy diamond that McBane wears is much like the Chinese tobacco box that Dunfer uses—both are commodities that are made possible by and associated with the labor of the racialized other that they ostensibly despise yet derive profit from. Like Dunfer, McBane is responsible for the death of those others, but his murders are motivated by nothing but hatred. There are no dialectical feelings of revulsion and attraction for McBane. McBane's antiblackness, standing as representative of the sentiment of poor white people in the South, is based on the most faithful subscription to what Nina Silber calls the "1890s cult of Anglo-Saxonism" (143), as his class and social standing depend on the exploitation and suffering of Black people in his employ as convict laborers. While the condition in the South that produced a figure such as McBane was certainly made possible by slavery, the violent subjection of Black people through terror and death, the novel insists, happened during and after Reconstruction, which unleashed the violent hatred of McBane. Described in association with a razor as a symbol of violence, McBane emblematizes the lethal antiblackness that amounted to capital for him, sustaining his very livelihood.

The novel pairs McBane with a Black character named Josh Green to contrast the violence represented by each. Like McBane, Green is described using the word *razor*, as he is said to always carry "a huge bowie-knife . . . which he had kept sharpened to a razor edge" for a "definite purpose" (Chesnutt, *Marrow* 309). That purpose is to kill McBane with the knife, as Green saw McBane's hoodless face on the night that his father was murdered by the Klan led by McBane.[9] Green deems it his life's purpose to kill McBane in order to avenge his father's death and his mother's resultant psychic breakdown. Green ultimately accomplishes this feat during the massacre when he leads a group of Black men to fight against the white terrorists, but he is also killed by McBane. Though the novel casts the two men as doubles, what is symbolized by Green's razor-sharp knife is completely different from the racist violence symbolized by McBane's razor. Green's knife acts as a vehicle of self-claimed agency, one that provides recourse to a murder committed with impunity, of which Green was an ineffectual witness. In a condition of sociality that deemed Green's father's life and Green's witness to be worthless and codified that proclaimed worthlessness into law, Green's knife—and by extension, the razor in the blackbody "coon songs"— counters that racial logic.

Implying that Green's knife "sharpened to a razor edge" represents self-protection in a violent system in which Black people are vulnerable to premature death at the hands of razor-wielding white people such as McBane, *The Marrow of Tradition* posits a mode of reading the razor in blackbody "coon songs" not as a symbol of Black people's innate predilection for violence but a structural critique of white supremacy. That Green's knife is not introduced in the novel until the very end during the race massacre, only when the Black residents of Wellington are driven to the point of self-defense, is important. Through McBane's razor and Green's knife, the novel suggests that the problem with the blackbody "coon songs" is not with the songs themselves but how they have been read, particularly by white people who have a preconceived notion of what Blackness is, based on the tradition of blackface minstrelsy. Using the novel form to stage an interventionist reading practice, Chesnutt ultimately teaches us how to read the "race question" in the South, characterized in the novel as a "great problem" (51).

In a chapter called "A Journey Southward," the novel begins to situate what was called the "Negro problem" in the South in the context of the larger violent history of the U.S. empire. The main plot of the chapter involves Dr. Miller, who is on a return journey home on a train after going to New York to buy supplies for his new hospital in Wellington. He runs into his old professor and mentor—a white man—and the two sit together, but as soon as they cross into Virginia, Miller is kicked out of the white car and forced to sit in the "colored" car. Outwardly, the chapter seems to be about the vagaries of the Jim Crow laws, as it adds contradictory instances such as when the white doctor protests that he will sit in the same car with Miller but is forbidden from doing so, while the same conductor who denied the white doctor does nothing to stop the belligerent McBane from going to Miller's car and using it as a spittoon while smoking there. The chapter is clearly referencing and restaging *Plessy v. Ferguson* (1896), which challenged segregated train cars in Louisiana but resulted in a ruling that deemed segregation to be constitutionally legal. But by inserting a reference to U.S. imperialism overseas and the figure of a Chinese worker, the novel also urges the reader to view the race question in the South through the incommensurability of antiblack violence established in slavery in the U.S. empire.

The chapter is presented mostly from Miller's point of view, thus making Miller exemplify a particular reader in the United States. Black, middle class, and professional, Miller embodies the answer to the "Negro problem" in the South. But Miller is an imperfect reader, particularly when it comes to the violence of the U.S. empire, and through him, the chapter puts forth a series of misreadings, or missed readings. After he is forced to sit in the segregated car, Miller decides to read the newspaper to pass the time and becomes "deep in an editorial which set forth in glowing language the inestimable advantages which would follow to certain recently acquired islands by the introduction of American liberty" (57). The description of "inestimable advantages" that "American liberty" promises is tinged with bitter irony when told from the viewpoint of someone who has just experienced American segregation. But the irony is doubled when we consider the Philippine-American War in particular, officially declared in 1899 after the end of the Spanish-American War in 1898, which was fought by Filipinos who wanted independence, not "American liberty," in the "recently acquired islands." In response to this demand by the Filipinos, who were derogatorily called "niggers," "savages," and "goo-goos," the United States annexed the Philippines, making the Filipino soldiers "insurgents," as errant children acting up against their benevolent caretaker.[10] The question that *The Marrow of Tradition* implicitly raises through the insertion of the newspaper article is this:

How is Miller reading and understanding the article's discussion of U.S. imperialism in glowing terms by getting "deep in" it? Does Miller make a connection between the Jim Crow train and U.S. imperialism overseas?

Miller does not make the connection, even though the novel sets the stage for him to do so by having McBane intrude in the segregated car and by interrupting the sentence describing Miller's newspaper reading: Miller was "deep in an editorial . . . when the rear door of the car opened to give entrance to Captain George McBane, who took a seat near the door and lit a cigar" (57). McBane's colonizing gesture paralleling the action of the U.S. empire abroad is not noted by Miller, who "detested heartily" McBane, merely as an "aggressive, offensive element among the white people" specific to the "New South" and not as a stand-in for the violent actions of the U.S. empire. McBane's presence is an opportunity to align U.S. imperialism with a new form of labor exploitation of Black people who were formerly enslaved, reflective of Du Bois's proclamation that "the exploitation of colored labor throughout the world thrives upon the approval of the United States, and the United States gives that approval because of the South" (*Black Reconstruction* 706). But Miller's reading of McBane is narrow and focused on himself, as he suspects that it was McBane who had alerted the conductor of Miller's presence in the white car and caused the latter's expulsion.

McBane's presence in the colored car points out a contradiction in the segregation law, that white people could access Black spaces but not the other way around. Earlier in the scene, the white doctor Burns had asked the white conductor if he could continue sitting with Miller in the Black car, to which the conductor had replied, "The beauty of the law lies in its strict impartiality—it applies to both races alike" (Chesnutt, *Marrow* 55). Remembering this reply, Miller complains of McBane's smoking to the conductor, who reluctantly tells McBane, "It's against the law for you to ride in the nigger car" (58). McBane refuses, stating, "I'll ride where I damn please. . . . I'll leave this car when I get good and ready, and that won't be till I've finished this cigar" (58). The conductor does nothing in response, exemplifying the inherent inequality built into the "separate but equal" segregation laws. Furthermore, Miller's futile effort to have McBane leave the segregated car could be compared to the fight for independence in the Philippines and other colonized spaces, but Miller does not make this connection. As if to underscore the connection that Miller does not articulate, when McBane finally leaves the car, Miller "[buries] himself again in his newspaper" (58), which means that the scene with McBane is bookended by the newspaper editorial about U.S. imperialism that is meant to act as an interpretive framework. Still, Miller gives no indication that he is reading the scene this way.

The departure of McBane brings Josh Green into the scene, and the novel emphasizes that Miller "had seen" and "recognized" him (59) as he hitched a ride on the train without paying.[11] However, Miller does not correctly read Green, either. Because Miller had previously read Green to be a "good-natured," "pleasure-loving negro," he cannot understand Green's look of "concentrated hatred almost uncanny in its murderousness" (59) directed at McBane in the white car. A representative Black worker in the novel, Green is victimized by McBane's rise in status during Reconstruction in a way that is incomparable to the humiliation Miller suffers from McBane's racism on the train. While Miller advocates for patience and legal restitution in response to white racism, Green has no such faith in the U.S. legal system. For Miller, Green's anger and hatred are incomprehensible, and he dismisses them as "very singular" (59). Miller ostensibly sees Green but ultimately does not see the connection between Green's situation and his own on a Jim Crow train as well as the larger connection to the newspaper editorial discussing U.S. imperialism. These connections that Miller fails to make serve as an important prelude to the scene with a Chinese worker that follows.

Immediately following Green's disappearance, the novel narrates what Miller observes and the connections that he makes—or does not make— based on that observation. It states:

> At the next station a Chinaman, of the ordinary laundry type, boarded the train, and took his seat in the white car without objection. At another point a colored nurse found a place with her mistress.
>
> "White people," said Miller to himself, who had seen these passengers from the window, "do not object to the negro as a servant. As the traditional negro,—the servant,—he is welcomed; as an equal, he is repudiated." (59)

At first, this scene seems to be a straightforward restaging of Justice John Harlan's lone dissenting statement in *Plessy v. Ferguson*.[12] In his opinion, Harlan criticized the Jim Crow laws as contradictory, pointing to two figures that Chesnutt later included in the scene observed by Miller. First,

Harlan cited the law promulgating that only "nurses attending children of the other race" are exempt from abiding the segregation law, and stated that "If a colored maid insists upon riding in the same coach with a white woman whom she has been employed to serve, and who may need her personal attention while traveling, she is subject to be fined or imprisoned for such an exhibition of zeal in the discharge of duty" (Plessy 554). Second, Harlan wrote, "There is a race so different from our own that we do not permit those belonging to it to become citizens of the United States. . . . I allude to the Chinese race. But, by the statute in question, a Chinaman can ride in the same passenger coach with white citizens of the United States, while citizens of the black race in Louisiana, many of whom, perhaps, risked their lives for the preservation of the Union" cannot (562). Based on this clear allusion to Harlan's dissent, Asian Americanist scholars have read the scene observed by Miller as reflecting Chesnutt's thoughts on the rulings of *Plessy*. Sanda Lwin argues that both Harlan and *The Marrow of Tradition* understand the "Chinaman" to be "[enjoying] an exceptional sort of mobility within the American racial landscape" (28), and the novel employs the figure as a "rhetorical foil" (17) to narrate the particulars of U.S. citizenship at the turn of the twentieth century. In contrast, Julia Lee argues that Chesnutt's train scene featuring the Chinese worker "levels the racialized logic of Harlan's decision," which assumes that it is only on the basis of race that Miller is removed from the white car and the Chinese worker is allowed to stay (66). Lee states that the "pairing of the Chinese laundryman *and* the black maid" in the scene demonstrates "how class overwhelms interpretations of . . . racial difference" (66; emphasis in original).

Assumed in Lwin's and Lee's arguments is that Miller is a reliable observer—or reader—in this scene, when in fact, Miller makes several assumptions and leaps that are unfounded. First, he sees a Chinese man and describes him as a "Chinaman, of the ordinary laundry *type*" (59; emphasis added), reflecting his reliance on the racial and class stereotype of the Chinese as laundry workers without explaining how he drew such a conclusion. If Chesnutt *was* referring to Harlan's dissent, the addition of the Chinese man's class is entirely his own.[13] Next, Miller sees a Black woman and a white woman and concludes that the former is a "nurse" and the latter is "her mistress." The "colored nurse," in Miller's point of view, gets transformed into "the traditional negro," who is a "servant" and a "he." This transformation is a profound misreading by Miller, not only because of the assumptions he makes about the Chinese man and Black woman as a laundry worker and a nurse, respectively, but more so because he conflates the two when they are not equal. The Chinese man "took his seat in the white car," whereas a "colored nurse found a place with her mistress." The fact that the latter is *with her mistress* is a crucial difference between the two figures—a difference that Miller elides by seeing "these passengers" as the singular "negro as a servant."[14] Conflating the two suits Miller's justification that he is excluded because of his class and the threat his position poses to white supremacy. His exclusion, as such, is where the injustice lies for him. This point of view is negated, however, when Miller finds himself joined by Black "laborers" (Chesnutt, *Marrow* 61) who board the colored section of the train. Though Miller feels warmth toward the workers initially, identifying them as "his people" (61), he quickly finds that "the air became too close" and leaves the car to get fresh air. He reasons that "these people were just as offensive to him as to the whites in the other end of the train" and adds that "if a classification of passengers on trains was at all desirable," it should be based on something "more logical and considerate," such as class, rather than a "brutal drawing of a color line" (61). Miller's faulty logic and hypocrisy are fully exposed here, as he implicitly admits that *his* segregation is more unjust, and certainly more unjustified, than that of the Black workers.

What Miller does not see in this scene is the specificity of antiblackness rooted in the history of chattel slavery. His misreading of the Black nurse as a servant and a "he," especially, is his misnaming of the Black woman, as discussed in Chapter 4 in reference to Hortense Spillers's argument that the legacy of ungendering perpetrated in chattel slavery lives on in the continued misrecognition and denigration of the Black woman. By pairing the Black woman with the Chinese man, Miller glosses over that legacy. However, even through Miller's limited class-biased observation, we see that the specificity of antiblackness cannot be completely expunged from this scene. After observing the Chinese man and the Black woman, Miller sees a dog board the train with its owner:

Miller wondered whether the dog would be allowed to ride with *his master*, and if not, what disposition would be made of him. He was a handsome dog, and Miller, who was fond of animals, would not have objected to the company of a dog, *as a dog*. He was nevertheless conscious of a queer sensation when he saw the porter take the dog by the collar and start in his own direction, and felt consciously relieved when the canine passenger was taken on past him into the baggage-car instead. (60; emphasis added)

Miller's description that the dog was with "his master" mirrors the earlier description of the "negro nurse" with "her mistress." Likewise, when he first sees Green on the train, Miller describes him as "[shaking] himself like a wet dog" after plunging his head in a "watering trough" (59). Miller's "conscious" awareness of a "queer sensation" when he thought the dog was going to join him sheds light on the unconscious way in which he used the same language to describe a dog that he did with humans. Miller cannot articulate the "queer sensation" and does not complete the thought that he did not mind the company of a dog "as a dog": if not as a dog, then as *what* would the dog have joined him? What is Miller's position that he saw the possibility of being grouped with a dog? More so than any other human figure in this scene, the nonhuman dog highlights the racial logic of slavery that equated Blackness with the nonhuman that is getting played out on the train, in the "journey southward." The animal calls to mind Frederick Douglass's description of the slave market previously mentioned in Chapter 4: "Men and women, old and young, married and single, were ranked with horses, sheep, and swine. There were horses and men, cattle and women, pigs and children, all holding the same rank in the scale of being, and were all subjected to the same narrow examination" (Douglass, *Narrative* 48). The Chinese character, who functions as the vehicle through which Miller misnames the Black woman, is not directly affected by this racial logic. As such, his character is not central to this scene; what needs to be stressed instead are the recognition and a correct reading of the specificity of Blackness in relation to slavery.

The Marrow of Tradition names blackface minstrelsy as one of the ways in which we can read the specificity and incommensurability of what Du Bois called the "strange meaning of being black" in the United States (*Souls* vii). As stated previously, when Chesnutt first decided to become a writer in 1880, he wrote in his journal, "I shall not record stale negro minstrel jokes, or worn out newspaper squibs on the 'man and brother.' I shall leave the realm of fiction, where most of this stuff is manufactured, and come down to hard facts" (Chesnutt, *Journals* 126). Chesnutt's indictment against the "realm of fiction" is in reference to the literary practice of borrowing from blackface minstrelsy, particularly by white writers such as Joel Chandler Harris and Thomas Nelson Page.[15] For Chesnutt, then, *The Marrow of Tradition* embodied his effort to incorporate "hard facts" to narrate the failures of Reconstruction to redress slavery as seen through a fictionalized race massacre based on an actual event. However, Chesnutt was against formidable competition in narrating the South. Even though Tourgée's Reconstruction novels were best sellers in the 1870s and 1880s, by the 1890s, the U.S. public was beginning to sympathize with the South and the former enslavers. As James Weldon Johnson stated succinctly, "The South lost the Civil War in 1865, but by 1900, in the fight waged on the Negro battle front, it had conquered the North" (*Black* 128).

One of the means by which the South conquered the North's sympathies for Southern white people, turning them against Southern Black people, was through the revisionist narratives of slavery in books and Northern magazines. The *Atlantic*—formerly the *Atlantic Monthly*—proudly boasts now that it was the first major literary magazine to publish a short story by a Black author, which was Chesnutt's "The Goopherd Grapevine" (1887), but it does not flaunt its publication history of stories sympathetic to the white South replete with Black caricatures that were printed around the same time as Chesnutt's story. Mirroring the "coon song" craze in popular culture and Nate Salsbury's rationale for thinking that something like his *Black America* would be successful, the post-Reconstruction period in the United States reverted to the racial logic of slavery for the dominant understanding of Blackness and made the material condition of Black lives something akin to slavery. It is little wonder, then, that historian Rayford Logan has labeled the period of post-Reconstruction as the "nadir" of Black status and rights in the United States (52). The 1890s, in particular, can be understood as a time when the political decisions made during Reconstruction, with a "look[] backward to slavery" (Du Bois, *Black Reconstruction* 143), manifested in the rise of the Jim Crow laws and state-sanctioned segregation, lynching, and white mobs that made Black life in the United States one of terror. Writing in this context, Chesnutt draws a connection between performing in blackface and lynching, characterizing both as "American" terror.

One of *The Marrow of Tradition*'s many subplots involves the Delameres, a white Southern aristocratic family overseen by a respected and aging patriarch John Delamere. Old Delamere has a nephew named Tom, a carefree and careless louse who drinks and gambles and stands to inherit all of Old

Delamere's wealth. Tom has a hobby of impersonating Sandy, Old Delamere's faithful Black servant, by stealing Sandy's clothes and blackening his face with "burnt cork" (Chesnutt, *Marrow* 223)—a practice used in minstrel shows. Dressed as Sandy, Tom performs the "cake walk" among Wellington's Black denizens for his own enjoyment.[16] When his performance is deemed so good that he wins first prize at the cake walk, he gets the idea to rob his wealthy aunt Polly Ochiltree while in blackface to settle a gambling debt that he was ordered to pay off at once when he was discovered cheating in a card game. Polly Ochiltree suffers a heart attack during the robbery, and eyewitness accounts locate "Sandy"—Tom in blackface—near the crime scene, which leads to the real Sandy's arrest and a white mob calling for his lynching.

Through Tom's actions, Chesnutt evacuates the purported humor from the blackface minstrel form. Tom's "prank" almost costs Sandy's life, and Sandy is only rescued at the last minute by Old Delamere, who finds out the truth about his nephew and commits perjury by falsely swearing that Sandy was with him on the night of the murder. Old Delamere's effective and noble, albeit illegal, gesture is in contrast to Josh Green's inability to be recognized as a reliable alibi, even though the truth is that Green was with Sandy at the time of the murder. The novel also subtly ties the practice of blackface performance with the sexual violence of slavery, as it implies that Sandy is related to the Delameres by blood, and the resemblance that Tom and Sandy bear to each other is so strong that Black and white people in the novel mistake Tom for Sandy when Tom wears Sandy's clothes.[17] Even Sandy thinks that he is seeing his own ghost when he runs into Tom in blackface. He decides to approach Tom about this, in an exchange that resembles a minstrel dialogue. Sandy asks, "Mistuh Tom . . . ef I wuz in yo' place, an' you wuz in my place, an' we wuz bofe in de same place, whar would I be?" (168). Characteristic of a minstrel exchange with Sandy cast as an end man and Tom as an interlocutor, Tom states "lightly," "I give it up, Sandy" (168), treating Sandy's question as a joke and expecting a punch line. But there is no punch line coming, except that of Sandy almost getting lynched. Tom's crime is covered up by the powerful white editor in town—Carteret—and the white mob gets appeased by Old Delamere's testimony for the time being until the massacre at the end of the novel. Old Delamere promptly dies of a heart attack before getting a chance to confront his lying and murdering nephew, and so Tom not only gets off scot-free but also inherits the family wealth.

The Marrow of Tradition raises the stakes of the violence associated with blackface minstrelsy by connecting that practice and the thwarted lynching in the South to U.S. overseas imperialism, this time making the connection explicit. The idea of a white man saving Sandy, who was placed in peril by another white man's "fun," informs the novel's meditation on the notion of the "white man's burden." The novel situates the happenings in the fictional Wellington as a part of U.S. imperialism that relies on a white supremacist racial logic, by stating, "The same argument that justified the conquest of an inferior nation could not be denied to those who sought the suppression of an inferior race" (238). The group of white people in Wellington who plot the race riot—one of whom is McBane—is likened to "the nation [as it] was rushing forward with giant strides toward colossal wealth and world-domination" (238). Chesnutt's critique of the minstrel form, therefore, was much broader than a critique of an individual such as Tom Delamere. It was a critique of the U.S. empire.

Though international in scope, *The Marrow of Tradition*'s exposition of the cold, hard fact of racism in the Jim Crow South emphasizes that this racism is specifically antiblack and located in the United States. This speci-ficity is fully displayed in the race massacre at the end of the novel, which does not affect the Chinese character who appears briefly on a Jim Crow train. Cutting across this rhetorical invocation of inferiority and "civilizing mission" of the U.S. empire is the murderous savagery of the Wellington Riot, marked by white rioters who yell, "Kill the niggers! Kill the damned niggers!" (298). The riot results in the burning down of the Black hospital founded by Miller—a sign of hope and "progress" that "lay smouldering in ruins, a melancholy witness to the fact that our boasted civilization is but a thin veneer, which cracks and scales off at the first impact of primal pas-sions" (310).[18] Even more dramatic than the destruction of the hospital is the death of Miller's son, killed by a stray bullet during the riot. The novel spares the description of Miller's son's death, focusing instead on the horror and grief of his mourning parents. In fact, Miller's son, who is described as a "little boy of six or seven" (64), is not given a name in the novel, though white child characters are. The unspecified age and namelessness mark Mill-er's son as a generalizable symbol of Black lives that do not matter in the novel during the riot, as "[a] dozen colored men lay dead in the streets of Wellington, inoffensive people, slain in cold blood because they had been bold enough to question the authority of those who had assailed them, or frightened enough to flee when they had been ordered to stand still" (303). Characterizing the riot as a "slaughter" (299) and comparing the murderous white people to "wol[ves] in a sheepfold" (298), Chesnutt again uses the language of nonhuman livestock to characterize the Black victims.[19] And his novel's insistence for the readers to recognize this specific dehumanized antiblackness and Black suffering is precisely what was not widely accepted by the U.S. reading public and also what got dismissed in William Dean Howells's 1901 review of the novel in the *North American Review*.

William Dean Howells, the Oriental Question, and the North American Review

Acknowledging his castaway position in a sea of literary whiteness, Chesnutt wrote to his good friend John P. Green about one year before the publication of *The Marrow of Tradition* to state, "I think you understand how difficult it is to write race problem books so that white people will read them" (Chesnutt, *"To Be"* 156). Chesnutt proved to be correct. White people—and Black people, it turns out—did not read his novel. *The Marrow of Tradition* sold only 3,276 copies during its first year of publication, 111 in 1902, and 0 from 1903 to 1905 (Chesnutt, *"To Be"* 172). In response to these dismal numbers, Chesnutt wrote, "If a novel which is generally acknowledged to be interesting, dramatic, well constructed, well written—all of which qualities have been pretty generally ascribed to *The Marrow of Tradition* . . . cannot sell 5,000 copies within three months after its publication, there is something radically wrong somewhere, and I do not know where it is unless it be the subject" (171). Chesnutt was correct that "there is something radically wrong somewhere," but that something was not just the subject of race. It was also that U.S. literature was a racist institution, with white men acting as gatekeepers. Writing at a time that he later labeled as "post-bellum pre-Harlem" (Chesnutt, "Post-bellum" 481), when the most popular cultural form was the "coon song" and Black writers such as Paul Laurence Dunbar and James Weldon Johnson were actively writing its lyrics, Chesnutt could not get his readers to see the "hard facts" of Black life in the U.S. empire.

The public reception of *The Marrow of Tradition* can also be attributed to a negative review by William Dean Howells, one of the most powerful literary figures in the United States at the time. Though it is difficult to state precisely how much of a factor Howells's review of *The Marrow of Tradition* played in the novel's lackluster sales, what is undeniable is that Howells was a commanding figure whose favorable review of Chesnutt's collection of short stories, *The Conjure Woman*, in 1900 had propelled Chesnutt's career, and a similar review could only have helped in 1901.

As a prominent figure in the elite New England literary circle, Howells was one of the most influential readers of Chesnutt's writings. Howells determined various authors' fates with his favorable, and unfavorable, reviews and placements in journals. He published Mark Twain's "A True Story" (1874) in the *Atlantic Monthly*, for example. Chesnutt, who once wrote in his journal that he has no "white friends," as the category to him was an impossibility as long as legal segregation and racism existed in the United States, admitted the weight of Howells's "friendship" in a letter to his editors. Betraying his frustration with *The Marrow of Tradition*'s lack of sales, Chesnutt stated, "My friend Mr. Howells, who has said many nice things about my writing—although his review of *The Marrow of Tradition* in the *North American Review* for December was not a favorable one, as I look at it—has remarked several times that there is no color line in literature" (Chesnutt, *"To Be"* 171). Howells had made such a claim about the color line in a positive review of *The Conjure Woman* in 1900, in which he contended that one should read Chesnutt's stories not from "racial interest" but more "simply and directly, as works of art, that they make their appeal, and we must allow the force of this quite independently of the other interest" (Howells, "Mr. Charles" 700). In addition, Howells wrote, "Our own more universal interest in him arises from the more than promise he has given in a department of literature where Americans hold the foremost place. In this there is, happily, no color line" (701). Given that Howells enthusiastically supported Twain's "A True Story" precisely because he liked Twain's use of the Black dialect, this "happy" denial of a color line was a privileged one that provided license for appropriation for white authors in U.S. literary realism while also providing lip service to U.S. liberalism and the spirit of inclusion.

A year later, this "friend," Howells, wrote a letter to novelist Henry B. Fuller mentioning that he had been reading *The Marrow of Tradition*. He wrote of Chesnutt, "You know he is a Negro, though you wouldn't know it from seeing him, and he writes of the black and white situation with an awful bitterness. But he is an artist almost of the first quality; as yet too literary, but promising things hereafter will scarcely be equaled in our fiction. Good Lord! How such a Negro must hate us" (Howells, *Life in Letters* 149). Howells's use of the word "bitterness" has an echo in his earlier review of Booker T. Washington's *Up from Slavery* (1901), in which Howells characterized Washington as an "exemplary citizen" and stated that "in [Washington's] heart there is no bitterness" (Howells, "Exemplary" 285). In that review, Howells had included Chesnutt in the same group as not only Washington but also Frederick Douglass and Paul Laurence Dunbar, men who wrote about the race question, according to Howells, with a "calm" that "saves them from bitterness" ("Exemplary" 248). The description of Chesnutt as writing with an "awful bitterness" therefore suggests that Chesnutt committed a breach in the tacit agreement Howells seems to have envisioned between Black (male) writers and white America. Certainly, Chesnutt's portrayal of the deadly white racism in *The Marrow of Tradition* was a departure from the dialect-filled "Uncle Julius" stories that so charmed Howells in Chesnutt's *The Conjure Woman*. As Matthew Wilson writes, "Chesnutt had judged white people in a way that no African American writer had ever before done in fiction" (141). However, Wilson's characterization, as well as Howells's statement that "such a Negro must hate us," reduces *The Marrow of Tradition* to an indictment of antiblackness that is the fault of white people only when in fact the novel's critique extends to exposing the afterlife of slavery in the larger structure of white supremacy in the U.S. empire. Howells himself betrays a glimmer of this understanding when he links his description of Chesnutt with U.S. imperialism, as he writes, "And then think of the Filipinos and the Cubans and Puerto Ricans whom we have added to our happy family. But I am talking treason" (*Life in Letters* 149). This recognition is similar to *The Marrow of Tradition*'s situating of antiblack racism in the larger workings of the U.S. empire; however, the key difference is Howells's position of privilege and whiteness, which makes him read the novel's critique of antiblackness as a personal attack and anticipates an extension of that attack by the "Filipinos and the Cubans and Puerto Ricans." As a staunch anti-imperialist, Howells reveals his anxiety that the newly colonized groups will bring further trouble to "our happy family," already unhappy because of Black people such as Chesnutt who were "bitter."

Moreover, the description of "our happy family" mirrors Howells's view of Chesnutt in "our fiction," indicating that his anxiety about Chesnutt's bitterness and the potential bitterness of the "Filipinos and the Cubans and Puerto Ricans" was really an anxiety about the U.S. literary tradition and whose voice rightfully belongs in it. Howells's review of *The Marrow of Tradition*, published one month after his letter to Fuller, can be read as an effort to alleviate this anxiety.

In the December 1901 issue of the *North American Review*, Howells proclaimed that *The Marrow of Tradition* "is, in fact, bitter, bitter" ("Psychological" 882). Given his repetition of the word "bitterness" in the review for *Up from Slavery*, also published in the *North American Review* in June 1901, Howells's readers may have understood that the characterization of Chesnutt's novel as "bitter, bitter" signaled its distinction from the accommodationist racial politics of Washington's. In the review of *The Marrow of Tradition*, Howells conceded that the novel has historical reasons to be so, "if wrong is to be repaid with hate," and "yet," he wrote, "it would be better if it was not so bitter" (882). Howells did not find any fault with Chesnutt's "aesthetics or ethics," stating, "No one who reads the book can deny that [it] is presented with great power" (883). Comparing *The Marrow of Tradition* to *The Conjure Woman*, which was mostly about the old plantation life in the South as told by a trickster figure named Uncle Julius, Howells stated that the novel was "less excellent in manner" (882) and concluded ambivalently that despite its limitations, "it is non the less [*sic*] a work of art" (883).

Given the lack of criticism on the artistry of Chesnutt's novel, Howells seems to have found issue with its racial politics and the urgency in its tone, which he could only interpret as "bitter." Howells's assessment is all the more revealing because he was considered an important ally of Black writers. In November 1913, Du Bois wrote an article in the *Crisis* titled "Howells and Black Folk," praising Howells for being "truthful" and for including Black characters in his literature. He also credited Howells with "discovering" Paul Dunbar and proclaimed that Howells was "among the first to sign the call" to make emancipation a "reality" for Black people through his practice of literary realism (*Writings*, 1147–48).[20] For his part, Howells ostensibly pushed Black writers to engage in realism and write against caricatured stereotypes, but he did this specifically through a nod to the minstrel form. In his review of *The Marrow of Tradition*, he implies that he is holding Chesnutt to a higher standard because Chesnutt is not only obviously talented but also "of that race which has, first of all, to get rid of the cakewalk, if it will not suffer from a smile far more blighting than any frown" ("Psychological" 882). Referring to the practice that originated in the Black captives' imitation of white people during slavery, which was incorporated into minstrel and vaudeville shows, Howells sees the responsibility of dismantling the antiblack stereotype—which he describes as "fighting a battle" (883)—as the burden of the Black writer, who should not rely on "cheap graces and poses of the jouster" (883). But Howells himself demonstrates that the responsibility was not solely on the part of the Black writer but instead on the white reader who could not help but read Black writing in light of the minstrel form. Even in his effusive review of Washington's *Up from Slavery*, for example, Howells suggested that Washington betrays an allegiance to the "ancestral Cakewalk" when he dedicates his book to "his 'wife, *Mrs.* Margaret James Washington,' and his 'brother, *Mr.* John H. Washington'" ("Exemplary" 280, 281; emphasis in original). Howells hints that Washington's dedication is an imitative pretension, even as he dismisses the idea that "nothing is less characteristic of the author than the cakewalk" (281). Despite his declaration that there was no color line in literature, mirroring Harlan's claim in his dissent on *Plessy* that the Constitution was color-blind, Howells could not help but see color, particularly in Black writers. And when Black writers went against the "exemplary" model of Booker T. Washington, Howells only saw bitterness. Howells's review of *The Marrow of Tradition*—his last review of Chesnutt's writings—apparently had a significant impact on Chesnutt. In a letter to a friend whose daughter decided to write a school report on Chesnutt's novel, Chesnutt stated that the novel "had a fair sale, but was criticized as being bitter" (Chesnutt, "*To Be*" 234). He added a caution that when the daughter writes the report, she should "eliminate anything that savors of rancor or bitterness" (234) in order to receive a high mark.

Taking up Howells as a representative of the reluctant white reading public in 1901, we might read his review of *The Marrow of Tradition* in comparison to another book that he was reviewing at the time. Specifically, Howells's review of Chesnutt's novel was part of a collection of reviews, and Howells even opened the review on Chesnutt with a direct comparison to another novel: "I wish that I could at all times praise as much the literature of an author who speaks for another colored race, not so far from us as the Japanese, but of as much claim upon our conscience, if not our interest"

("Psychological" 881–82). If Chesnutt's novel affected Howells's conscience and the other book piqued his interest, Howells ultimately favored the latter. The book that Howells reviewed immediately before *The Marrow of Tradition* was *A Japanese Nightingale* (1901), a "pretty novelette" (881) by Onoto Watanna, who is better known in Asian North American literary studies as one of the "Eaton sisters."[21]

Unlike her sister Edith Eaton, who wrote under the name Sui Sin Far, aligned with the Chinese heritage of their mother,[22] Winnifred Eaton assumed a Japanese identity and name, as "Onoto Watanna."[23] It was believed to be more fashionable to be Japanese at this time, when Chinese women were categorically labeled as "prostitutes" in the discourse of Chinese slavery and Chinese men continued to be racialized as the "heathen Chinee" or the unassimilable "coolie." Winnifred Eaton's adoption of a Japanese name therefore speaks to the same logic that may have pushed John Isham to incorporate Japaneseness in—and name his grand spectacle—*Oriental America*. Howells's review of *A Japanese Nightingale* reveals this Orientalist marketing of the perceived Asian foreignness, especially concerning how the novel portrays a race "so far from us as the Japanese" ("Psychological" 881), reminiscent of Harlan's characterization of the Chinese as a race "so different from our own."

A Japanese Nightingale takes place mostly in an exoticized landscape of Japan. Even though the female protagonist Yuki's "half-caste" identity is central to the novel, *A Japanese Nightingale* treats race as insignificant. Possibly because of such omission of the "color line," in his estimation of the novel and its characters, Howells stated glowingly, "Yuki herself is of a surpassing lovableness" ("Psychological" 881). He added, "Nothing but the irresistible charm of the American girl could, I should think, keep the young men who read Mrs. Watana's [*sic*] book from going out and marrying Japanese girls. They are safe from this, however, for the reason suggested, and therefore it can be safely commended at least to young men intending fiction, as such a lesson in the art of imitating nature as has not come under my hand for a long while" (881). In this effusive review, Howells comes one step short of endorsing interracial marriages wholesale as he claims, cryptically, "They are safe from this." Since the pronoun "they" can refer to both the "Japanese girls" and "[American] young men," it is unclear who will be saved from intermarriage by the "irresistible charm of the American girl." The mention of "Japanese girls," "young men," and especially the "American girl" thwarting miscegenation is safely distanced from the anti-Asian sentiments of this period, materialized in exclusionary and antimiscegenation laws that targeted Asian men as potential threats to white workers and white women (see Koshy).

The notion that Onoto Watanna's novel was an outstanding realist work of literature among all the books that Howells was reviewing causes one to wonder about the relationship between Howells's understanding of "bitter" and "real," as Howells had no such unmitigated praise for Chesnutt. Instead, Howells concluded the review of *The Marrow of Tradition* ambiguously and somewhat ominously by stating that "No one who reads the book can deny that the case is presented with great power, or fail to recognize in the writer a portent of the sort of negro equality against which no series of hangings and burnings will finally avail" ("Psychological" 883). Contrary to the notion that "there is, happily, no color line" in literature, Howells's final review of Chesnutt reveals that "equality" for a writer who is racialized as "Negro" is itself racialized. Howells could not but see Chesnutt as a "Negro writer."[24]

The pairing and contrasting of *A Japanese Nightingale* and *The Marrow of Tradition* by Howells speaks to a representative way of thinking about race as simply Black and white, and divorcing Asians from the binary. This racial thinking exoticizes the "Asian" category as a foreign, culturally (nonracial) other identity. The Orientalist focus on foreignness, which allows Howells to designate *A Japanese Nightingale* paternalistically as a "pretty novelette," also serves to trivialize depictions of antiblackness as "bitter." At the same time that Howells considers *The Japanese Nightingale* quaint and exotic, he deems it completely different from *The Marrow of Tradition*, which, as bitter as it supposedly was, was of a race of "much claim on our conscience, if not our interest."

What should be clear from Howells's criticism in the *North American Review* is not just that Asians and questions about Asians were prevalent at this time, but also that those questions occupied the same space in public discourse about the larger race question concerning Black people but were rarely treated as related issues. In the same volume of *North American Review* that contained Howells's review of *The Marrow of Tradition*, James Phelan, a San Francisco mayor well known for his vocal anti-Chinese politics, explained why the Chinese Exclusion Act of 1882 should not be repealed in 1902. His article, "Why the Chinese Should Be Excluded," was in fact a response to the Chinese ambassador Ho Yow's article, "Chinese Exclusion, a Benefit or a Harm?," which was also published in *North Ameri-*

can Review in September 1901, three months before Howells's reviews. In response to Yow's appeal to worker solidarity—"It is my profound hope that the laboring people of America will now see these questions in the light of truth, and that they may become aroused to the injury which these laws are doing them" (330)—James Phelan argued that the Chinese question was "not a mere labor question, nor a race question. It is an American question" (667). Nationalizing the Chinese question in the process, Phelan warned his readers that the Chinese were migrating from California to the rest of the country, citing the destruction resulting from the Civil War as a reason to stop Chinese immigration as well as Chinese internal migration. "The drastic remedies of the war should be a warning today," he wrote, and if slavery had caused such destruction, Chinese "coolie" labor would surely usher in the same result again (672). But even though Phelan connected coolie labor with slavery, he was decidedly unambiguous about the "new" aspect of the Chinese question, deeming that the problems wrought by slavery had ended in Reconstruction. The comparison of Chinese labor to slavery during Reconstruction found its way to public debate about Chinese immigration again at the turn of the twentieth century. These arguments in Phelan's article and Yow's article, as well as Marrion Wilcox's article in September 1900, "The Filipino's Vain Hope of Independence," which likened the Philippines to the reconstructing South after the Civil War, were all part of the same cultural forum as Howells's reviews of *The Japanese Nightingale* and *The Marrow of Tradition* in the *North American Review*. None of these articles discussed the ongoing antiblack racism and the deadly violence of lynching and deprivation of liberty that were part of the everyday Black life in the South. In contrast, *The Marrow of Traditions* makes visible connections among these texts through its remembrance of Reconstruction and its aftermath. The novel attests that the ongoing and deadly antiblack racism was a result of the failures of Reconstruction, which coincided with Chinese exclusion and the casting of the Chinese as a race "so different from our own" as well as U.S. imperialism overseas. This message of the novel provides the critical lens through which to read other cultural productions in the U.S. empire during this time, particularly in the long afterlife of blackface minstrelsy.

. . .

After *The Marrow of Tradition*, Chesnutt published another novel, *The Colonel's Dream* (1905), but after that, he could not find a publisher for his new

fictional writings. In contrast, Sui Sin Far and Onoto Watanna continued
to publish until close to their deaths in 1914 and 1954, respectively. Likewise, Bret Harte, Mark Twain, and Ambrose Bierce published prolifically
their entire lives. Twain, in particular, began publishing "Chapters from My
Autobiography" serially in the *North American Review* in 1906, in which he
professed his love of blackface minstrelsy. Though Chesnutt outlived Harte,
Twain, Bierce, and Sui Sin Far, *The Colonel's Dream* would be the last new
fictional publication in his lifetime.[25] I close this chapter—and book—by
reflecting on Chesnutt's exclusion from U.S. literature and the historical
context in which he was writing through a reading of two scenes from *The
Colonel's Dream*, a novel narrated in the vein of Tourgée's *A Fool's Errand*,
featuring the white title character who returns to the post-Reconstruction
South in the hopes of rebuilding it and rectifying its race relations.

In the novel, Chesnutt describes the following scene at a dinner party at
the colonel's house in the South:

> The conversation languished for a moment, and then one of the young
> ladies said something about music, and one of the young men remarked
> that he had brought over a new song. . . . Graciella went to the piano and
> with great boldness of touch struck the bizarre opening chords and then
> launched into the grotesque words of the latest New York "coon song," one
> of the first and worst of its kind, and the other young people joined in the
> chorus. (*Colonel's Dream* 49)

Listening to the young people sing enthusiastically, the white colonel thinks
the song is a travesty of a "plantation song of the olden time . . . sung
by the tired slaves at the end of their day of toil" (49), which he used to
enjoy listening to. Reminiscent of Du Bois's description of sorrow songs,
the colonel's response to the song criticizes blackface minstrelsy and its latest iteration at the turn of the twentieth century in the "coon song" that
made a mockery out of an expression of Black suffering in slavery. As such,
the colonel perceives the song as "hackneyed" and having "no music" at all
(49). Still, he thinks, "In a metropolitan music hall, gaudily bedecked and
brilliantly lighted, [the song] would have been tolerable from the lips of a
black-face comedian. But in this quiet place, upon this quiet night, and in
the colonel's mood, it seemed like a profanation" (49–50). What we see in
this scene is the colonel's recognition of Black suffering in slavery. We also
see the colonel's recognition that the "coon song" dissociates the history of

white performance of blackface from the history of Black suffering and slavery. Yet, the colonel essentially admits that such violence would have been "tolerable" if the conditions were right—in a fancy music hall with the right lighting. Only when the violence implicated in such performance intrudes into his personal space does the song *seem* like a profanation. The colonel is a white ally figure, but even he is seduced by blackface minstrelsy. So the place of hope to counter that seduction, the novel suggests, is the "quiet place," likely a place where one would read literature, since for Chesnutt, literature is the antithesis of minstrelsy. More specifically, Black literature, Chesnutt seems to suggest through not just *The Colonel's Dream* but his other writings, such as *The Marrow of Tradition*, is key to challenging representations by a "black-face comedian." This notion of the literary functioning as the antithesis of minstrelsy can be seen in other Black literary writings—most poignantly in Paul Laurence Dunbar's poem "We Wear the Mask," in which the speaker says, "We wear the mask that grins and lies, / It hides our cheeks and shades our eyes,— / With torn and bleeding hearts we smile" (71). As the writer of the lyrics to many "coon songs," Dunbar expresses in the poem what may have been behind the masks worn by many blackbody performers.

Recalling the fact that Chesnutt saw literature as the ideal means to challenge antiblack racism pervasive in every aspect of Black life in the United States—not just on the minstrel stage—when he first contemplated a writing career, *The Colonel's Dream* meditates on that optimism twenty-five years later. The novel features a subplot that was originally a short story called "The Dumb Witness." The story was rejected by various magazines before its inclusion in the book. It involves a white man and a Black female captive named Viney, living in the South before the war. In the short story, the man's name is Malcolm Murchison; in the novel, his name is Malcolm Dudley. The woman's name remains the same, without a last name, much like the Black female characters in Sui Sin Far's "Away Down in Jamaica," discussed in Chapter 4. Malcolm is Viney's enslaver. It is implied that Malcolm and Viney were in a romantic relationship until Malcolm decides to marry a wealthy white widow from the North. When he tells Viney of his plans, in both stories, Viney begs for him to reconsider. When he does not, Viney goes to the widow and tells her something that causes the widow to break off the engagement. Malcolm finds out about what Viney did and hires an overseer to whip her. At this time, the war breaks out. Malcolm's wealthy uncle stops by the house with two bags of gold that he wants Malcolm to keep for him. Only Viney is home at the time, so the uncle leaves a letter for Malcolm, stating that Viney knows where the gold is. In the short story, Viney is referred to in the letter as "our blood" (Chesnutt, "Dumb Witness" 166), whereas the novel simply says "our girl Viney" (Chesnutt, *Colonel's Dream* 127). Because Viney was so severely beaten by the overseer, she loses her ability to speak. In an attempt to get the gold, however, Malcolm tries everything to get her to communicate. He even hires a teacher to teach her to write but to no avail. Slowly, the frustrated desire for the gold, as well as Viney's silence, drives Malcolm mad.

Unlike the short story, the novel explains that the name "Viney" is a "Negro corruption of Lavinia" (Chesnutt, *Colonel's Dream* 171). This explanation is significant because Lavinia is also a character in William Shakespeare's violent tragedy *Titus Andronicus*. Lavinia is the eponymous character's second daughter, who is abducted by his enemies and raped.[26] To prevent her from divulging what happened, the men cut off her tongue and hands. Without the ability to speak or write, she points to Ovid's *Metamorphosis*, which features the myth of Philomel, to convey what happened to her.[27] When Titus Andronicus deciphers her cryptic insistence of pointing to Philomel, he gives her a stick, with which she writes down the names of her rapists using her mouth and what the play describes as her "stumps" (Shakespeare 129). This prompts Titus Andronicus to vow for and carry out his revenge. In the next act, however, Titus Andronicus kills Lavinia, reasoning that he wanted to end her shame and his sorrow. Since her rape, or her "shame" according to Titus Andronicus, was not known before she pointed to the mythology of Philomel, it could be argued that Lavinia's own testimony ends up destroying her. If we make a leap from Shakespeare to Chesnutt, we might even argue that Lavinia's pointing to the "canonical" text of Ovid to seek justice is a metaphor for the limits of a Black author's relationship to dominant white literature in the effort to call out antiblackness. In the end, Lavinia's recourse to literature is what brings her short-lived victory as well as death, which can be read as either her ultimate demise or a transcendence of her rape.

Like her namesake Lavinia, Viney endures violence at the hand of a man. Likewise, Viney and Lavinia are both punished for speaking the truth. But unlike Lavinia, Viney is able to act on her punishment, since unlike Lavinia's silence, Viney's is self-imposed—in both the story and the novel, Viney never actually loses her speech. Instead of pointing to a book to tell her story, Viney performs an inability to read and write. In "The Dumb Witness," Viney stays silent until Malcolm dies. At that point, she reveals where the gold has been hidden (in the chair where Malcolm had been sitting for all of these years), and the story ends on a note of resolution. In the novel, however, Viney breaks her silence at Malcolm's deathbed. She tells him (not in "Negro dialect," which Chesnutt pondered over and ultimately used in Viney's dialogue in "The Dumb Witness"), "You had me whipped. . . . Do you remember that? You had me whipped—whipped—whipped—by a poor white dog I had despised and spurned! You had said that you loved me, and you had promised to free me—and you had me whipped! But I have had my revenge!" (Chesnutt, *Colonel's Dream* 273). She then reveals that Malcolm's uncle had come back for the gold: "The money was here one hour, but in that hour you had me whipped, and for that you have spent twenty-five years in looking for nothing—something that was not here!" (274).

This secret, that Viney was silent about nothing, is her revenge in the novel, and it points to both the power of silence and the exigency of representing something that does not exist, "something that was not here." Viney's assigned task of adequately representing what was not there to begin with captures Chesnutt's own work of writing a novel about Blackness. In a culture in which the "strange meaning of being black" was so closely tied to the caricature performed on the minstrel stage, which had ramifications on actual Black life and death, what sort of a recourse existed for the Black writer in literature? Unlike Viney in "The Dumb Witness," Viney in *The Colonel's Dream* dies immediately after Malcolm's death. As it is for Shakespeare's Lavinia, the moment that she chooses to break her silence is not a moment of triumph for her but an end. Accordingly, Chesnutt's literary career might be understood as a self-imposed silence, an unwillingness to play the part of a "Negro writer," like Booker T. Washington, in fiction. In both this silence and Viney's death in the novel, we see Chesnutt's refusal to be misread. This refusal is an indictment of U.S. literature and empire, which have depended on the misreading of what it means to be Black. With such an indictment grounding our reading practice, we can begin to see the incommensurability of Blackness defined through but ultimately exceeding the minstrel form in the afterlife of slavery.

Notes

1. Tavia Nyong'o argues cogently that "blackface minstrelsy" is an "inadequate modern shorthand" that does not consider the "complex performance genealogy" of Black impersonation (105). In line with Nyong'o's work, which complicates the shorthand, my employment of the term seeks to further trouble its genealogy.

2. *American Publication* lists the publication year of the song as 1869, but the booklet for the song says it is 1870. Also, the name is listed as Harry E. Lorraine on the song cover, but the Library of Congress lists the songwriter's name as Harry F. Lorraine.

3. I am grateful for the community-sourced guideline on writing about slavery that recommends terms such as "enslaved," "captive," and "enslaver," counter to the more commonplace designations. See Foreman.

4. See E. Williams; C. Robinson; Baptist; W. Johnson, "The Pedestal"; Roediger, *How Race Survived*; Beckert; Beckert and Rockman; and Singh.

5. For scholarship on the history of Black performances as critiques of minstrelsy, see D. Brooks; McMillan. In a similar vein, Sylvia Wynter argues that the minstrel stereotype was created to marginalize and contain the "incredible inventiveness of black culture" ("Sambos and Minstrels" 149).

6. Evidencing the limits of white antislavery activism, the Hutchinson Family included a depiction of Douglass as a caricatured "runaway slave" in one of their songbooks, which prompted Douglass to take charge of his own representations through photography. See Nyong'o 146.

7. Nyong'o's work presents a nuanced study of Douglass's relationship to minstrelsy. See Nyong'o 123–34.

8. In the play, a Black enslaved man refuses to dance, negating the demand of a white man who is looking to purchase him. See Brown, *The Escape*.

9. This is also cited in Hartman, *Scenes* 46.

10. For the variations of the "Jim Crow" songs, see Lhamon 95–136.

11. The Chinese and Native peoples were not included in the 1860 census.

12. The mining songs also expressed violence toward Native people. The lyrics following the description of the murder of a Chinese man read, "Then he [Joaquin Murietta] went to Sonora, / where he killed eleven more, / And a big Digger Indian, / which made the twenty-four" (History of Music Project, *San Francisco* 44).

13. For the history of Chinese railroad workers, see Chang, *Ghosts*; and Chang and Fishkin. For a study that situates the workers' history in the context of continental imperialism and railroad colonialism, see Karuka.

14. On the history of Chinese drive-outs, see Pfaelzer.

15. For a discussion on the significance of the removal of the Chinese workers in national memorialization of the completion of the transcontinental railroad in photographs, see Eng.

16. On the history of the Chinese workers in the North Adams shoe factory, see A. Lee, *A Shoemaker's Story*. For a contemporary fictionalization of the workers, see Shepard.

17. The notion that the history of the United States is a development narrative of the frontier was most influentially expounded in Frederick Jackson Turner's "The Significance of the Frontier in American History" (1893), which came to be better known as simply the Frontier Thesis (and was later published as a book). In it, Turner stated that "when American history comes to be rightly viewed it will be seen that the slavery question is an incident" (*Frontier* 24).

18. Sui Sin Far called herself a "pioneer" for her Eurasian racial identity ("Leaves" 129), and some of the earliest scholars of her works linked the label with her writings. See Solberg and Ling. In 1928, the NAACP recognized Charles Chesnutt for his "pioneer work as a literary artist depicting the life and struggles of Americans of Negro descent" with its most distinguished award, the Spingarn Medal (Gates and Higginbotham 114). Chesnutt was customarily—and incorrectly—called the first African American novelist in the early twentieth century.

CHAPTER 1. THE "HEATHEN CHINEE" AND TOPSY
IN BRET HARTE'S NARRATIVES OF THE WEST

1. On Whitman's representations of Blackness influenced by minstrelsy, see I. Wilson.

2. Harte was criticizing the lukewarm reception that the San Francisco audience had for Artemus Ward, probably the most popular humorist in the United States in the 1860s.

3. Eric Lott also uses the term "racial conscious." See "Love and Theft."

4. Harte was not unique in evoking Topsy in his literary creations. For a discussion of how Stowe's Topsy influenced the characterizations in Louisa May Alcott's *Little Women*, see Abate.

5. See Fenn; J. Foster; E. Kim; and W. Wu. See also Tchen 196–197; and Takaki 222–229. In his important *Orientals: Asian American in Popular Culture*, Robert G. Lee has a chapter called "The 'Heathen Chinee' on God's Free Soil" but does not discuss Harte or his poem.

6. For various arguments on how Harte's "Plain Language" should be read, see Métraux; Penry; Romeo, "Irony Lost"; and Scharnhorst, "Plain Language," "Ways That Are Dark." For a discussion on the significance of "Plain Language" as a dialect poem, see Nurhussein.

7. On the significance of the West during Reconstruction, see Emberton; S. Smith; Bottoms; Paddison; Richardson; and West.

8. According to Gary Scharnhorst, by 1995, the poem had been reprinted ninety-eight times, mostly prior to 1940. See Scharnhorst, *Bret Harte: A Bibliography*, 41–44.

9. For plays inspired by the "heathen Chinee," see D. Williams, *The Chinese Other*; and Hyde. For an analysis of theatrical representations of the Chinese, see D. Williams, *Misreading*. The popularity of Harte based on the "heathen Chinee" inspired the rise of the "frontier drama," featuring characters found in his stories, including the Chinese worker figure. See Daly; and R. Hall, *Performing*.

10. The economic depression in California from 1869 to 1871 and the larger population of the Chinese compared to the Black population in San Francisco also factored into the anti-Chinese sentiment in California generally and among Black Californians specifically.

11. As the editor of the *Overland Monthly*, Harte also published "The Chinese Labor Problem" by Charles Wolcott Brooks, which argues for the merits of Chinese labor, particularly in comparison to Black "heathen barbarians" (415). See Brooks, "The Chinese Labor Problem."

12. Harte wrote a poem protesting antiblack discrimination, called "The Executive Committee to the Colored Population" (1866), satirizing white liberals who denied Black people from participating in a citywide event in San Francisco, but he never discussed slavery directly or included Black characters in his stories prior to 1875. For a possible explanation of Harte's avoidance of the topic of slavery, see Scherting.

13. As Yong Chen notes, U.S. census and immigration records roundly assigned "Ah," an informal prefix much like adding a "ny" after "John," as the official first name of the majority of the Chinese entering the United States (53). See also Bonner 33.

14. Bernstein builds on W. B. Worthern's and Diana Taylor's notions of the "archival" and the "repertoire" to develop her own argument about the latter. See Bernstein 12.

15. Bret Harte published an essay by Henry George in the *Overland Monthly* in 1868 that touches on the "Chinese question" that he would develop more fully in the *New-York Tribune* in 1869. See George, "What the Railroad."

16. On the various illustrations accompanying Harte's poem, see Scharnhorst, "Ways."

17. On the specificity of the violence of the anti-Chinese exclusionary politics, see Lew-Williams. For Black testimonies of racial violence after emancipation, see K. Williams.

18. To the best of my knowledge, Margaret Hosmer is actually the first to have written about the Chinese in fiction. See her novel *Story of a Chinese Boy* (1867) and *You-Sing, the Chinaman in California: A True Story of the Sacramento Flood* (1868). Originally from Philadelphia, Hosmer lived in California in the late 1850s and from 1864 to the late 1870s. She coedited the *Golden Era* with Bret Harte. Mark Twain also wrote about a Chinese character in his serialized short story, "Goldsmith's Friend Abroad Again," first published in October 1870, which I discuss in Chapter 2. See Twain, *Contributions*.

19. On the mines in nineteenth-century California as homosocial spaces, see Susan Johnson.

20. For an especially acerbic review of *Gabriel Conroy*, see Nadal. On the charge that a particularly "brutal" review was anonymously penned by Twain, see Young (45).

21. Derived from the language of either the Wyandotte or Haudenosaunee (Iroquois) peoples, "Kentucky" is also the home of Uncle Tom in *Uncle Tom's Cabin*, and the novel also has a chapter called "Kentuck." See Klotter and Friend.

22. When Harte published "Wan Lee, the Pagan" in a short story collection, the first story included was titled "The Pagan Child," about a white girl raised in the mines. See Harte, *Wan Lee, the Pagan, and Other Stories*. Moreover, Harte wrote a letter in 1871 describing a meeting with the official illustrator for "Plain Language" and stated, "I gave him several ideas about the 'Heathen Chinee' and his *Pagan* brother—the California miner" (Harte, *Letters* 12; emphasis added).

23. Topsy's statement of "never born" is in contrast with the opening line of many narratives of Black captives, including that of Frederick Douglass's. On the significance of the opening line, see Olney. On a discussion of Douglass's opening statement in particular, see Sharpe, *Monstrous* 7.

24. The word *huckleberry* also appears in a poem that Mark Twain was accused of writing in imitation of "Plain Language from Truthful James" in 1871. Though it is impossible to prove that the word had a secret meaning between Harte and

Twain, their shared use of it to refer to male child characters who share the writers' own biographical traits seems to be more than a coincidence. On the significance of the huckleberry in Twain's writing, see Colwell.

25. Ambrose Bierce, discussed in Chapter 3, also worked as a printer's devil as a young man. On the significance of the rise of the printing industry in Mark Twain's literary career, see Michelson.

26. On the trope of vagrancy in *Adventures of Huckleberry Finn* and "Three Vagabonds of Trinidad," see Hsu, "Vagrancy."

27. On the significance of Jack Hamlin's character in Harte's writings, see Buckland.

28. The riot could also be referencing the anti-Native Wiyot Massacre of 1860, which Harte wrote about as the assistant editor for the *Northern Californian*. See Harte, "Indiscriminate." See also G. Stewart, *Bret Harte* and "Bret Harte on the Frontier" (270).

29. In a reprint of the story, the exclamation points are taken out.

30. An example of such a childlike Black adult character, who bears a close resemblance to Topsy, is Pete in Harte's novel, *Gabriel Conroy* (1875). Similar to Augustine, who makes Topsy read aloud for his enjoyment in *Uncle Tom's Cabin*, Jack Hamlin has Pete do the same: as Hamlin "always made the reader repeat the more difficult words, he extracted from this diversion a delicious enjoyment, which Pete never suspected" (*Gabriel Conroy* 215). Harte's other caricatured Black characters can be seen in "A Protégée of Jack Hamlin's" (1882).

CHAPTER 2. MARK TWAIN'S CHINESE CHARACTERS
AND THE FUNGIBILITY OF BLACKNESS

1. For a discussion of Stewart's contradictory and perplexing relationship to the Chinese, see McClain 39–40.

2. The mutually prickly relationship between the two men began in Nevada and ended unpleasantly in Washington, D.C., when Twain was a personal secretary of Stewart's and reported for Western newspapers on the congressional hearings.

3. Twain is famously remembered as saying, "I am not an American; I am *the* American," though this quotation was originally spoken by someone else. See "I Am Not an American."

4. For his part, Twain got his revenge in his writing through an unflattering portrait (a badly drawn caricature of Stewart with an eye patch) of Stewart in *Roughing It*. Twain also spoke frequently about his days as a personal secretary to the senator in his autobiography.

5. 1850 Cal. Stat., chap. 99, § 14.

6. For Howells's account of his friendship with Mark Twain, see Howells, *My Mark Twain*.

7. According to the Twain biographer DeLancey Ferguson, "All that [Twain] was to say and write for the rest of his life was to be merely an expansion and consolidation of this San Francisco achievement" (Ferguson 113). See also Zmijewski. Twain would later add "Our Fellow Savages of the Sandwich Islands" to the title of his lecture (Fatout 4).

8. See notices from the Newark *Daily Advertiser* for Tuesday, December 8, 1868, available at Railton's page, http://twain.lib.virginia.edu/huckfinn/mnstrads.html.

9. On the connection between Twain and Maguire and how concerned Twain was about the ticket sales to his lectures, see Takashima.

10. The judge in San Francisco who initially instructed the jury to acquit Tom Maguire was Lorenzo Sawyer, who would go on to write a letter to historian H. H. Bancroft in 1886, saying, "The Chinese are vastly superior to the negro, but they are a race entirely different from ours and never can assimilate and I don't think it desirable that they should. . . . If they would never bring their women here and never multiply and we would never have more than we can make useful, their presence would always be an advantage to the State . . . so long as the Chinese don't come here to stay. . . . When the Chinaman comes here and don't bring his wife here, sooner or later he dies like a worn out steam engine; he is simply a machine, and don't leave two or three or half dozen children to fill his place" (qtd. in Peffer 67).

11. Black performers of minstrelsy were not accepted until after emancipation, with the most famed minstrel troupe being the Callender's Minstrels. As Misha Berson writes, while "white minstrel groups were having a field day [as] San Francisco went minstrel-crazy in the 1850s and early 1860s," Black troubadours were having a hard time making a living (81).

12. For a discussion of "Chinese looks," see Metzger, *Chinese Looks*.

13. This scene calls to mind Eric Hayot's argument about the ways in which the figure of the "Mandarin" came to serve as the barometer of the European sympathetic subject of modernity. See Hayot.

14. On the limits of white empathy that tries to imagine the suffering of the racialized other, see Hartman, *Scenes*.

15. Twain's vicious anti-Native racism was not unique to him. As the editor of *Overland Monthly*, Bret Harte published an essay very similar in tone in 1868. See Cremony.

16. In the November 1870 issue, Twain took "history" out of the note to state, "Fancy is not needed to give variety to a Chinaman's sojourn in America" (*Contributions* 91).

17. The Burlingame Treaty was reversed by the Chinese Exclusion Act in 1882.

18. For an illuminating discussion of how *Dred Scott* serves as a throughline in the U.S. empire-state, see Moon-Kie Jung, *Beneath* 70–81; Moon-Kie Jung et al. 11–20.

19. Ah Song Hi's "freemen," like "freedmen," excludes women, specifically Black women, from the category.

20. See Romeo, "Comic Coolie," for a detailed study of Charles Parsloe.

21. Twain scholars such as Randall Knoper and Hsuan Hsu have provided insightful readings of *Ah Sin*. Knoper reads the character of Ah Sin through the lens of mimicry, while Hsu argues that the "Chinese laundryman's motives and strategies—along with the formal incoherence of the text as a whole—represent historically informed responses to the debates precipitated by *People v. Hall*" (Hsu, *Sitting* 43).

22. In the play, Twain recycled a description of the Chinese worker that he had used in at least two of his previous works: Ah Sin setting the table as a domestic worker mirrors exactly a story that Twain wrote in San Francisco in the 1860s about an imitative Chinese servant and also a scene from *Roughing It*.

23. I thank the anonymous reviewer at Stanford University Press for this information.

24. Twain's description of Rachel is reminiscent of the description of a Black woman whom Harte encounters while on his lecture circuit in Kansas: "I've seen but one that interested me—an old negro wench. She was talking and laughing outside my door the other evening, but her laugh was so sweet and unctuous and musical—so full of breadth and goodness—that I went outside and talked to her while she was scrubbing the stairs. She laughed as a canary bird sings—because she couldn't help it" (Harte, *Letters of Bret Harte* 28). Because the description is from a letter that Harte wrote to his wife Anna, it is unlikely that Twain would have seen it unless Harte shared the impression with him after they reconciled in 1871. Remarkable here is that both men are describing women who had been enslaved, whose present affect is utter joy despite their past condition.

25. Sharon McCoy notes that the song is featured again in Twain's unpublished novel, *No. 44, the Mysterious Stranger: Being an Ancient Tale Found in a Jug and Freely Translated from the Jug*, which he worked on intermittently from 1897 to 1908 (McCoy "I Ain'").

26. James Baldwin's "Going to Meet the Man" is also a powerful rejoinder to Twain's characterization of the white lynching mob. See Baldwin.

27. This definition of carnival draws on Mikhail Bakhtin's concept. More applicable here is Nyong'o's theorization of "carnivalesque." Expanding on Bakhtin, Nyong'o explains that the term denotes "carnival as refracted in the commodity mirror and transfigured by the commercial nexus" (108).

CHAPTER 3. AMBROSE BIERCE'S CRITIQUE OF BLACKFACE
MINSTRELSY AND ANTI-CHINESE RACISM

1. Bierce's *The Cynic's Word Book* (1906) is often cited as the first iteration of *The Devil's Dictionary*. The words associated with minstrelsy are not found in the former.

2. See W. Wu; E. Kim; R. Lee; Okihiro; Lee-Keller; Hsu, *Sitting in Darkness*; and Cynn.

3. Though Harte published Bierce's nonfictional writings in the *Overland Monthly*, he had already left for the East when "The Haunted Valley" was published in July 1871.

4. Peter Davis, email correspondence with the author, October 1, 2010.

5. Bierce associated the term ambivalently with scientific progress and modernity, as he wrote in "The Age Romantic" (1902): "Science and invention have made our world a spectacular extravaganza, a dream of delight to the senses and the mind," but human beings will always throw "a longing look backward to the barbarism to which eventually [they] will return" (*Collected Works* 9:316).

6. Because of the Treaty of Guadalupe Hidalgo, Mexicans in California were legally categorized as white, though they were not recognized as such culturally. On the racialized sexualization of Mexican women, especially by white eugenicists, see Kitch, 207–8.

7. For an elaboration on nineteenth-century Asian American masculinity, see R. Lee and Cheung. See also Shah, *Contagious Divides* and *Stranger Intimacy*.

8. On the practice of cross-dressing in San Francisco, see Boag and Sears.

9. The term "grotesque essence" refers to the collection of minstrel plays by Gary Engle.

10. The *Oxford English Dictionary* has two entries for the word *queer* as a noun, the secondary of which states, "A homosexual; *esp.* a male homosexual." It attributes such use of the word to the Marquess of Queensberry's letter submitted during the trial of Oscar Wilde in 1894. See Cynn. For an explanation of the term, see University of Pittsburgh.

11. Bierce was not a stranger to romance between two men, interracial or otherwise. In an 1872 letter to Charles Stoddard, who is thought to have been gay, Bierce stated, "Tell me about everybody, won't you, and about your last voyage. Did you fall in love with another nigger boy." See Joshi and Schultz 7.

12. See Gary Okihiro's reading of the story in *Common Ground*, which views Gopher and Ah Wee as two women.

13. In *The Complete Short Stories of Ambrose Bierce*, divided into three worlds— horror, war, and tall tales—"The Haunted Valley" is placed in the world of horror. See Bierce, *Complete*.

14. Stoler is writing in particular about the presence of the U.S. empire in North American history (1).

15. On the nineteenth-century history of Chinese in California, see Chan, *This Bittersweet Soil*, and Ngai.

16. The article also states that the wooden shoes that the Chinese were known to wear will give way to U.S.-made shoes and will only be used to "kindle a fire for

barbecuing a rat dinner." Other modes of fashion will be adopted by the Chinese, and once that happens, the only distinction will be "the copper color, the narrow angular eyes, the peculiar gibberish and beardless faces" (2).

17. This account of minstrel history in San Francisco was written by Frank Dumont, who wrote plays influenced by minstrelsy featuring Chinese characters, such as *Little Miss Nobody* (1897), containing the first line, "Get out, ye yaller-faced nigger, get out!" (9).

18. For a critique of the notion that early antebellum minstrelsy was antislavery, see Nyong'o; and D. Jones, "Black Politics." See also D. Jones, *Captive Stage*.

19. The performance of "A Negro's Appeal" has a complex relationship to minstrelsy and the abolitionist movement in the United States because it was written as an antislavery song originally called "The Negro's Complaint" by a British poet William Cowper in 1793. See Joseph Jones.

20. The story was first published in 1874 in London and published in the *San Francisco Examiner* in 1877 as "The Night-Doings at 'Deadman's.'"

CHAPTER 4. REPRESENTATIONS OF GENDER AND SLAVERY IN SUI SIN FAR'S EARLY FICTIONS

1. In writings about Sui Sin Far, some scholars refer to her last name as "Far," while others refer to her as "Sui." In her autobiographical essay, Sui Sin Far suggests that "Far" is the last name, as she is referred to as a little girl as "Miss Sui" and as "Miss Far" as an adult. See Sui Sin Far, "Leaves" 125, 129. Following Annette White-Parks's claim that "Sui Sin Far" means "narcissus" in Cantonese—and that "meaning depends on the sequence, 'Sui Sin Far,' and does not work if the sequence is broken" (White-Parks xvii), I use the full name Sui Sin Far, the iteration of her pen name at the end of her life, throughout this chapter. I also use Sui Sin Far instead of Edith Eaton for the same reason that I use Mark Twain instead of Samuel Clemens when discussing Twain's writings.

2. Blackburn Harte himself had a high opinion of Bret Harte. In "The Rumor of Genius," he included Bret Harte in an "early group of American writers of genius," calling Harte's story "The Luck of Roaring Camp," in particular, "incomparable" (qtd. in Doyle 112).

3. Sui Sin Far's serialized travel writings in the *Los Angeles Express*, detailing a journey across the United States and published under the identity of a Chinese man named "Wing Sing," closely resemble Mark Twain's serialized "Goldsmith's Friend Abroad Again," featuring a Chinese character named Ah Song Hi, as well as *Roughing It*.

4. The editorial also mentions Ambrose Bierce, siding with his misogynistic characterization of women writers producing "hysterical fiction" as part of a "Shrieking Sisterhood," and describing a charming young woman in contrast,

who is most likely Sui Sin Far's sister, Grace, married to Walter Blackburn Harte (W. Harte, "Bubble and Squeak" 215).

5. The depiction of the Chinese representation that appeals to "one's sense of ludicrous and mysterious" could be a rejoinder to Bierce's "The Haunted Valley," in which the narrator responds to a Chinese worker's epitaph that identifies the worker as both a "Chinaman" and a "she" as "ludicrous transition of gender and sentiment" (91) and discloses no definitive knowledge about the mystery of the worker's life or death.

6. For some of the earlier scholarship that cautions against "reclaiming" Sui Sin Far as an Asian American pioneer, see Beauregard; Nguyen; and Shih. For scholarship that places Sui Sin Far in a transnational framework, see Chapman, "A 'Revolution in Ink'"; Pan; and Wong. For an innovative reading of Sui Sin Far through the sentimental genre, see Song. For Afro-Asian connections in Sui Sin Far, see Wong; J. Lee; Yao; and Cutter, "Sex." On reading Sui Sin Far's writings about Jamaica as part of Caribbean American regionalism, see Goudie.

7. In addition to *Becoming Sui Sin Far*, see Chapman, "Finding Edith Eaton." June Howard also merits mention for her rediscovery of "The Son of Chung Wo." See her "Introduction to 'The Son of Chung Wo,' by Sui Sin Far (Edith Maude Eaton)."

8. As James Doyle writes, "Advertisements for the *Land of Sunshine* appear in the *Fly Leaf*, which may indicate that [Blackburn] Harte knew the magazine through his contacts with [Edwin] Markham or Bierce and suggested that Eaton offer her work to it" (96). Edwin Markham was a Californian poet and was one of Blackburn Harte's closest friends. See Doyle 50.

9. Contrary to common knowledge, slavery existed in Canada for two hundred years. See Cooper.

10. Sui Sin Far wrote an essay called "The Chinese Woman in America" in which the word *slave* does not appear. The short stories that feature the word *slave* are "Ku Yum" (1896), "The Daughter of a Slave" (1897), "A Chinese Ishmael" (1899), "The Prize China Baby" (1905), and "The Son of Chung Wo" (1910).

11. I found similarities in the stories written by Sui Sin Far and by Edith King Latham (a white woman) around this time, both in the *Land of Sunshine*. Remarkably, Latham's short story, "While the Honorables Slept," features "an old slave woman" named "Seen Fah" (303).

12. In 1868, Stanton summarily declared, "According to man's idea, as set forth in his creeds and codes, marriage is a condition of slavery." See Stanton, "Miss Becker" 178.

13. The issue of the *Anti-slavery Bugle* containing Robinson's version of Truth's speech can be viewed at https://chroniclingamerica.loc.gov/lccn/sn83035487/1851-06-21/ed-1/seq-4.

14. On how the Black female captive is also excluded from the categorization of the "Black worker" during slavery, specifically Du Bois's in *Black Reconstruction*, see Hartman, "The Belly."

15. Spillers specifically discusses the "misnaming" of Black women as matriarchs in *The Negro Family: The Case for National Action* (1965), better known as the Moynihan report.

16. On the discussion of the Chinese workers during Reconstruction debates, see Aarim-Heriot; Moon-Ho Jung; Torok; and Wong. On the comparison of Chinese and Black stereotypes in the nineteenth-century United States, see Spoehr; and D. Caldwell.

17. Though Black and Chinese men were most often racialized in comparison to one another, the labor of Chinese men was sometimes compared with Black women's. See Woodville's short story, "Chang-How and Anarky." Also see Hunter 78–79.

18. See R. Ferguson for an instructive discussion of how the "universalization of heteropatriarchy produces the prostitute as the other of heteropatriarchal ideals . . . [who] names social upheavals of capital as racialized disruptions" (9–10).

19. See also Cho, *Uncoupling* 77–102. On Chinese female sex workers in nineteenth-century California who were variously "free, indentured, [and] enslaved," see Hirata.

20. The discourse on nineteenth-century Chinese sex workers can be studied alongside the cultural figure of the white female prostitute, which emerged as the embodiment of slavery after emancipation. Debates about white slavery and the Mann Act emerged later. See Stanley. I thank Moon-Ho Jung for this clarification.

21. Sui Sin Far's stories "Lin John" and "Woo-Ma and I" feature women who are most likely engaged in sex work, but they are never labeled as "slaves" or "prostitutes."

22. To my knowledge, the only other Black character in Sui Sin Far's stories is the "old mulatto Jewess" in "Her Chinese Husband." See Sui Sin Far, "Her Chinese Husband" 82.

23. This reading of Ku Yum's character alongside minstrel songs about "Black" women is in line with Lisa Lowe's argument in *Intimacies* that the Chinese woman figure might be read as serving a triangulating and disciplinary function to regulate Black femininity in relation to white femininity in colonial archives. I thank Elda Tsou for this observation.

24. Waitman Barbe (1864–1925) was a white West Virginian writer and literary critic. He is said to have corresponded widely with major literary figures of his time such as William Dean Howells, Julia Ward Howe, and Richard Harding Davis. See Torsney. After inquiring into a collection of his papers at the West Virginia and

Regional History Center at the West Virginia University, I was told that there is no correspondence between Barbe and Sui Sin Far (or Walter Blackburn Harte).

25. On race in "The Bohemian Girl," see Romines.

26. On how "yellow" became a racial category, see Keevak.

27. While the sentence "I too am of the 'brown people' of the earth" has been read as proof of Sui Sin Far's solidarity and identification with Blackness, I would argue that she is identifying here with multiraciality and not Blackness. As was customary in Jamaica at the time, she seems to distinguish between "black" and "brown," identifying mostly with the latter. An evidence for this can be seen in "Leaves" when she confronts a racist white man for being anti-Chinese while sidestepping altogether the antiblackness in his statement that "a Chinaman is, in my eyes, more repulsive than a nigger" (129). Nonetheless, it is undeniable that Sui Sin Far's racial politics seems to have changed in the course of her writing career, particularly by the time and after she wrote "Leaves" in 1909. In her journalistic writings from Jamaica in 1896–1897, I found more ambivalence than convincing overtures toward identification with Blackness. For insightful discussions of Sui Sin Far's time in Jamaica, particularly the fact that "her acceptance as a journalist depended on her being perceived as white" (Ferens 78), see Ferens 68–78; and Chapman, *Becoming* xlii–xlv.

28. For a reading of "Away Down in Jamaica" that underscores the role of the U.S.-Jamaican relationship at the turn of the twentieth century, see Goudie.

29. We should read Phil's Canadian nationality—as well as Sui Sin Far's—by remembering the history of chattel slavery in Canada, particularly the close ties between Montreal and Jamaica as British colonies. See Nelson; and Elgersman.

30. The mention of "black buzzards" calls to mind a popular African American song of the time that features a crow and a blackbird saying to each other that white people hate them because they are the color black. See White 203–4. Phil is usually read as a sympathetic figure (Cutter, "Sex" 87; Chapman, *Becoming* xlv), but his characterization of Jamaica is suspect, specifically in his labeling it as "beastly" and his description of the "black member in white clothes" in the Jamaican Legislative Council (Eaton 4).

31. The story underscores this point about gender trumping race when it points to a Black member of the Jamaican legislature. Sui Sin Far was probably overestimating the power of Black members of the council, however. See Ferens.

32. Kathleen is described elsewhere in the story using the adjective "fair" (Eaton 13), as is Phil (13), so their whiteness is meant to be unambiguous in the story. On the basis of Sui Sin Far's reference to a "poor black maid" of a hotel where she was staying in Jamaica (Sui Sin Far, "Leaves" 130), we might guess that Sui Sin Far's hotel maid served as a prototype for Rachel's character.

33. For a discussion of the mammy figure in twentieth-century United States, see McElya.

34. I thank Katie Van Heest for pointing out this connection.

35. Calling to mind Frantz Fanon's theorization of the "zone of nonbeing," Clarissa's position demands a reworking of the concept, as Fanon understood it as a condition of Black masculinity. See Fanon 2. I thank Moon-Kie Jung for making this connection.

36. This narrative structure is common in Sui Sin Far's fiction, as the first-person (or plural first-person) narrators who are introduced in the beginning of the story are quickly supplanted by omniscient third-person narrators as in "The Chinese Ishmael," "The Story of Tin-A," and "The Smuggling of Tie Co."

37. Legree thinks that it is Emmaline who is singing but does not dare go upstairs to check.

38. In the rest of the hymn that "Away Down in Jamaica" does not cite, it is proclaimed that parents and children will not be *united* at the judgment seat of Christ but rather will "part to meet no more" (Stowe, *Uncle* 487). If the hymn was indeed "common among the slaves," the words of the song must have been directed not at the singers themselves who are Christian, but at those who are not, who will experience eternal separation from their loved one who are not Christian and vice versa. In short, the "mourning" in question is not necessarily *our* mourning but *their* mourning, the mourning of the unsaved and unbelievers. So even though the singing—as well as a lock of hair from a previous scene—makes Legree "shudder to think what if the form of his dead mother should suddenly appear to him" (487), the lyrics are actually saying something completely opposite: that he and his devout Christian mother will "meet no more." This, then, is a scene of Legree's misreading of the hymn.

39. Unlike the Black Rachel in Sui Sin Far's story, the white Rachel in *Uncle Tom's Cabin* has a last name.

40. Given the history of Sui Sin Far's mother, who *was* kidnapped in China, and the Eatons' family connection to England, *if* Sui Sin Far had read *Wuthering Heights*, this is a detail that would have stuck with her.

41. For a history of the Chinese in Jamaica, see Lee-Loy.

42. Here I am thinking of Christina Sharpe's reminder that "while all modern subjects are post-slavery subjects fully constituted by the discursive codes of slavery and post-slavery, post-slavery subjectivity is largely borne by and readable on the (New World) *black* subject" (*Monstrous* 3; emphasis in original).

43. In addition to "The Daughter of a Slave," "The Three Souls of Ho Kiang: A Story of the Pacific Coast," a story that Sui Sin Far wrote in October 1899 for the *Traveler* magazine, was changed to "The Three Souls of Ah Son Nan," and "A

White Woman Who Married a Chinaman," originally published in the *Independent* in March 1910, was changed to "The Story of One White Woman Who Married a Chinese" in *Mrs. Spring Fragrance*.

44. Evidencing a sense of religious solidarity, in "Her Chinese Husband" (1910), a Chinese character thinks that "the stories in the Bible were more like Chinese than American stories" and states, "If you had not told me what you have about the Bible I should say that it was composed by the Chinese" (358).

45. Du Bois's essay and *Souls* are an elaboration on his "Strivings of the Negro People," published in the *Atlantic Monthly* in 1897 and in which he first introduced the concept of the veil.

46. Sui Sin Far's short story collection, *Mrs. Spring Fragrance*, was published by A. C. McClurg and Company, which also published Du Bois's *Souls* in 1903 and, more than other publishers, books by women and writers of color (White-Parks 197).

47. This proclamation by the woman, herself a singular ethnic and racial figure, anticipates the last line regarding the son of an "American Negro" and a princess from India in Du Bois's novel *Dark Princess* (1928), as their baby is described as a "Messenger and Messiah to all the Darker Worlds" and declared to be a prophet (301).

CHAPTER 5. READING THE MINSTREL TRADITION
AND U.S. EMPIRE THROUGH CHARLES CHESNUTT'S
THE MARROW OF TRADITION

1. For the history of Black musical theater, see Riis, *Just Before Jazz*.

2. On Asians occupying an interstitial space in the South and the binary racial logic in the United States, see Bow; and Loewen.

3. For a discussion of Du Bois's *The Souls of Black Folk* in the context of the popularity of blackface minstrelsy, see Herring.

4. For a picture of Bob Cole in whiteface as Willie Wayside, see Sampson, *Ghost* 150.

5. The show *In Dahomey* (1903) was another important precedence in Black theater. A play about U.S. Black imperialism in Africa, it featured a minor Chinese character named Mee Sing and included a song called "My Luzon," in reference to an island in the Philippines. It was also a collaboration of many of the top names in the business, such as Will Marion Cook, Paul Laurence Dunbar, Alex Rogers, Bert Williams, James Weldon Johnson, Bob Cole, and Rosamond Johnson. See Riis, *The Music and Scripts of "In Dahomey."* Also see D. Brooks.

6. While New York City had the largest Black population in the North, it was certainly not free of antiblack racism. See Hartman's rendering of the race riot in

the Tenderloin in 1900, which was a "major catalyst in the making of Harlem" (*Wayward* 174).

7. Wellington is the fictionalized name of Wilmington, North Carolina, where the Riot of 1898 took place; an estimated twenty black residents of Wilmington were massacred by a white mob. Prior to the publication of *The Marrow of Tradition*, the Wilmington Riot (called Wilmington Massacre by many) was also fictionalized by David Bryant Fulton, who wrote under the pen name Jack Thorne. See Thorne.

8. On the importance of reading the novel as a critique of Reconstruction, see Roe.

9. Josh Green states that the Ku Klux Klan men "had masks on" but that one man's—McBane's—fell off, so he was able to see his face (Chesnutt, *Marrow* 111). The reference to masks draws a connection to blackface minstrelsy and its inherent violence. For a different understanding of wearing masks as a Black performative practice, see Dunbar.

10. The label of Filipinos as America's "little brown brothers"—and later as "American nationals"—as well as the shifting view of America for Filipinos (initially as "redeemers," as Emilio Aguinaldo proclaimed, then as enemies) complicates this scene even more. See Kramer.

11. Eric Sundquist notes the importance of Green and Miller riding in the same section of the car (444), but assumed in that reading is Green's consent to segregation, which is missing in the novel. Unlike Miller, who paid for a first-class ticket, Green does not pay to be on the train.

12. For a reading of *Plessy v. Ferguson* as producing the legal category of radical racial alterity in the figure of the "Asiatic," see Phan.

13. On the "complicated attitude" that Chesnutt had toward the Chinese, see Thomas 353n33.

14. Chesnutt also conflates the Chinese with the "Negro question" in 1928 when he discusses the case of Martha Lum, a Chinese American girl whose father sued her high school in Mississippi for segregation on the grounds that Martha was not "colored" and that the country did not provide a separate school for Chinese American children. See Chesnutt, *Charles W. Chesnutt: Essays* 497.

15. Perplexingly, Harris actually saw himself as breaking away from the minstrel tradition, though Chesnutt would have disagreed. In a letter to Booker T. Washington, written in November 1901 after the publication of *The Marrow of Tradition*, Chesnutt stated, "It has been the writings of Harris and Page and others of that ilk which have furnished my chief incentive to write something upon the other side of this very vital question" (Chesnutt, *"To Be"* 167).

16. The cake walk was a popular component of many "coon shows." It reached its peak in the show *Clorindy: The Origins of the Cake Walk* (1899), by Will Marion

Cook and Paul Dunbar. In James Johnson's *Autobiography of an Ex–Colored Man*, the narrator states that Black people should be proud of the cake walk as a distinctly Black art form.

17. This subplot of the novel is very close to that of Mark Twain's *Pudd'nhead Wilson* concerning the Delacroix family. The "Black" character (whose mother is "one sixteenth" Black [15] and whose father is white) in Twain's novel is also named Tom.

18. As a restitution to Sandy and the Black race (and a punishment for Tom), Old Delamere decides to leave all of his wealth to Dr. Miller and his hospital and changes his will accordingly. Upon his death, however, his (white) lawyer decides that this change in the new will is not prudent and uses the old will, which leaves everything to Tom. The novel does not state explicitly that the final will was destroyed.

19. Earlier in the novel, Carteret describes Black captives during the Civil War as "running hither and thither like sheep without a shepherd" (44).

20. Considering how *not* effusive Du Bois was about Chesnutt in accusing the latter for abandoning his writing for a more lucrative career in court writing, this article's praise for Howells is especially noteworthy. See *Writings*, 1147–48.

21. Perhaps in a pointed dig at Howells's comparison between *The Marrow of Tradition* and a "pretty novelette," Chesnutt characterized Howells's *An Imperative Duty* (1891), a novel about interracial romance, as "very pretty" in a speech delivered in 1916. See Andrews 330.

22. Edith and Winnifred Eaton's father was an English merchant who had a fascination for China. Their mother, who was Chinese, was a converted Christian who had been educated in England.

23. In personal communications, Mary Chapman has shared with me that Winnifred Eaton's adoption of a Japanese name was not wholly opportunistic given her family history, particularly the existence of a Japanese uncle. Mary Chapman, email correspondence with the author, August 4, 2017.

24. William Andrews writes that Howells's final review of Chesnutt was influenced by how he understood Black people to be based on the model advocated by Booker T. Washington. He states that when "*The Marrow of Tradition* posed a most serious challenge in Howells's eyes to the whole idea fostered by the example of Booker T. Washington that blacks were a forgiving, patient, even submissive race" (337), Howells stopped reviewing the novel as a literary work but understood it as an indictment against Chesnutt's character.

25. Harte died in 1902; Twain, in 1910; Bierce, circa 1914 (he disappeared in Mexico during the Mexican Revolution); Sui Sin Far, in 1914; and Chesnutt, in 1932. A number of Chesnutt's unpublished manuscripts have since been published.

26. Lavinia's rapists are the sons of Tamora, an empress who is cast as foreign and sexualized, in contrast to Lavinia, who is cast as virginal and pure.

27. Philomel is another female character who suffers violence from a man. In Greek mythology, Philomel is abducted and raped by her brother-in-law, Tereus. He keeps her imprisoned to hide his crime, but she weaves her story into a tapestry. Her sister Procne sees this and rescues Philomel. They run away from Tereus and, while fleeing, get turned into birds—Procne into a swallow and Philomel into a nightingale.

Bibliography

Aarim-Heriot, Najia. *Chinese Immigrants, African Americans, and Racial Anxiety in the United States, 1848–1882.* Urbana: University of Illinois Press, 2003.

Abate, Michelle Ann. "Topsy and Topsy-Turvy Jo: Harriet Beecher Stowe's *Uncle Tom's Cabin* and/in Louisa May Alcott's *Little Women.*" *Children's Literature,* vol. 34, no. 1, 2006, pp. 59–82.

Aldrich, Thomas Bailey. "Literary Items." *Every Saturday,* vol. 10, 1871, p. 19.

Allen, James. *Without Sanctuary: Lynching Photography in America.* Santa Fe: Twin Palms, 2000.

Ammons, Elizabeth. *Conflicting Stories: American Women Writers at the Turn of the Twentieth Century.* New York: Oxford University Press, 1992.

"Amusements, Etc." *Daily Alta California,* November 24, 1870, p. 1.

Andrews, William L. "William Dean Howells and Charles W. Chesnutt: Criticism and Race Fiction in the Age of Booker T. Washington." *American Literature,* vol. 48, no. 3, 1976, pp. 327–39.

Baldwin, James. "Going to Meet the Man." *Going to Meet the Man.* New York: Dial Press, 1965, pp. 227–49.

Baptist, Edward E. *The Half That Has Never Been Told: Slavery and the Making of American Capitalism.* New York: Basic Books, 2014.

Barbe, Waitman. "To M'lle Bohemia." *Fly Leaf,* vol. 1, no. 3, 1896, p. 13.

Beauregard, Guy. "Reclaiming Sui Sin Far." *Re/Collecting Early Asian America: Essays in Cultural History,* edited by Josephine Lee, Imogene L. Lim, and Yuko Matsukawa, Philadelphia: Temple University Press, 2002, pp. 340–54.

Beckert, Sven, and Seth Rockman, editors. *Slavery's Capitalism: A New History of American Economic Development.* Philadelphia: University of Pennsylvania Press, 2016.

Beckert, Sven. *The Empire of Cotton.* New York: Vintage Books, 2014.

Bell, Bernard W. "Twain's 'Nigger' Jim: The Tragic Face Behind the Minstrel Mask." *Mark Twain Journal,* vol. 23, 1985, pp. 10–17.

Bernstein, Robin. *Racial Innocence: Performing American Childhood from Slavery to Civil Rights.* New York: New York University Press, 2011.

Berrett, Anthony J. "Huckleberry Finn and the Minstrel Show." *American Studies,* vol. 27, no. 2, 1986, pp. 37–49.

Berson, Misha. *The San Francisco Stage: From Gold Rush to Golden Spike, 1849–1869.* San Francisco: San Francisco Performing Arts Library and Museum, 1989.

Bierce, Ambrose. "The Affair at Coulter's Notch." *The Collected Works of Ambrose Bierce,* vol. 2, *In the Midst of Life: Tales of Soldiers and Civilians,* New York: Neale, 1891.

———. *The Collected Works of Ambrose Bierce,* vol. 3, *Can Such Things Be?* New York: Neale, 1910.

———. *The Collected Works of Ambrose Bierce,* vol. 9, *Tangential Views,* New York: Neale, 1911.

———. *The Complete Short Stories of Ambrose Bierce.* Edited by Ernest Jerome Hopkins, Lincoln: University of Nebraska Press, 1984.

———. "The Haunted Valley." *Overland Monthly,* vol. 7, no. 1, 1871, pp. 88–95.

———. (D.G.) "The Strange Night-Doings at Deadman's." *London Sketch-Book,* vols. 1–2, March 1874, pp. 67–70.

———. "An Occurrence at Owl Creek Bridge." *San Francisco Examiner,* July 13, 1890, pp. 11–12.

———. *The Unabridged Devil's Dictionary.* Edited by David E. Schultz and S. T. Joshi, Athens: University of Georgia Press, 2000.

Bingham, Edwin R. *Charles F. Lummis: Editor of the Southwest.* San Marino, CA: Huntington Library, 1955.

Blackhawk, Ned. *Violence over the Land: Indians and Empires in the Early American West.* Cambridge, MA: Harvard University Press, 2008.

Blair, Elizabeth. "The Strange Story of the Man Behind 'Strange Fruit.'" *National Public Radio,* September 5, 2012.

Blassingame, John W. *Slave Testimony: Two Centuries of Letters, Speeches, Interviews, and Autobiographies.* Baton Rouge: Louisiana State University Press, 1977.

Blight, David W. *Race and Reunion: The Civil War in American Memory.* Cambridge, MA: Belknap Press of Harvard University Press, 2001.

Boag, Peter. *Re-dressing America's Frontier Past.* Berkeley: University of California Press, 2011.

Bonner, Arthur. *Alas! What Brought Thee Hither? The Chinese in New York, 1800–1950*. Madison, NJ: Fairleigh Dickinson University Press, 1997.

Bottoms, Michael D. *An Aristocracy of Color: Race and Reconstruction in California and the West, 1850–1890*. Norman: University of Oklahoma Press, 2013.

Bow, Leslie. *Partly Colored: Asian Americans and Racial Anomaly in the Segregated South*. New York: New York University Press, 2010.

"Bret Harte." *Baltimore Sun*, May 7, 1902, p. 4.

"Bret Harte's Books." *Every Saturday*, January 14, 1871, p. 26.

Briggs, Charles Frederick. "Uncle Tomitudes." *Putnam's Monthly*, January 1, 1853, pp. 97–102.

Brontë, Charlotte. *Jane Eyre*. 1847. Philadelphia: Porter and Coates, 1900.

Brontë, Emily. *Wuthering Heights*. 1847. New York: Norton, 2003.

Brooks, Charles Wolcott. "The Chinese Labor Problem." *Overland Monthly*, vol. 3, no. 5, 1869, pp. 407–19.

Brooks, Daphne. *Bodies in Dissent: Spectacular Performances of Race and Freedom, 1850–1910*. Durham, NC: Duke University Press, 2006.

Broussard, Albert S. "Civil Rights, Racial Protest, and Anti-slavery Activism in San Francisco, 1850–1865," https://www.nps.gov/goga/learn/historyculture/upload/Civil-Rights-Racial-Protest-Anti-Slavery-Activism-in-San-Francisco-1850-1865.pdf. Accessed July 31, 2019.

Brown, William Wells. *Clotel: or, The President's Daughter*. New York: Modern Library, 2000.

————. *The Escape; or, A Leap for Freedom: A Drama in Five Acts*. Philadelphia: Rhistoric, 1969.

Buckland, Roscoe L. "Jack Hamlin: Bret Harte's Romantic Rogue." *Western American Literature*, vol. 8, no. 3, 1973, pp. 111–22.

Buckley, James. *Buckley's Ethiopian Melodies*. New York: P. J. Cozens, 1853.

Bureau of the Census. *Population of the United States in 1860*. Washington, DC: Government Printing Office, 1864, https://www2.census.gov/prod2/decennial/documents/1860a-02.pdf.

Byrd, Jodi A. *The Transit of Empire: Indigenous Critiques of Colonialism*. Minneapolis: University of Minnesota Press, 2011.

Caldwell, Dan. "The Negroization of the Chinese Stereotype in California." *Southern California Quarterly*, vol. 53, no. 2, June 1971, pp. 123–31.

Caldwell, Erskine. *The Stories of Erskine Caldwell*. Athens: University of Georgia Press, 1996.

Carby, Hazel V. *Reconstructing Womanhood: The Emergence of the Afro-American Woman Novelist*. New York: Oxford University Press, 1987.

Cather, Willa Sibert. "The Bohemian Girl." *McClure's Magazine*, vol. 39, August 1912, pp. 421–43.

Chan, Sucheng. "Exclusion of Chinese Women, 1870–1943." *Entry Denied: Exclusion and the Chinese Community in America, 1882–1943*, edited by Sucheng Chan, Philadelphia: Temple University Press, 1991.

———. *This Bittersweet Soil: The Chinese in California Agriculture, 1860–1910*. Berkeley: University of California Press, 1986.

Chang, Gordon H. *Fateful Ties: A History of America's Preoccupation with China*. Cambridge, MA: Harvard University Press, 2015.

———. *Ghosts of Gold Mountain: The Epic Story of the Chinese Who Built the Transcontinental Railroad*. Boston: Houghton Mifflin Harcourt, 2019.

Chang, Gordon H., and Shelley Fisher Fishkin. *The Chinese and the Iron Road: Building the Transcontinental Railroad*. Stanford, CA: Stanford University Press, 2019.

Chapman, Mary M. "A 'Revolution in Ink': Sui Sin Far and Chinese Reform Discourse." *American Quarterly*, vol. 60, no. 4, 2008, pp. 975–1001.

———. "Finding Edith Eaton." *Legacy: A Journal of American Women Writers*, vol. 29, no. 2, 2012, pp. 263–69.

———, editor. *Becoming Sui Sin Far: Early Fiction, Journalism, and Travel Writing by Edith Maude Eaton*. Montreal: McGill-Queen's University Press, 2016.

———. "Sui Sin Far in Solidarity with the 'Brown People of the Earth.'" Paper presented at Association for Asian American Studies Annual Conference, San Francisco, CA, March 30, 2018.

Charles, Christopher A. D. "Skin Bleachers' Representations of Skin Color in Jamaica." *Journal of Black Studies*, vol. 40. no. 2, 2009, pp. 153–70.

Chen, Yong. *Chinese San Francisco, 1850–1943: A Trans-Pacific Community*. Stanford, CA: Stanford University Press, 2000.

Chesnutt, Charles W. *Charles W. Chesnutt: Essays and Speeches*. Edited by Joseph R. McElrath et al. Stanford, CA: Stanford University Press, 1999.

———. *The Colonel's Dream*. 1905. Upper Saddle River, NJ: Gregg Press, 1968.

———. "The Dumb Witness." *The Conjure Woman, and Other Conjure Tales*, edited by Richard H. Brodhead, Durham, NC: Duke University Press, 1993, pp. 158–71.

———. "The Goopherd Grapevine." *Atlantic Monthly*, vol. 60, August 1887, pp. 254–60.

———. *The Journals of Charles W. Chesnutt*. Edited by Richard H. Brodhead, Durham, NC: Duke University Press, 1993.

———. *The Marrow of Tradition*. 1901. Ann Arbor: University of Michigan Press, 1969.

———. "Post-bellum—Pre-Harlem." *The Portable Charles W. Chesnutt*, edited by William L. Andrews, New York: Penguin Books, 2008, pp. 481–87.

———. *"To Be an Author": Letters of Charles W. Chesnutt, 1889–1905.* Edited by Joseph R. McElrath Jr. and Robert C. Leitz III, Princeton, NJ: Princeton University Press, 1997.

Cheung, Floyd. "Anxious and Ambivalent Representations: Nineteenth-Century Images of Chinese American Men." *Journal of American Culture*, vol. 30, no. 3, 2007, pp. 293–309.

"The China Boys." *Daily Alta California*, May 12, 1851, p. 2.

"A Chinaman's Tail." *Buckley's Ethiopian Melodies #4.* New York: Philip J. Cozans, 1857, p. 66.

"Chinese Immigration to California." *New-York Tribune*, September 29, 1854, p. 4.

Cho, Yu-Fang. *Uncoupling American Empire: Cultural Politics of Deviance and Unequal Difference, 1890–1910.* Albany: State University of New York, 2013.

———. "'Yellow Slavery,' Narratives of Rescue, and Sui Sin Far/Edith Maude Eaton's 'Lin John' (1899)." *Journal of Asian American Studies*, vol. 12, no. 1, 2009, pp. 35–63.

Christy, George, and Charles White. *Christy's and White's Ethiopian Melodies: Containing Two Hundred and Ninety-One of the Best and Most Popular and Approved Ethiopian Melodies Ever Written.* Philadelphia: T. B. Peterson and Brothers, 1854.

Chude-Sokei, Louis. *The Last "Darky": Bert Williams, Black-on-Black Minstrelsy, and the African Diaspora.* Durham, NC: Duke University Press, 2006.

Cole, Bob, and Billy Johnson. *No Coons Allowed!* New York: Howley, Haviland, 1897.

———. *The Wedding of the Chinee and the Coon.* New York: Howley, Haviland, 1897.

Colwell, James L. "Huckleberries and Humans: On the Naming of Huckleberry Finn." *PMLA*, vol. 86, no. 1, 1971, pp. 70–76.

Congressional Globe, 41st Congress, 2nd Session, 1870.

Congressional Globe, 41st Congress, 3rd Session, 1871.

Conlogue, William. "A Haunting Memory: Ambrose Bierce and the Ravine of the Dead." *Studies in Short Fiction*, vol. 28, Winter 1991, pp. 21–28.

Cooper, Afua. *The Hanging of Angélique: The Untold Story of Canadian Slavery and the Burning of Old Montréal.* Athens: University of Georgia Press, 2007.

Coulombe, Joseph L. "Mark Twain's Native Americans and the Repeated Racial Pattern in 'Adventures of Huckleberry Finn.'" *American Literary Realism*, vol. 33, no. 3, 2001, pp. 261–79.

Cremony, J. C. "The Apache Race." *Overland Monthly*, vol. 1, no. 3, 1868, pp. 201–9.

Cutter, Martha. "Sex, Love, Revenge, and Murder in 'Away Down in Jamaica': A Lost Short Story by Sui Sin Far (Edith Eaton)." *Legacy: A Journal of American Women Writers*, vol. 21, no. 1, 2004, pp. 85–89.

————. "Sui Sin Far's Letters to Charles Lummis: Contextualizing Publication Practices for the Asian American Subject at the Turn of the Century." *American Literary Realism*, vol. 38, no. 3, 2006, pp. 259–75.

Cynn, Christine. "'[T]he Ludicrous Transition of Gender and Sentiment': Chinese Labor in Ambrose Bierce's 'The Haunted Valley.'" *Journal of Asian American Studies* 19, no. 2, 2016, pp. 237–62.

Daly, Augustin. *Horizon*. Cambridge: ProQuest Information and Learning, 2003.

Davis, J. Frank. "Tom Shows." *Scribner's Magazine*, vol. 67, 1925, pp. 350–60.

Day, Iyko. *Alien Capital: Asian Racialization and the Logic of Settler Colonial Capitalism*. Durham, NC: Duke University Press, 2016.

"Death of 'Billy' Emerson." *New York Times*, February 24, 1902, p. 3.

Deloria, Philip J. *Playing Indian*. New Haven, CT: Yale University Press, 1998.

Dormon, James H. "Shaping the Popular Image of Post-Reconstruction American Blacks: The 'Coon Song' Phenomenon of the Gilded Age." *American Quarterly*, vol. 40, no. 4, 1988, pp. 450–71.

Douglass, Frederick. "The Hutchinson Family.—Hunkerism." *North Star*, October 27, 1848, http://utc.iath.virginia.edu/minstrel/miar03bt.html.

————. *Narrative of the Life of Frederick Douglass*. Oxford: Oxford University Press, 1999.

Dred Scott v. Sandford. 60 U.S. 393 (1857).

Doyle, James. *The Fin de Siècle Spirit: Walter Blackburn Harte and the American/Canadian Literary Milieu of the 1890s*. Toronto: ECW Press, 1995.

Driscoll, Kerry. *Mark Twain among the Indians and Other Indigenous Peoples*. Oakland: University of California Press, 2018.

Du Bois, W. E. Burghardt. *Black Reconstruction in America*. 1935. New York: Atheneum, 1962.

————. "The Color Line Belts the World." *W. E. B. Du Bois on Asia: Crossing the World Color Line*, edited by Bill V. Mullen and Cathryn Watson, Jackson: University Press of Mississippi, 2005, pp. 33–34.

————. *Dark Princess: A Romance*. 1928. Millwood, NY: Kraus-Thomson Organization, 1976.

————. *The Souls of Black Folk: Essays and Sketches*. Chicago: A. C. McClurg, 1903.

————. "The Souls of White Folk." *Independent*, vol. 69, no. 3220, 1910, pp. 339–42.

————. "Strivings of the Negro People." *Atlantic Monthly*, vol. 80, 1897, pp. 194–98.

————. *W. E. B. Du Bois: Writings*. New York: Library of America, 1986.

Duckett, Margaret. *Mark Twain and Bret Harte*. Norman: University of Oklahoma Press, 1964.

Dumont, Frank. *Little Miss Nobody: A Comedy-Drama in Three Acts.* Philadelphia: Penn, 1900.

Dunbar, Paul Laurence. "We Wear the Mask." *The Complete Poems of Paul Laurence Dunbar,* New York: Dodd, Mead, 1922, p. 71.

Eaton, Edith. "Away Down in Jamaica." *The Metropolitan,* March 19, 1898, pp. 4, 13.

Edholm, M. G. C. "A Stain on the Flag." *Californian Illustrated Magazine,* vol. 1, no. 3, 1892, p. 159.

Elgersman, Maureen G. *Unyielding Spirits: Black Women and Slavery in Early Canada and Jamaica.* New York: Garland, 1999.

Emberton, Carole. "Unwriting the Freedom Narrative: A Review Essay." *Journal of Southern History,* vol. 82, no. 2, 2016, pp. 377–94.

Eng, David L. *Racial Castration: Managing Masculinity in Asian America.* Durham, NC: Duke University Press, 2001.

Engle, Gary D. *This Grotesque Essence: Plays from the American Minstrel Stage.* Baton Rouge: Louisiana State University Press, 1978.

Equal Justice Initiative. "Lynching in America: Confronting the Legacy of Racial Terror." 2017, https://lynchinginamerica.eji.org/report.

Estavan, Lawrence, editor. *San Francisco Theatre Research,* vol. 2, *Tom Maguire, Dr. David G. (Yankee) Robinson, M. B. Levitt,* San Francisco: Work Projects Administration, 1938.

———, editor. *San Francisco Theatre Research,* vol. 13, *Minstrelsy,* San Francisco: Work Projects Administration, 1939.

Fanon, Frantz. *The Wretched of the Earth.* New York: Grove Press, 1966.

Fatout, Paul. *Mark Twain Speaking.* Iowa City: University of Iowa Press, 1976.

Fenn, William Purviance. *Ah Sin and His Brethren in American Literature.* Peking, China: College of Chinese Studies and California College in China, 1933.

Ferens, Dominika. *Edith and Winnifred Eaton: Chinatown Missions and Japanese Romances.* Urbana: University of Illinois Press, 2002.

Ferguson, DeLancey. *Mark Twain: Man and Legend.* New York: Russell and Russell, 1943.

Ferguson, Roderick A. *Aberrations in Black: Toward a Queer of Color Critique.* Minneapolis: University of Minnesota Press, 2004.

Fishkin, Shelley Fisher. *Was Huck Black? Mark Twain and African-American Voices.* New York: Oxford University Press, 1993.

Foner, Philip S. *Mark Twain: Social Critic.* 1958. New York: International, 1966.

Foreman, P. Garielle, et al. "Writing About Slavery? Teaching About Slavery?" https://docs.google.com/document/d/1A4TEdDgYslX-hlKezLodMIM71 My3KTN0zxRv0IQTOQs/mobilebasic. Accessed October 18, 2019.

Foster, John Burt. "China and the Chinese in American Literature, 1850–1950." PhD dissertation, University of Illinois, 1952.

Foster, Stephen Collins. *Minstrel Songs, Old and New: A Collection of World-Wide, Famous Minstrel and Plantation Songs.* Boston: Oliver Ditson, 1882.

———. *Oh! Susanna: As Sung by the Ethiopian Serenaders.* Baltimore: F. D. Benteen, 1849.

Franklin, Ben, Jr. "The Yellow Girl." *Fly Leaf,* vol. 1, no. 1, 1895, pp. 10–15.

Fulton, Joe B. *The Reconstruction of Mark Twain: How a Confederate Bushwhacker Became the Lincoln of Our Literature.* Baton Rouge: Louisiana State University Press, 2010.

Gates, Henry Louis, Jr., and Evelyn Brooks Higginbotham. *Harlem Renaissance Lives from the African American National Biography.* Oxford: Oxford University Press, 2009.

George, Henry. "The Chinese Question." *New York Tribune,* May 1, 1869, pp. 1–2.

———. "What the Railroad Will Bring Us." *Overland Monthly,* vol. 1, no. 4, 1868, pp. 297–306.

Ghartey-Tagoe Kootin, Amma Y. "Lessons in Blackbody Minstrelsy: Old Plantation and the Manufacture of Black Authenticity." *TDR: The Drama Review,* vol. 57, no. 2, 2013, pp. 102–22.

Gillette, William. *Retreat from Reconstruction, 1869–1879.* Baton Rouge: Louisiana State University Press, 1979.

Gilmore, Ruth Wilson. *Golden Gulag: Prisons, Surplus, Crisis, and Opposition in Globalizing.* Berkeley: University of California Press, 2007.

Glisan, Rodney. *Journal of Army Life.* San Francisco: A. L. Bancroft, 1874.

Goddu, Teresa A. *Gothic America: Narrative, History, and Nation.* New York: Columbia University Press, 1997.

Goudie, Sean X. "Toward a Definition of Caribbean American Regionalism: Contesting Anglo-America's Caribbean Designs in Mary Seacole and Sui Sin Far." *American Literature,* vol. 80, no. 2, 2008, pp. 293–322.

Graf, Fritz. *Greek Mythology: An Introduction.* Baltimore: Johns Hopkins University Press, 1993.

Green, Alan W. C. "'Jim Crow,' 'Zip Coon': The Northern Origins of Negro Minstrelsy." *Massachusetts Review,* vol. 11, no. 2, Spring 1970, pp. 385–97.

Greenslet, Ferris. *The Life of Thomas Bailey Aldrich.* Boston: Houghton Mifflin, 1908.

Greyser, Naomi. "Affective Geographies: Sojourner Truth's Narrative, Feminism, and the Ethical Bind of Sentimentalism." *American Literature,* vol. 79, no. 2, 2007, pp. 275–305.

Gunning, Sandra. *Race, Rape, and Lynching: The Red Record of American Literature, 1890–1912.* New York: Oxford University Press, 1996.

Haley, Sarah. *No Mercy Here: Gender, Punishment, and the Making of Jim Crow Modernity.* Chapel Hill: University of North Carolina Press, 2016.

Hall, Lisa Kahaleole. "Strategies of Erasure: U.S. Colonialism and Native Hawaiian Feminism." *American Quarterly,* vol. 60, no. 2, June 2008, pp. 273–80.

Hall, Roger Allan. "'Black America': Nate Salsbury's 'Afro-American Exhibition.'" *Educational Theatre Journal,* vol. 29, no. 1, 1977, pp. 49–60.

———. *Performing the American Frontier, 1870–1906.* Cambridge: Cambridge University Press, 2001.

Haney López, Ian. *White by Law: The Legal Construction of Race.* New York: New York University Press, 1996.

Harris, Helen L. "Mark Twain's Response to the Native American." *American Literature,* vol. 46, no. 4, 1975, pp. 495–505.

Harte, Bret. *Bret Harte's California: Letters to the Springfield Republican and Christian Register, 1866–67.* Edited by Gary Scharnhorst, Albuquerque: University of New Mexico Press, 1990.

———. "Brown of Calaveras." *Overland Monthly,* vol. 4, no. 3, 1870, pp. 284–90.

———. "The Christmas Gift that Came to Rupert." *Overland Monthly,* vol. 6, no. 1, 1871, pp. 88–92.

———. "Current Literature." *Overland Monthly,* vol. 3, no. 4, 1869, pp. 389–92.

———. "The Executive Committee to the Colored Population." *San Francisco Chronicle,* June 18, 1869, p. 3.

———. *Gabriel Conroy.* Boston: Houghton, Mifflin, 1882.

———. *The Heathen Chinee.* Illustrated by Joseph Hull. Chicago: Western News, 1870.

———. "The Iliad of Sandy Bar." *Overland Monthly,* vol. 5, no. 5, 1870, pp. 479–85.

———. "Indiscriminate Massacre of Indians." *Northern Californian,* February 29, 1860, p. 1.

———. "The Latest Chinese Outrage." *Spirit of the Times,* February 2, 1878, p. 705.

———. *The Lectures of Bret Harte.* Edited by Charles Meeker Kozlay, Brooklyn, NY: C. M. Kozlay, 1909.

———. *The Letters of Bret Harte.* Edited by Geoffrey Bret Harte, Boston: Houghton Mifflin, 1926.

———. "The Luck of the Roaring Camp." *Overland Monthly,* vol. 1, no. 2, 1868, pp. 183–89.

———. "The Outcasts of Poker Flat." *Overland Monthly*, vol. 2, no. 1, 1869, pp. 41–47.

———. "Plain Language from Truthful James." *Overland Monthly*, vol. 5, no. 3, 1870, pp. 287–88.

———. *A Protégée of Jack Hamlin's and Other Stories*. Boston: Houghton Mifflin, 1894.

———. *The Queen of the Pirate Isle*. Illustrated by Kate Greenaway, London: Chatto and Windus, 1886.

———. "The Reveille." *The Complete Poetical Works of Bret Harte*, Boston: Houghton, Mifflin, 1903, pp. 86–87.

———. "The Rise of the 'Short Story.'" *Cornhill Magazine*, vol. 7, no. 37, 1899, pp. 1–8.

———. "Tennessee's Partner." *Overland Monthly*, vol. 3, no. 4, 1869, pp. 360–65.

———. "The Three Vagabonds of Trinidad." *Punch*, June 6, 1900, pp. 411–14.

———. *Two Men of Sandy Bar*. Boston: Houghton, Mifflin, 1904.

———. "Wan Lee, the Pagan." *Scribner's*, vol. 8, no. 5, 1874, pp. 552–59.

———. *Wan Lee, the Pagan, and Other Stories*. London: Ward, Lock, 1876.

———. *The Writings of Bret Harte*, vol. 20. Boston: Houghton, Mifflin, 1914.

Harte, Walter Blackburn. "Bubble and Squeak." *Lotus*, vol. 2, no. 6, 1896, pp. 212–18.

———. "A Tribute to Ambrose Bierce." *The Biblio*, vol. 4, 1924, pp. 680–81.

Hartman, Saidiya. "The Belly of the World: A Note on Black Women's Labors." *Souls*, vol. 18, no. 1, 2016, pp. 166–73.

———. *Lose Your Mother: A Journey Along the Atlantic Slave Route*. New York: Farrar, Straus and Giroux, 2008.

———. *Scenes of Subjection: Terror, Slavery, and Self-Making in Nineteenth-Century America*. New York: Oxford University Press, 1997.

———. *Wayward Lives, Beautiful Experiments: Intimate Histories of Social Upheaval*. New York: W. W. Norton, 2019.

Harvey, Charles. *De Yaller Gal wid de Kinky Hair*. New York: Tom Maguire Music, 1896.

Haverly, Jack. *Negro Minstrels: A Complete Guide*. 1902. Upper Saddle River, NJ: Literature House/Gregg Press, 1969.

Hayot, Eric. *The Hypothetical Mandarin: Sympathy, Modernity, and Chinese Pain*. Oxford: Oxford University Press, 2009.

"The Heathen Chinee in British Columbia." *Canadian Illustrated News*, April 26, 1879, p. 1.

Herring, Scott. "Du Bois and the Minstrels." *MELUS*, vol. 22, no. 2, 1997, pp. 3–17.

Hill, Errol G., and James V. Hatch. *A History of African American Theatre.* New York: Cambridge University Press, 2003.

Hirata, Lucie Cheng. "Free, Indentured, Enslaved: Chinese Prostitutes in Nineteenth-Century America." *Signs: Journal of Women in Culture and Society,* vol. 5, no. 1, 1979, pp. 3–29.

History of Music Project. *Music of the Gold Rush Era.* 1939. Edited by Cornel Lengyel. New York: AMS Press, 1972.

———. *A San Francisco Songster, 1849–1939.* 1939. Edited by Cornel Lengyel. New York: AMS Press, 1972.

Hong, Grace Kyungwon, and Roderick A. Ferguson, editors. *Strange Affinities: The Gender and Sexual Politics of Comparative Racialization.* Durham, NC: Duke University Press, 2011.

Hosmer, Margaret. *Story of a Chinese Boy.* Philadelphia: American Sunday-School Union, 1867.

———. *You-Sing, the Chinaman in California: A True Story of the Sacramento Flood.* Philadelphia: Presbyterian Publication Committee, 1868.

Howard, George. "Oh, I'se So Wicked." 1854, http://utc.iath.virginia.edu/songs/sowickedf.html.

Howard, J. D. "Cook and Stevens." *Indianapolis Freeman,* October 23, 1909, p. 5.

Howard, John Tasker. "Stephen Foster and His Publishers." *Musical Quarterly,* vol. 20, no. 1, January 1934, pp. 77–95.

Howard, June. "Introduction to 'The Son of Chung Wo,' by Sui Sin Far [Edith Maude Eaton]." *Legacy: A Journal of American Women Writers,* vol. 28, no. 1, 2011, pp. 115–25.

Howells, William Dean. "An Exemplary Citizen." *North American Review,* vol. 173, June 1901, pp. 280–88.

———. *Life in Letters of William Dean Howells,* vol. 2. Edited by Mildred Howells, Garden City, NJ: Doubleday, Doran, 1928.

———. "Mr. Charles W. Chesnutt's Stories." *Atlantic Monthly,* vol. 85, no. 511, 1900, pp. 699–701.

———. *My Mark Twain.* New York: Harper and Brothers, 1910.

———. "A Psychological Counter-current in Recent Fiction." *North American Review,* vol. 173, no. 541, 1901, pp. 872–88.

Hsu, Hsuan L. *Sitting in Darkness: Mark Twain's Asia and Comparative Racialization.* New York: New York University Press, 2015.

———. "Vagrancy and Comparative Racialization in Huckleberry Finn and 'Three Vagabonds of Trinidad.'" *American Literature: A Journal of Literary History, Criticism, and Bibliography,* vol. 81, no. 4, December 2009, pp. 687–717.

Hudson, Lynn M. "Entertaining Citizenship: Masculinity and Minstrelsy in Post-emancipation San Francisco." *Journal of African American History*, vol. 93, no. 2, 2008, pp. 174–97.

Huhndorf, Shari M. *Going Native: Indians in the American Cultural Imagination.* Ithaca, NY: Cornell University Press, 2001.

Hunter, Tera W. *To 'Joy My Freedom: Southern Black Women's Lives and Labors After the Civil War.* Cambridge, MA: Harvard University Press, 1998.

Hu-Dehart, Evelyn. "Chinese Coolie Labor in Cuba in the Nineteenth Century: Free Labor or Neoslavery?" *Contributions in Black Studies*, vol. 12, January 1993, pp. 38–54.

Hyde, Stuart W. "The Chinese Stereotype in American Melodrama." *California Historical Society Quarterly*, vol. 34, no. 4, 1955, pp. 357–67.

"I Am Not an American; I Am the American." Mark Twain House and Museum blog, June 30, 2011, marktwainhouse.blogspot.com/2011/06/i-am-not-american-i-am-american.html.

Johnsen, Leigh Dana. "Equal Rights and the 'Heathen "Chinee"': Black Activism in San Francisco, 1865–1875." *Western Historical Quarterly*, vol. 11, no. 1, 1980, pp. 57–68.

Johnson, James Weldon. *Black Manhattan.* New York: Da Capo Press, 1991.

———. *The Autobiography of an Ex-Colored Man.* Boston: Sherman, French, 1912.

Johnson, Susan Lee. *Roaring Camp: The Social World of the California Gold Rush.* New York: W. W. Norton, 2000.

Johnson, Sylvester. *The Myth of Ham in Nineteenth-Century American Christianity: Race, Heathens, and the People of God.* New York: Palgrave Macmillan, 2004.

Johnson, Walter. *Soul by Soul: Life Inside the Antebellum Slave Market.* Cambridge, MA: Harvard University Press, 1999.

———. "The Pedestal and the Veil: Rethinking the Capitalism/Slavery Question." *Whither the Early Republic: A Forum on the Future of the Field*, edited by John Lauritz Larson and Michael A. Morrison, Philadelphia: University of Pennsylvania Press, 2005, pp. 149–58.

Jones, Douglas A., Jr. "Black Politics but Not Black People: Rethinking the Social and 'Racial' History of Early Minstrelsy." *TDR: The Drama Review*, vol. 57, no. 2, 2013, pp. 21–37.

———. *The Captive Stage: Performance and the Proslavery Imagination of the Antebellum North.* Ann Arbor: University of Michigan Press, 2014.

Jones, Jacqueline. *Labor of Love, Labor of Sorrow: Black Women, Work, and the Family, from Slavery to the Present.* New York: Basic Books, 2010.

Jones, Joseph. "The 'Distress'd' Negro in English Magazine Verse." *Studies in English*, vol. 17, July 8, 1937, pp. 88–106.

Joshi, S. T., and David E. Schultz. *A Much Misunderstood Man: Selected Letters of Ambrose Bierce*. Columbus: Ohio State University Press, 2003.

Jun, Helen Heran. *Race for Citizenship: Black Orientalism and Asian Uplift from Pre-emancipation to Neoliberal America*. New York: New York University Press, 2011.

Jung, Moon-Ho. *Coolies and Cane: Race, Labor, and Sugar Production in the Age of Emancipation*. Baltimore: Johns Hopkins University Press, 2006.

Jung, Moon-Kie. *Beneath the Surface of White Supremacy: Denaturalizing U.S. Racisms Past and Present*. Stanford, CA: Stanford University Press, 2015.

———. "The Enslaved, the Worker, and Du Bois's Black Reconstruction: Toward an Underdiscipline of Antisociology." *Sociology of Race and Ethnicity*, vol. 26, no. 2, 2019, pp. 157–68.

Jung, Moon-Kie, João H. Costa Vargas, and Eduardo Bonilla-Silva, editors. *State of White Supremacy: Racism, Governance, and the United States*. Stanford, CA: Stanford University Press, 2011.

Kanellakou, Chris. "Mark Twain and the Chinese." *Mark Twain Journal*, vol. 12, no. 1, 1963, pp. 7–9.

Kang, Laura Hyun Yi. *Compositional Subjects: Enfiguring Asian/American Women*. Durham, NC: Duke University Press, 2002.

Kaplan, Amy. *The Anarchy of Empire in the Making of U.S. Culture*. Cambridge, MA: Harvard University Press, 2002.

Karuka, Manu. *Empire's Tracks: Indigenous Nations, Chinese Workers, and the Transcontinental Railroad*. Oakland: University of California Press, 2019.

Keevak, Michael. *Becoming Yellow: A Short History of Racial Thinking*. Princeton, NJ: Princeton University Press, 2011.

Kim, Daniel Y. *Writing Manhood in Black and Yellow: Ralph Ellison, Frank Chin, and the Literary Politics of Identity*. Stanford, CA: Stanford University Press, 2005.

Kim, Elaine H. *Asian American Literature: An Introduction to the Writings and Their Social Context*. Philadelphia: Temple University Press, 1982.

Kim, Ju Yon. *The Racial Mundane: Asian American Performance and the Embodied Everyday*. New York: New York University Press, 2015.

Kingston, Maxine Hong. *China Men*. New York: Vintage, 1980.

Kitch, Sally L. *The Specter of Sex: Gendered Foundations of Racial Formation in the United States*. Albany: State University of New York Press, 2009.

Klotter, James C., and Craig Thompson Friend. *A New History of Kentucky*, 2nd ed. Lexington: University Press of Kentucky, 2018.

Knoper, Randall. *Acting Naturally: Mark Twain in the Culture of Performance*. Berkeley: University of California Press, 1995.

Kolb, Harold H. "The Outcast of Literary Flat: Bret Harte as Humorist." *American Literary Realism, 1870–1910*, vol. 23, no. 2, 1991, pp. 52–63.

Koshy, Susan. *Sexual Naturalization: Asian Americans and Miscegenation*. Stanford, CA: Stanford University Press, 2004.

Kramer, Paul A. *The Blood of Government: Race, Empire, the United States, and the Philippines*. Chapel Hill: University of North Carolina Press. 2006.

Lai-Henderson, Selina. *Mark Twain in China*. Stanford, CA: Stanford University Press, 2015.

Latham, Edith King. "While the Honorables Slept." *Land of Sunshine*, vol. 12, no. 5, 1900, pp. 303–05.

Lee, Anthony W. *A Shoemaker's Story: Being Chiefly About French Canadian Immigrants, Enterprising Photographers, Rascal Yankees, and Chinese Cobblers in a Nineteenth-Century Factory Town*. Princeton, NJ: Princeton University Press, 2008.

Lee, Erika. *At America's Gates: Chinese Immigration During the Exclusion Era, 1882–1943*. Chapel Hill: University of North Carolina Press, 2003.

Lee, Julia H. *Interracial Encounters: Reciprocal Representations in African American and Asian American Literatures, 1896–1937*. New York: New York University Press, 2011.

Lee, Robert G. *Orientals: Asian Americans in Popular Culture*. Philadelphia: Temple University Press, 1999.

Lee-Keller, Hellen. "Civilizing Violence: 'The Haunted Valley.'" *Ambrose Bierce Project Journal*, vol. 2, no. 1, Fall 2006, http://ambrosebierce.org/journal2lee-keller.html.

Lee-Loy, Anne-Marie. "An Antiphonal Announcement: Jamaica's Anti-Chinese Legislation in Transnational Context." *Journal of Asian American Studies*, vol. 18, no. 2, June 2015, pp. 141–64.

Levine, Caroline. *Forms: Whole, Rhythm, Hierarchy, Network*. Princeton, NJ: Princeton University Press, 2015.

Lew-Williams, Beth. *The Chinese Must Go: Violence, Exclusion, and the Making of the Alien in America*. Cambridge, MA: Harvard University Press, 2018.

Lhamon, W. T. *Jump Jim Crow: Lost Plays, Lyrics, and Street Prose of the First Atlantic Popular Culture*. Cambridge, MA: Harvard University Press, 2003.

Ling, Amy. "Edith Eaton: Pioneer Chinamerican Writer and Feminist." *American Literary Realism*, vol. 16, 1983, pp. 287–98.

Loewen, James. *The Mississippi Chinese: Between Black and White*. Cambridge, MA: Harvard University Press, 1971.

Logan, Rayford W. *The Negro in American Life and Thought: The Nadir, 1877–1901*. New York: Dial Press, 1954.

Lorraine, Harry F. *Nigger Versus Chinese*. St. Louis, MO: Balmer and Weber, 1870.

Lott, Eric. "Love and Theft: The Racial Unconscious of Blackface Minstrelsy." *Representations* 39, Summer 1992, pp. 23–50.

————. *Love and Theft: Blackface Minstrelsy and the American Working Class.* New York: Oxford University Press, 1993.

Lowe, Lisa. *The Intimacies of Four Continents.* Durham, NC: Duke University Press, 2015.

Lwin, Sanda Mayzaw. "'A Race So Different from Our Own': Segregation, Exclusion, and the Myth of Mobility." *AfroAsian Encounters: Culture, History, Politics*, edited by Heike Raphael-Hernandez and Shannon Steen, New York: New York University Press, 2006, pp. 17–33.

Lye, Colleen. "The Afro-Asian Analogy." *PMLA*, vol. 123, no. 5, 2008, pp. 1732–36.

————. *America's Asia: Racial Form and American Literature, 1893–1945.* Princeton, NJ: Princeton University Press, 2005.

"Mark Twain as 'Heathen Chinee.'" *Mark Twain Journal*, vol. 38, no. 1, 2000, p. 9.

McClain, Charles J. *In Search of Equality: The Chinese Struggle Against Discrimination in Nineteenth-Century America.* Berkeley: University of California Press, 1994.

McCoy, Sharon D. "'I Ain' No Dread Being': The Minstrel Mask as Alter Ego." *Centenary Reflections on Mark Twain's No. 44, The Mysterious Stranger*, edited by Joseph Csicsila and Chad Rohman, Columbia: University of Missouri Press, 2009, pp. 13–40.

————. "'The Trouble Begins at Eight': Mark Twain, the San Francisco Minstrels, and the Unsettling Legacy of Blackface Minstrelsy." *American Literary Realism*, vol. 41, no. 3, 2009, pp. 232–48.

McCullough, Joseph B. "Mark Twain and the Hy Slocum–Carl Byng Controversy." *American Literature*, vol. 43, no. 1, 1971, pp. 42–59.

McElderry, Bruce R., Jr. "Introduction." *Contributions to "The Galaxy," 1868–1871*, by Mark Twain, Gainesville, FL: Scholars' Facscimile and Reprints, 1961, pp. ix–xx.

McElya, Micki. *Clinging to Mammy: The Faithful Slave in Twentieth-Century America.* Cambridge, MA: Harvard University Press, 2007.

McMillan, Uri. *Embodied Avatars: Genealogies of Black Feminist Art and Performance.* New York: New York University Press, 2015.

McNutt, James C. "Mark Twain and the American Indian: Earthly Realism and Heavenly Idealism." *American Indian Quarterly*, vol. 4, no. 3, 1978, pp. 223–42.

Meer, Sarah. *Uncle Tom Mania: Slavery, Minstrelsy, and Transatlantic Culture in the 1850s.* Athens: University of Georgia Press, 2005.

"Meeting of the Chinese Residents of San Francisco." *Alta California*, December 10, 1849, p. 1.

Melamed, Jodi. "Racial Capitalism." *Critical Ethnic Studies*, vol. 1, no. 1, 2015, pp. 76–85.

Melville, Herman. "Bartleby." *The Piazza Tales*, New York: Dix and Edwards, 1856, pp. 31–107.

Merwin, Henry Childs. *The Life of Bret Harte, with Some Account of the California Pioneers*. Boston: Houghton Mifflin, 1911.

Métraux, Daniel A. "How Bret Harte's Satirical Poem 'The Heathen Chinee' Helped Inflame Racism in 1870s America." *Southeast Review of Asian Studies*, vol. 33, 2011, pp. 173–78.

Metzger, Sean. "Charles Parsloe's Chinese Fetish: An Example of Yellowface Performance in Nineteenth-Century American Melodrama." *Theatre Journal*, vol. 56, no. 4, 2004, pp. 627–51.

———. *Chinese Looks: Fashion, Performance, Race*. Bloomington: Indiana University Press, 2014.

Michelson, Bruce. *Printer's Devil: Mark Twain and the American Publishing Revolution*. Berkeley: University of California Press, 2006.

Moon, Krystyn R. *Yellowface: Creating the Chinese in American Popular Music and Performance, 1850s–1920s*. New Brunswick, NJ: Rutgers University Press, 2005.

Morgan, Jennifer L. *Laboring Women: Reproduction and Gender in New World Slavery*. Philadelphia: University of Pennsylvania Press, 2004.

Morris, Roy, Jr. *Ambrose Bierce: Alone in Bad Company*. New York: Crown, 1995.

Morrison, Toni. *Playing in the Dark: Whiteness and the Literary Imagination*. New York: Vintage Books, 1993.

"Mortality Among Actors." *Alta California*, December 10, 1849, p. 2.

Mount, Nick. *When Canadian Literature Moved to New York*. Toronto: University of Toronto Press, 2005.

Moy, James S. *Marginal Sights: Staging the Chinese in America*. Iowa City: University of Iowa Press, 1993.

Moynihan, Daniel P. *The Negro Family: The Case for National Action*. Washington, DC: U.S. Department of Labor, 1965.

"Mr. Francis Bret Harte." *Every Saturday*, vol. 2, no. 55, 1871, pp. 42–43.

Murdock, Charles A. *A Backward Glance at Eighty: Recollections and Comments*. San Francisco: P. Elder, 1921.

"Musical—Theatrical." *Daily Alta California*, August 28, 1853, p. 2.

"Musical—Theatrical." *Daily Alta California*, August 20, 1854, p. 2.

Nadal, E. S. "*The Luck of Roaring Camp, and Other Sketches; East and West Poems; Condensed Novels; Gabriel Conroy* by Bret Harte." *North American Review*, vol. 124, no. 254, 1877, pp. 81–90.

Nelson, Charmaine A. *Slavery, Geography and Empire in Nineteenth-Century Marine Landscapes of Montreal and Jamaica*. London: Routledge, 2016.

Newcomb, Bobby. *Billy West's 'Banjo Solo' Songster*. New York: Robert M. DeWitt, 1873.

Newhouse, Wade. "Reeking Black Skin: Race, War, and Ideology in Ambrose Bierce's 'The Affair at Coulter's Notch.'" *ABP Journal*, vol. 1, no. 1, 2005. http://www.ambrosebierce.org/journal1newhouse.html.

Newman, Louise Michele. *White Women's Rights: The Racial Origins of Feminism in the United States*. New York: Oxford University Press, 1999.

Ngai, Mae M. "Chinese Gold Miners and the 'Chinese Question' in Nineteenth-Century California and Victoria." *Journal of American History*, vol. 101, no. 4, 2015, pp. 1082–1105.

Nguyen, Viet Thanh. *Race and Resistance: Literature and Politics in Asian America*. New York: Oxford University Press, 2002.

Nissen, Axel. *Bret Harte: Prince and Pauper*. Jackson: University Press of Mississippi, 2000.

Northup, Solomon. *Twelve Years a Slave: Narrative of Solomon Northup, a Citizen of New-York, Kidnapped in Washington City in 1841, and Rescued in 1853*. Edited by David Wilson, Chapel Hill: University of North Carolina at Chapel Hill Library, 2011.

Nurhussein, Nadia. *Rhetorics of Literary: The Cultivation of American Dialect Poetry*. Columbus: Ohio State University Press, 2013.

Nyong'o, Tavia. *The Amalgamation Waltz: Race, Performance, and the Ruses of Memory*. Minneapolis: University of Minnesota Press, 2009.

Okihiro, Gary Y. *Common Ground: Reimagining American History*. Princeton, NJ: Princeton University Press, 2001.

Olney, James. "'I Was Born': Slave Narratives, Their Status as Autobiography and as Literature." *Callaloo*, no. 20, Winter 1984, pp. 46–73.

Ou, Hsin-yun. "Mark Twain's Racial Ideologies and His Portrayal of the Chinese." *Concentric: Literary and Cultural Studies*, vol. 36, no. 2, September 2010, pp. 33–59.

Paddison, Joshua. *American Heathens: Religion, Race, and Reconstruction in California*. Berkeley and Los Angeles: Huntington Library Press and University of California Press, 2012.

Pan, Arnold. "Transnationalism at the Impasse of Race: Sui Sin Far and U.S. Imperialism." *Arizona Quarterly*, vol. 66, no. 1, 2010, pp. 87–114.

Patterson, Orlando. *Slavery and Social Death: A Comparative Study*. Cambridge, MA: Harvard University Press, 1985.

———. *The Sociology of Slavery: An Analysis of the Origins, Development and Structure of Negro Slave Society in Jamaica*. Rutherford, NJ: Fairleigh Dickinson University Press, 1969.

Peffer, George Anthony. *If They Don't Bring Their Women Here: Chinese Female Immigration Before Exclusion*. Urbana: University of Illinois Press, 1999.

Penry, Tara. "The Chinese in Bret Harte's *Overland*: A Context for Truthful James." *American Literary Realism*, vol. 43, no. 1, 2010, pp. 74–82.

People v. Hall. 4 Cal. 399 (1854).

Pettit, Arthur G. *Mark Twain and the South*. Lexington: University Press of Kentucky, 1974.

Pfaelzer, Jean. *Driven Out: The Forgotten War Against Chinese Americans*. Berkeley: University of California Press, 2008.

Phan, Hoang Gia. "'A Race So Different': Chinese Exclusion, the Slaughterhouse Cases, and Plessy v. Ferguson." *Labor History*, vol. 45, no. 2, May 2004, pp. 133–63.

Phelan, James D. "Why the Chinese Should Be Excluded." *North American Review*, vol. 173, no. 540, 1901, pp. 663–76.

Plessy v. Ferguson. 163 U.S. 537 (1896).

Podell, Leslie. "Compare the Two Speeches." Sojourner Truth Project, https://www.thesojournertruthproject.com/compare-the-speeches. Accessed July 31, 2019.

Pollard, Edward A. *The Lost Cause: A New Southern History of the War of the Confederates*. 1867. New York: Bonanza Books, 1974.

"Proceedings of the City Court—Negro Samuel Robinson vs. Edward Townsend." *Baltimore Sun*, November 9, 1837, p. 2.

Rawick, George, editor. *The American Slave: A Composite Autobiography*, vol. 9. Westport, CT: Greenwood, 1973.

Reddy, Chandan. *Freedom with Violence: Race, Sexuality, and the US State*. Durham, NC: Duke University Press, 2011.

Rice, Edward Leroy. *Monarchs of Minstrelsy: From 'Daddy' Rice to Date*. New York: Kenny, 1911.

Richards, Jason. *Imitation Nation: Red, White, and Blackface in Early and Antebellum US Literature*. Charlottesville: University of Virginia Press, 2017.

Richardson, Heather Cox. *West from Appomattox: The Reconstruction of America After the Civil War*. New Haven, CT: Yale University Press, 2007.

Riis, Thomas Laurence. *Just Before Jazz: Black Musical Theater in New York, 1890–1915*. Washington, DC: Smithsonian Institution Press, 1989.

———, editor. *The Music and Scripts of "In Dahomey."* Madison, WI: A-R Editions, 1996.

Robinson, Cedric. *Black Marxism: The Making of the Black Radical Tradition*. Chapel Hill: University of North Carolina Press, 2004.

Robinson, Elaine L. *Gulliver as Slave Trader: Racism Reviled by Jonathan Swift*. Jefferson, NC: McFarland, 2006.

Robinson, Marius R. "Sojourner Truth." *Anti-slavery Bugle*, June 21, 1851, p. 160.

Roe, Jae H. "Keeping an 'Old Wound' Alive: *The Marrow of Tradition* and the Legacy of Wilmington." *African American Review*, vol. 33, no. 2, 1999, pp. 231–43

Roediger, David R. *How Race Survived U.S. History: From Settlement and Slavery to the Obama Phenomenon.* New York: Verso, 2008.

————. *Wages of Whiteness: Race and the Making of the American Working Class.* New York: Verso, 1991.

Romeo, Jacqueline. "Comic Coolie: Charles T. Parsloe and Nineteenth-Century American Frontier Melodrama." PhD dissertation, Tufts University, 2008.

————. "Irony Lost: Bret Harte's Heathen Chinee and the Popularization of the Comic Coolie as Trickster in Frontier Melodrama." *Theatre History Studies*, vol. 26, 2006, pp. 108–36.

Romines, Ann. "Losing and Finding 'Race': Old Jezebel's African Story." *Cather Studies*, vol. 8, 2010, pp. 396–411.

Saffle, Michael. "Eastern Fantasies on Western Stages: Chinese-Themed Operettas and Musical Comedies in Turn-of-the-Last-Century London and New York." *China and the West: Music, Representation, and Reception*, edited by Michael Saffle and Hon-Lun Yang, Ann Arbor: University of Michigan Press, 2017, pp. 87–118.

Said, Edward. *Culture and Imperialism.* New York: Vintage Books, 1994.

"Sambo's 'Dress to He Bredren." Library of Congress, https://www.loc.gov/resource/amss.as112220/?st=text. Accessed July 30, 2019.

Sampson, Henry T. *Blacks in Blackface: A Sourcebook on Early Black Musical Shows.* Lanham, MD: Scarecrow Press, 2014.

————. *The Ghost Walks: A Chronological History of Blacks in Show Business, 1865–1910.* Metuchen, NJ: Scarecrow Press, 1988.

"Saturday Morning, June 4." *Daily Alta California*, June 4, 1853, p. 2.

Savage, W. Sherman. *Blacks in the West.* Westport, CT: Greenwood Press, 1976.

Saxton, Alexander. "Blackface Minstrelsy." *Inside the Minstrel Mask: Readings in Nineteenth-Century Blackface Minstrelsy*, edited by Annemarie Bean, James V. Hatch, and Brooks McNamara, Hanover, NH: University Press of New England for Wesleyan University Press, 1996, pp. 67–85.

————. *Indispensable Enemy: Labor and the Anti-Chinese Movement.* Berkeley: University of California Press, 1995.

Scharnhorst, Gary. *Bret Harte: A Bibliography.* Lanham, MD: Scarecrow Press, 1995.

————. "The Bret Harte–Mark Twain Feud: An Inside Narrative." *Mark Twain Journal*, vol. 31, no. 1, 1993, pp. 29–32.

————. *Bret Harte: Opening the American Literary West.* Norman: University of Oklahoma Press, 2000.

————. *The Life of Mark Twain: The Early Years, 1835–1871*. Columbia: University of Missouri Press, 2018.

————. "Plain Language from Truthful James." *American History Through Literature, 1870–1920*. Detroit: Charles Scribner's Sons, 2006, pp. 843–46.

————. "'Ways That Are Dark': Appropriations of Bret Harte's 'Plain Language from Truthful James.'" *Nineteenth-Century Literature*, vol. 51, no. 3, 1996, pp. 377–99.

Scherting, Jack. "Bret Harte's Civil War Poems: Voice of the Majority." *Western American Literature*, vol. 8, 1973, pp. 133–42.

Schmidt, Barbara. "'Hy Slocum' Identified." *TwainQuotes.com*, http://www.twain quotes.com/HySlocum.html. Accessed July 30, 2019.

S.D., Trav. *No Applause—Just Throw Money: The Book That Made Vaudeville Famous*. New York: Farrar, Straus and Giroux, 2006.

Sears, Clare. "All that Glitters: Trans-ing California's Gold Rush Migrations." *GLQ: A Journal of Lesbian and Gay Studies*, vol. 14, nos. 2–3, 2008, pp. 383–402.

————. *Arresting Dress: Cross-Dressing, Law, and Fascination in Nineteenth-Century San Francisco*. Durham, NC: Duke University Press, 2015.

Shah, Nayan. *Contagious Divides: Epidemics and Race in San Francisco's Chinatown*. Berkeley: University of California Press, 2001.

————. *Stranger Intimacy: Contesting Race, Sexuality, and the Law in the North American West*. Berkeley: University of California Press, 2011.

Shakespeare, William. *Titus Andronicus*. New York: Dover, 2015.

Shankman, Arnold. "Black on Yellow: Afro-Americans View Chinese-Americans, 1850–1935." *Phylon*, vol. 39, no. 1, 1978, pp. 1–17.

Sharpe, Christina Elizabeth. *In the Wake: On Blackness and Being*. Durham, NC: Duke University Press, 2016.

————. *Monstrous Intimacies: Making Post-slavery Subjects*. Durham, NC: Duke University Press, 2010.

Shepard, Karen. *The Celestials*. Portland, OR: Tin House Books, 2013.

Shih, David. "The Seduction of Origins: Sui Sin Far and the Race for Tradition." *Form and Transformation in Asian American Literature*, edited by Zhou Xiaojing and Samina Najmi, Seattle: University of Washington Press, 2005.

Silber, Nina. *The Romance of Reunion: Northerners and the South, 1865–1900*. Chapel Hill: University of North Carolina Press, 1993.

Singh, Nikhil Pal. "On Race, Violence, and So-Called Primitive Accumulation." *Social Text*, vol. 34, no. 3, 2016, pp. 27–50.

Slout, William L. *Burnt Cork and Tambourines: A Source Book of Negro Minstrelsy*. Rockville, MD: Wildside Press, 2007.

Smallwood, Stephanie. *Saltwater Slavery: A Middle Passage from African to American Diaspora*. Cambridge, MA: Harvard University Press, 2007.

Smith, Matthew J. *Liberty, Fraternity, Exile: Haiti and Jamaica After Emancipation*. Chapel Hill: University of North Carolina Press, 2014.

Smith, Stacey L. *Freedom's Frontier: California and the Struggle over Unfree Labor, Emancipation, and Reconstruction*. Chapel Hill: University of North Carolina Press, 2013.

Solberg, S. E. "Sui Sin Far/Edith Eaton: The First Chinese-American Fictionist." *MELUS*, vol. 8, no. 1, 1981, pp. 27–39.

Song, Min Hyoung. "Sentimentalism and Sui Sin Far." *Legacy: A Journal of American Women Writers*, vol. 20, nos. 1–2, 2003, pp. 134–52.

Sotiropoulos, Karen. *Staging Race: Black Performers in Turn of the Century America*. Cambridge, MA: Harvard University Press, 2006.

Speer, William. *The Oldest and the Newest Empire: China and the United States*. Hartford, CT: S. S. Scranton, 1870.

Spillers, Hortense J. "Mama's Baby, Papa's Maybe: An American Grammar Book." *Diacritics*, vol. 17, no. 2, 1987, pp. 65–81.

Spoehr, Luther W. "Sambo and the Heathen Chinee: Californians' Racial Stereotypes in the Late 1870s." *Pacific Historical Review*, vol. 42, no. 2, 1973, pp. 185–204.

Stanford, Leland. *Inaugural Address of Leland Stanford*. Sacramento, CA: Benj. P. Avery, 1862.

Stanton, Elizabeth Cady, et al. *History of Woman Suffrage*, vol. 1, 2nd ed. Rochester, NY: Charles Mann, 1889.

———. "Miss Becker on the Difference in Sex." *The Selected Papers of Elizabeth Cady Stanton and Susan B. Anthony*, vol. 2, *Against an Aristocracy of Sex, 1866 to 1873*, edited by Ann D. Gordon, New Brunswick, NJ: Rutgers University Press, 2000, pp. 176–83.

Stewart, George R. *Bret Harte, Argonaut and Exile*. Boston: Houghton Mifflin, 1931.

———. "Bret Harte on the Frontier: A New Chapter of Biography." *Southwest Review*, vol. 11, no. 3, 1926, pp. 265–73.

Stewart, William M. *Reminiscences of Senator William M. Stewart, of Nevada*. New York: Neale, 1908.

Stoler, Ann Laura, editor. *Haunted by Empire: Geographies of Intimacy in North American History*. Durham, NC: Duke University Press, 2006.

Stowe, Harriet Beecher. *Oldtown Folks*. Boston: Fields, Osgood, 1869.

———. *Uncle Tom's Cabin; Or, Life Among the Lowly*. 1852. Cambridge, MA: Belknap Press of Harvard University Press, 2009.

Sui Seen Far, "The Daughter of a Slave." *Short Stories*, vol. 25, 1897, pp. 218–23.

———. "The Gamblers." *Fly Leaf*, vol. 1, no. 3, 1896, pp. 14–18.

———. "Ku Yum." *Land of Sunshine*, vol. 5, no. 1, 1896, pp. 29–31.

Sui Sin Fah. "A Chinese Ishmael." *Overland Monthly*, vol. 34, no. 199, 1899, pp. 43–49.

———. "Lin John." *Land of Sunshine*, vol. 10, no. 2, 1899, pp. 76–77.

Sui Sin Far. "The God of Restoration." *Mrs. Spring Fragrance*, edited by Hsuan L. Hsu, Peterborough, Ontario: Broadview Press, 2011, pp. 136–41.

———. "Her Chinese Husband." *Independent*, vol. 69, no. 3220, 1910, pp. 358–61.

———. "Its Wavering Image." *Mrs. Spring Fragrance and Other Writings*, edited by Amy Ling and Annette White-Parks, Urbana: University of Illinois Press, 1995, pp. 61–66.

———. "Leaves from the Mental Portfolio of a Eurasian." *Independent*, vol. 66, no. 3138, 1909, pp. 125–32.

———. *Mrs. Spring Fragrance*. Edited by Hsuan L. Hsu, Peterborough, Ontario: Broadview Press, 2011.

———. "The Son of Chung Wo." *Legacy: A Journal of American Women Writers*, vol. 28, no. 1, 2011, pp. 127–35.

———. "Tian Shan's Kindred Spirit." *Mrs. Spring Fragrance*, edited by Hsuan L. Hsu, Peterborough, Ontario: Broadview Press, 2011, pp. 152–58.

———. "A White Woman Who Married a Chinaman." *Independent*, vol. 68, no. 3197, 1910, pp. 518–23.

Sundquist, Eric J. *To Wake the Nations: Race in the Making of American Literature*. Cambridge, MA: Belknap Press of Harvard University Press, 1993.

Swinton, John. "The New Issue: The Chinese-American Question." *New-York Tribune*, June 30, 1870, pp. 1–2.

Takaki, Ronald. *Iron Cages: Race and Culture in 19th-Century America*. New York: Oxford University Press, 1979.

Takashima, Mariko. "The Impacts of the Performances of Maguire and Risley's Imperial Japanese Troupe on Mark Twain's Lectures in San Francisco and New York in 1866 and 1867." *Bulletin of the Faculty of Representational Studies*, vol. 14, 2014, pp. 79–96.

Tchen, Jack Kuo Wei. *New York Before Chinatown: Orientalism and the Shaping of American Culture, 1776–1882*. Baltimore: Johns Hopkins University Press, 1999.

"Theater, Holliday Street—Jim Crow's Speech." *Baltimore Sun*, November 9, 1837, p. 2.

"Theatrical and Musical." *Daily Alta California*, May 12, 1852, p. 2.

Thomas, Brook. *The Literature of Reconstruction: Not in Plain Black and White*. Baltimore: Johns Hopkins University Press, 2017.

Thorne, Jack (David Bryant Fulton). *Hanover; Or, The Persecution of the Lowly: A Story of the Wilmington Massacre*. 1900. Chapel Hill: Academic Affairs Library, University of North Carolina, 2001.

Toll, Robert C. *Blacking Up: The Minstrel Show in Nineteenth-Century America*. New York: Oxford University Press, 1974.

Torok, John Hayakawa. "Reconstruction and Racial Nativism: Chinese Immigrants and the Debates on the Thirteenth, Fourteenth, and Fifteenth Amendments and Civil Rights Laws." *Asian Law Journal*, vol. 3, 1996, pp. 55–103.

Torsney, Cheryl B. "Waitman Barbe." *e-WV: The West Virginia Encyclopedia*, September 25, 2012, http://www.wvencyclopedia.org/articles/346.

Truth, Sojourner. *Narrative of Sojourner Truth*. 1850. Edited by Olive Gilbert, Salem, NH: Ayer, 1992.

Turner, Frederick Jackson. *The Frontier in American History*. New York: Holt, Rinehart, and Winston, 1962.

Twain, Mark. *Adventures of Huckleberry Finn*. New York: Charles L. Webster, 1885.

———. *The Adventures of Tom Sawyer*. 1876. Hartford, CT: American, 1884.

———. *Autobiography of Mark Twain*, vol. 2, *Mark Twain Papers*. Berkeley: University of California Press, 2013.

———. *The Celebrated Jumping Frog of Calaveras County: And Other Sketches*. New York: American News, 1867.

———. "Chapters from My Autobiography: XIII." *North American Review*, vol. 184, no. 610, 1907, pp. 449–63.

———. *The Complete Essays by Mark Twain*. Edited by Charles Neider, Garden City, NJ: Double Day, 1963.

———. *Contributions to "The Galaxy," 1868–1871*. Edited by Bruce R. McElderry Jr., Gainesville, FL: Scholars' Facsimile and Reprints, 1961.

———. *The Innocents Abroad; or, The New Pilgrim's Progress*. 1869. New York: Harper and Row, 1911.

———. "Mark Twain's 'Day at Niagara.'" *Daily Alta California*, September 5, 1869, p. 3.

———. *Mark Twain's Letters*, vol. 4, *1870–1871*, edited by Victor Fischer and Michael B. Frank. Berkeley: University of California Press, 1995.

———. *Mark Twain's Letters to His Publishers, 1867–1894*. Edited by Hamlin Hill, Berkeley: University of California Press, 1967.

———. *Mark Twain's Travels with Mr. Brown*. New York: Alfred A. Knopf, 1940.

———. *Mark Twain to Mrs. Fairbanks*. Edited by Dixon Wecter, San Marino, CA: Huntington Library, 1978.

———. *Pudd'nhead Wilson: A Tale*. London: Chatto and Windus, 1894.

———. *Roughing It*. Chicago: Sun-Times Media Group, 1872.

———. "A True Story, Repeated Word for Word as I Heard It." *Atlantic Monthly*, vol. 34, no. 205, November 1874, pp. 591–94.

———. *The Works of Mark Twain*, vol. 14, *Early Tales and Sketches*, vol. 1, *1851–1864*, edited by Edgar Marquess Branch et al., Berkeley: University of California Press, 1979.

———. *The Works of Mark Twain*, vol. 15, *Early Tales and Sketches*, vol. 2, *1864–1865*, edited by Edgar Marquess Branch, Robert H. Hirst, and Harriett E. Smith, Berkeley: University of California Press, 1981.

Twain, Mark, and Bret Harte. *Ah Sin: A Dramatic Work*. San Francisco: Book Club of California, 1961.

Twain, Mark, and William D. Howells. *Mark Twain–Howells Letters: The Correspondence of Samuel L. Clemens and William D. Howells, 1872–1910*. Edited by Henry Nash Smith and William M. Gibson, Cambridge, MA: Belknap Press of Harvard University Press, 1960.

Twain, Mark, and Charles Dudley Warner. *The Gilded Age: A Tale of To-day*. Hartford: American, 1873.

"Typescript of Letter to Editor of *The Examiner* Concerning Death of Billy Emerson." *Billy Emerson*, MS Thr 556 (55), American Minstrel Show Collection, 1823–1947, Harvard Theatre Collection, Houghton Library, Harvard University, Cambridge, MA.

University of Pittsburgh. "Keyword: Queer." http://keywords.pitt.edu/keywords _defined/queer.html. Accessed July 31, 2019.

Von Sneidern, Maja-Lisa. "'Wuthering Heights' and the Liverpool Slave Trade." *ELH*, vol. 62, no. 1, Spring 1995, pp. 171–96.

Watson, James L., editor. *Asian and African Systems of Slavery*. Berkeley: University of California Press, 1980.

Weber, Jordan. "Reconstructing Whiteness in Ambrose Bierce." MA thesis, DePaul University, 2017.

West, Elliott "Reconstructing Race." *Western Historical Quarterly*, vol. 34, no. 1, February 2003, pp. 6–26.

Wheat, Carl I. "'California's Bantam Cock': The Journals of Charles E. De Long, 1854–1863." *California Historical Society Quarterly*, vol. 8, no. 3, September, 1929, pp. 193–213.

———. "'California's Bantam Cock': The Journals of Charles E. De Long, 1854–1863." *California Historical Society Quarterly*, vol. 8, no. 4, December 1929), pp. 337–63.

Wheeler, H. H. *Up-to-Date Minstrel Jokes*. Boston: W. H. Baker, 1902.

White, Newman Ivey, and Frank Clyde Brown. *The Frank C. Brown Collection of North Carolina Folklore: The Folklore of North Carolina, Collected by Dr. Frank C. Brown During the Years 1912 to 1943, in Collaboration with the North Carolina Folklore Society*. Durham, NC: Duke University Press, 1952.

Whitehead, Colson. *The Underground Railroad: A Novel*. New York: Doubleday, 2016.

White-Parks, Annette. *Sui Sin Far/Edith Maude Eaton: A Literary Biography*. Urbana: University of Illinois Press, 1995.

Wild, Willie. "Letter from California." *Daily Picayune*, July 11, 1869, p. 12.

Williams, Bert. "Chink, Chink, Chinaman." Chicago: Will Rossiter, 1909.

Williams, Dave. *The Chinese Other, 1850–1925: An Anthology of Plays*. Lanham, MD: University Press of America, 1997.

———. *Misreading the Chinese Character: Images of the Chinese in Euroamerican Drama to 1925*. New York: Peter Lang, 2000.

Williams, Eric Eustace. *Capitalism and Slavery*. Chapel Hill: University of North Carolina Press, 1994.

Williams, Kidada E. *They Left Great Marks on Me: African American Testimonies of Racial Violence from Emancipation to World War I*. New York: New York University Press, 2012.

Wilson, Ivy G. *Specters of Democracy: Blackness and the Aesthetics of Politics in the Antebellum U.S.* New York: Oxford University Press, 2011.

Wilson, Matthew. *Whiteness in the Novels of Charles W. Chesnutt*. Jackson: University Press of Mississippi, 2004.

Wittmann, Matthew. "Empire of Culture: U.S. Entertainers and the Making of the Pacific Circuit, 1850–1890." PhD dissertation, University of Michigan, 2010.

Wolfe, Patrick. "Land, Labor, and Difference: Elementary Structures of Race." *American Historical Review*, vol. 106, no. 3, 2001, pp. 866–905.

———. "Settler Colonialism and the Elimination of the Native." *Journal of Genocide Research*, vol. 8, no. 4, 2006, pp. 387–409.

Wong, Edlie L. *Racial Reconstruction: Black Inclusion, Chinese Exclusion, and the Fictions of Citizenship*. New York: New York University Press, 2015.

Woodville, Jennie. "Chang-How and Anarky." *Lippincott's Magazine of Popular Literature and Science*, July 1878, pp. 114–18.

Wu, Cynthia. *Chang and Eng Reconnected: The Original Siamese Twins in American Culture*. Philadelphia: Temple University Press, 2012.

Wu, William F. *The Yellow Peril: Chinese Americans in American Fiction, 1850–1940*. Hamden, CT: Archon Books, 1982.

Wynter, Sylvia. "Afterword: Beyond Miranda's Meanings; Un/Silencing the 'Demonic Ground' of Caliban's 'Woman.'" *Out of the Kumbla: Caribbean Women and Literature*, edited by Carol Boyce Davies and Elaine Savory Fido, Trenton, NJ: Africa World, 1990, pp. 355–72.

———. "Sambos and Minstrels." *Social Text*, no.1, 1979, pp. 149–56.

Yao, Christine "Xine." "Black-Asian Counterintimacies: Reading Sui Sin Far in Jamaica." *J19: The Journal of Nineteenth-Century Americanists*, vol. 6, no. 1, 2018, pp. 197–204.

Young, James Harvey. "Anna Dickinson, Mark Twain, and Bret Harte." *Pennsylvania Magazine of History and Biography*, vol. 76, no. 1, 1952, pp. 39–46.

Yow, Ho. "Chinese Exclusion, a Benefit or a Harm?" *North American Review*, vol. 173, no. 538, 1901, pp. 314–30.

Yun, Lisa. *The Coolie Speaks: Chinese Indentured Laborers and African Slaves in Cuba*. Philadelphia: Temple University Press, 2008.

Zehr, Martin. "Mark Twain, 'The Treaty with China,' and the Chinese Connection." *Journal of Transnational American Studies*, vol. 2, no. 1, 2010, https://escholarship.org/uc/item/5t02n321.

Zesch, Scott. *The Chinatown War: Chinese Los Angeles and the Massacre of 1871*. New York: Oxford University Press, 2012.

Zmijewski, David. "Mark Twain and Hawaiian Politics: The Attack on Harris and Staley." *Mark Twain Journal*, vol. 31, no. 2, 1993, pp. 11–27.

Index